Damned
If She Does,
Damned
If She Doesn't

Damned
If She Does,
Damned
If She Doesn't

Rethinking the
Rules of the Game
That Keep Women
from Succeeding
in Business

Lynn Cronin
& Howard Fine

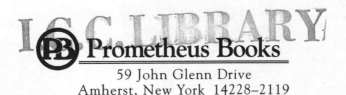

Prometheus Books

59 John Glenn Drive
Amherst, New York 14228–2119

Published 2010 by Prometheus Books

Inquiries should be addressed to
Prometheus Books
59 John Glenn Drive
Amherst, New York 14228–2119
VOICE: 716–691–0133
FAX: 716–691–0137
WWW.PROMETHEUSBOOKS.COM

14 13 12 11 10   5 4 3 2 1

Library of Congress Cataloging-in-Publication Data

Cronin, Lynn, 1951–
    Damned if she does, damned if she doesn't : rethinking the rules of the game that keep women from succeeding in business / by Lynn Cronin and Howard Fine.
        p. cm.
    Includes bibliographical references and index.
    ISBN 978-1–61614–174–5 (pbk.)
    1. Sex discrimination against women—United States. 2. Businesswomen—United States. 3. Sex discrimination in employment—United States. I. Fine, Howard, 1952– II. Title.

HQ1237.5.U6C76 2010
650.1082—dc22

                                                                        2010003632

Printed in the United States of America

For Drew and Lee,
our pride and joy of the past,
our faith and hope for the future.

CONTENTS

8 CONTENTS

ACKNOWLEDGMENTS

Writing this book has been a major undertaking for the two of us. We could not have met such a challenge without the assistance and support of many people.

First and foremost, thank you to the multitude of business-women and businessmen who have shared their stories with us over the years. Through their experiences, we have gained perspective and insight on the gender issues that persist in the corporate world. While we are limited in our ability to recognize these individuals by name for reasons of confidentiality, we hope all of them realize the value of what they've confided in us and our sincere appreciation for their input.

Thank you to Jessica Faust, our agent. She and her staff at BookEnds, LLC, have been a steadying, reassuring force steering us through the intricacies of the publishing world. Thank you also to Mary Ann Naples, a literary agent who took time to give us essential early feedback and counsel, even though our book was not within the realm of her practice. She helped us more than she knows.

Thank you to Linda Regan, our editor, to Ann O'Hear, and to all the staff at Prometheus Books. The confidence they expressed in us—two first-time authors—provided a foundation that anchored our efforts and allowed us to move this project to completion. Their professionalism, efficiency, and depth of support were truly impressive.

Thank you to the New York Public Library. This institution, so often taken for granted, is an incredible resource to have at our fingertips. We are fortunate and grateful to live in a city that provides such a comprehensive, accessible library system to all its residents.

Finally, thank you to our family. Our parents, Patricia and Matthew Cronin and Ceil Fine, have been unwavering in their support of our efforts. Though many people questioned the wisdom of our undertaking the project of writing this book, our parents never expressed any doubt or lack of interest. Their continuous love and support are special gifts we always cherish. Lynn's sister, Laureen Harris, has been an almost daily source of solace, humor, and counsel. Her value cannot be overestimated. And, of course, our children—Drew and Lee. They are not only our pride and joy but our inspiration. Throughout this project, they have been with us, tolerating our highs and lows and supporting us with their love and understanding. They are the best.

INTRODUCTION

But I've never been content to agonize when I could analyze instead.

SARAH BLAFFER HRDY,
*MOTHER NATURE: A HISTORY OF MOTHERS,
INFANTS, AND NATURAL SELECTION*

Sitting in yet another diversity training seminar, Lynn Cronin and Howard Fine listened as the leader, a partner in a renowned global human resources consulting firm, confessed, "I have been consulting in corporate diversity for over twenty years, and I am sorry to say, women have not made much progress since I started."

Lynn leaned over to Howard and whispered, "If not much progress has been made, maybe we need to change how we are looking at this problem." That moment was the genesis of this book.

Forty-five years after Betty Friedan's *The Feminine Mystique*, women have yet to achieve parity with men in the workplace. Men continue to make more money than women, and women's representation in the higher management ranks continues to lag behind men's. Our own odyssey through the corporate world confirms what we were told at corporate diversity training. After thirty years of working in and consulting to corporate America, we still find the experience of work more difficult for women than for men. But the question is "Why?"

We entered the business world at the same time, a young man and a young woman of the same age with similar, if somewhat esoteric, backgrounds. Both of us were and are Fellows of the Society of Actuaries who took our training in the mathematics of employee healthcare and pension plans and then broadened our focus to consult on a wide range of corporate human resource issues. While on a few occasions we worked for the same consulting firm at the same time, our career paths diverged with different degrees of success and failure. Generally speaking, though, Howard's pay increases tended to be larger, his job opportunities bigger, and his advancement faster than Lynn's. Initially, we attributed our differing patterns to our respective abilities and limitations, as well as to the different organizations we worked for. And, no doubt, these were factors. But we both had a nagging sense that the differences were larger than they should be.

One of the major advantages of being married for more than thirty years is that we are a man and a woman who can speak candidly to each other. After having spent so much of our working lives together, we decided to take an unvarnished look at our differing work experiences. Our examination of this sensitive subject was part intellectual exercise, part marital therapy, and part parental edification—we have a daughter and a son entering the business world and wanted to see if there were lessons from our careers that we could use to counsel them. Our free-flowing analysis took us to fascinating places. We began to sort through experiences gathered over the years from friends, acquaintances, and business associates, as well as our own experiences and those we noted in the course of our plethora of consulting assignments. We are fortunate and grateful to have children whose friends also shared their perspectives with us as they began to enter the business world, thereby giving us a multigenerational perspective. After talking to so many, we began to see that the disparities between men and women at work are due to more than just their individual strengths and weaknesses. We became convinced that the problem is systemic, and that corporate culture is the culprit.

So we decided to write this book in an attempt to move forward the discussion of gender issues in the business world. Our personal experiences, our discussions with others, and our analysis of the role of gender in business led us to insights that we wanted to share. We have found that the vast majority of men and women in business strongly believe that there should be equality of the sexes at work. As a result, we don't think the inequalities that persist are due to the individual prejudices or biases of men and women. Nor are they due to the inability of women to compete on the same level as men. Contrary to the myriad self-help books exhorting women to work harder, smarter, or wiser, no amount of individual effort on the part of women will overcome the challenges they uniquely face in the business world. Rather, we believe the problem with male/female relationships in corporate America is embedded in the protocols of business.

The corporate system—the way the business world operates—generates rules of behavior that create common guidelines for what is acceptable and what is not. These basic, respected rules of business work well for men but can inadvertently create paradoxes that put women in no-win situations and limit their opportunity to succeed in a manner comparable to men. Exploring these parity paradoxes in depth led us to the roots of the continuing gender conflict in business.

Our book begins with both anecdotal and statistical proof of women's stalled progress in the business world. Though the first two chapters may look a little dry, they provide the foundation necessary to achieve deeper insight into the problem. Chapter 3 represents a breakthrough in our thinking. In this chapter, we explore how contemporary corporate cultures can be influenced by the "man's world" of business of the past. With this enhanced understanding, we begin to see gender issues in business in an entirely new light. We then analyze five respected rules of business and the paradoxes they pose for women. On the surface, these fundamental rules—be a team player, find mentors and win advocates, demonstrate commitment, bond with co-workers, be prudent in challenging the power structure —certainly seem laudable and are apparently gender neutral, applying equally to men and women. But when women attempt to follow the rules, they often run into impossible dilemmas that men don't encounter.

When faced with these parity paradoxes, women cannot excel. They are frustrated by a system that passes them over for promotions, steers them to "female" jobs or departments, or simply pays them lower wages. Relative to comparably talented men, they are at least a half step behind. No wonder so many women choose to start their own businesses or leave corporate life altogether.

But we think the system can be changed to allow women to break through. In our final chapter, we present the concept of a *coed company*—a model of corporate culture that achieves gender equality and eliminates parity paradoxes. The coed company is the cultural antidote to the parity paradoxes.

Our goal in writing *Damned If She Does, Damned If She Doesn't: Rethinking the Rules of the Game That Keep Women from Succeeding in Business* is to shed light on the dilemmas women face. Gender limitations in the corporate world are real—women continue to earn less than men, women's progress in climbing the corporate ladder has stalled, and even some men are mystified by the persistence of gender inequity. All the statistics we present are current and the stories are true, though at the request of the storytellers, we have changed names and modified the circumstances to preserve their anonymity. We hope that businessmen and businesswomen who read our analysis will learn that they, individually, are not to blame for the gender inequities that persist, but that they, individually, can make a difference.

We are at a unique and exciting time in American history. With our first nonwhite president ensconced in the White House, we are rethinking many aspects of our society. Health-care, energy, the role of government, and the structure of the financial world are all under review. It is time to take a fresh look at gender issues in the business world and, building on the progress we've made to date, take the final step toward true gender equality at work. We present this book to all the men and women who genuinely hope to resolve the continuing gender conflict in corporate America. Together, we can change hope into reality.

Chapter 1

STILL STUCK ON AN UNLEVEL PLAYING FIELD

DISJOINTED IMAGES

The restaurant was humming with conversation. Men and women from the halls of corporate America were engaged in a hallowed ritual: the business lunch—a time when deals are advanced, successes are celebrated, networks are built, and, sometimes, unguarded opinions are shared. At one table Howard sat with two other men, Robert, a tall, dark-haired asset manager, and Stephan, a trim, graying senior human resources (HR) executive. While the predefined purpose for their meeting was to discuss how Robert's new investment fund could be marketed to employee 401(k) plans, the conversation took an interesting twist.

"By the way, how's your son doing? Didn't he graduate from college last year?" Stephan asked Robert, intermingling the personal with the professional in the time-honored tradition of business bonding.

"Yeah, he graduated. But he's having a tough time finding a good job. It's very competitive out there now. Frankly, I think he'd be having an easier time of it if he was female," replied Robert.

"Why do you say that?" inquired Howard.

"Well, I think women have an advantage nowadays. The talented women are courted and treated with kid gloves. My son was a strong student, but guys like him don't get anything special."

"You know, I can understand how you feel," Stephan, the HR professional, thoughtfully concurred. "In my company, we go out of our way to recruit women with high potential and go to great lengths to celebrate their promotions. Can't say we do that for men."

Three blocks up Sixth Avenue, while Robert, Stephan, and Howard were enjoying their dessert, Lynn was sitting in a diversity training class led by Marilyn, a middle-aged woman with a grandmotherly manner. The session was a required course in the management development program of the entertainment company Lynn was working for. Marilyn, a consultant with a renowned human resources firm, was recognized as an expert on corporate diversity and was frequently quoted in the press as a pioneer in the field. Standing in front of the seventeen managers from a cross-section of departments, Marilyn began with a sobering question: "How many of you believe that men have an advantage over women at work?" Every woman in the room hesitantly raised her hand. Marilyn continued, "I have been getting the same response from women for decades." The women in the group nodded knowingly in agreement.

These are two perspectives from what purportedly is the same world. One portrays a work environment where the pendulum has swung too far, where women's fight for equality has resulted in a reverse sense of inequity. The other shows a degree of frustration, a weary resignation that after years of effort the fight is far from over. This contrast raises questions about the true state of gender equity in business and whether the sexes will ever agree.

Entering a local Barnes & Noble bookstore, we were confronted with more disjointed images. In the periodical section, a photograph of the stunning, dark-haired beauty Gina Bianchini graced the cover of *Fast Company* next to the heading "This

CEO Has Silicon Valley Buzzing."[1] Her youth and T-shirted casualness attested to the power and triumph of today's businesswoman. Annually, *Fortune* trumpets the "The Power 50: 50 Most Powerful Women in Business"; the magazine stated in 2007 that "ten editions of the Most Powerful Women list prove it: Women have come a long way (don't say "baby")—and they're not slowing down."[2] Moving down the aisle to the management section, we found book after self-help book on what women need to do differently to succeed in business. The message hasn't changed much in thirty years. Both in the recently published books and in those from the 1970s, women are seen as outsiders trying to break into the world of business. But in order to succeed, they simply need to be smarter and wiser in the way they work. The undeviating, not-so-subtle message is that if women would just learn to do what men do, the problems of today's businesswomen would disappear.

But if the solution is so simple, why do working women continue to need so much coaching? Instead of being inspired, why do most women roll their eyes at photographs of female executives who have reached the top rung of the corporate ladder? And why do most businesswomen continue to feel a keen sense of inequity, while so many businessmen feel that the playing field has not only been leveled but may be tilting in favor of women? The polarity of these points of view makes us wonder: just where are we today?

DAY-TO-DAY INEQUITIES

While business magazine covers showing high-flying female executives paint a vivid image of women's success in the workplace today, it's the everyday anecdotal experiences of working women that provide a truer picture. Individual stories like Kim's are parables for what women encounter throughout corporate America.

Craig, a St. Louis office manager, wanted to fire Kim. "She

is so hard to work with," he thought. "Always challenging, excessively vocal. Ever since the merger last year, she has been just a pain." Though he couldn't dispute her talent and commitment—she had a proven, twenty-year track record with clients—he, along with several other senior leaders, accused Kim of having a negative attitude and being a primary contributor to the recent dysfunction in the office.

"This doesn't seem right," lamented Kim to the regional manager, Craig's boss, when he was visiting their office and sharing with her the feedback from her peers. "I'm a senior person here and I care about what's happening. When poor decisions are made, decisions I'm expected to live by, shouldn't I speak up? Haven't I earned the right to express my opinion? Sure, I may have lost my cool a couple times, but who hasn't around here lately? Things are so tense. Why am I being singled out?"

After listening to Kim, the regional manager intervened and stopped Craig from firing her that day. But though her job was saved, her career at that company was not. Within eighteen months of her conversation with the regional manager, she decided her reputation had suffered so much damage that she wasn't able to do her job effectively. Her peers and subordinates simply weren't giving her the degree of respect they had given her in the past. Kim decided she needed to leave the organization.

Kim's story is one of many. Listening to women throughout the business world, we hear murmurings of disquiet, feelings of discomfort and unease with the current work environment. Most women will quickly acknowledge that the blatant harassment and overt discrimination so prevalent in the past have virtually vanished. No longer is there a daily need to express a sense of outrage and intense anger at flagrant inequities. Yet things are still not quite right. Today a more subtle malaise prevails—a troublesome awareness that equality with men has not been achieved, coupled with a nagging suspicion that the situation is not getting any better.

The continuing sense of inequity many women feel is fueled by a series of day-to-day slights that may individually be dismissed as occasional bad experiences. But cumulatively, over time, these slights leave women feeling they are treated unfairly and more harshly than men. Kim's tale is a good example. Too often, women feel that their mistakes and shortcomings are magnified relative to men's. While there are no perfect employees—everyone has strengths and weaknesses—the women we speak with feel that their foibles are treated more severely and with less tolerance than those of men. Their male co-workers will lose their tempers, bungle an assignment, or turn in a submission late with few or no consequences, while women who trip up in the same way receive a heavy reprimand or a note in their personnel files. This inconsistent treatment leaves many a woman wondering "Why me?"

Even more disheartening than the "Why me?" treatment, though, is its converse: "Why not me?" Time and again, women feel that their successes are minimized in comparison to those of their male counterparts. One saleswoman saw it this way: "When I win a new account, my managers are pleased. But when one of the guys wins, everyone shoots off fireworks." Whether it is a major sales win or the development of an innovative concept, working women see that their contributions don't receive the community recognition that those of their male co-workers do. "You're not as good as you think you are" is the tacit or even explicit message of the feedback they receive.

Certainly, some companies go out of their way to celebrate the successes of individual women, especially their promotions. Josey remembered the time her investment bank convened a luncheon at a four-star restaurant for all the newly named female vice presidents. "The head of human resources stood up in front of us to say how pleased the bank was that they were elevating so many women. That, with this round of promotions, our bank had the highest percentage of female officers of all our competitors." Josey paused, then continued: "Look, I appreciate the bank's efforts, but something in the way it was said left me and most of the other women in the room pissed. We have worked hard—really hard—for this company. We earned those promotions. They made it sound like we were promoted just because we were women." These women were left with the sense that the company was praising itself more than the women it was promoting. To them, the company was essentially saying, "See how progressive we are? Aren't we a good company to be doing this for women?" Whereas the women receiving the promotions felt that their elevations were hard earned and long overdue.

Women have told us that it is not only the formal but the informal recognition that goes disproportionately to men in the corporate world. The pat-on-the-back praise that comes from a boss or a peer doesn't flow their way as frequently, or is given almost begrudgingly. The casual compliment ("nice job") is what many employees say keeps them motivated and coming to work each day. Though the lack of acknowledgment is a fairly trifling matter, it is deeply felt by these women.

These relatively small slights can catch women by surprise, or become clearer in hindsight. Debra, a member of the new generation of women entering the business world, recalled a particular incident occurring within two years of her being hired for her first job. Coming out of the Ivy League, she landed a position with a youthful, vibrant, and successful New York management consultancy. The company sported a modern, open office design, high technology enabling employees to work from anywhere at any time, and a supportive culture with work buddies and career mentors. Debra hit the ground running as soon as she started the job. It was a work-hard, play-hard environment, and Debra found herself excelling.

After a year and a half, those joining the company at the same time as Debra had their first opportunity for promotion. In this company, employees had to nominate themselves by submitting their names for consideration and a written rationale for why they should be promoted. Though Debra's semiannual reviews said that she was performing as well as or better than anyone else in her "class," she thought it a bit premature to self-nominate so early in her employment with the company. She presumed her peers would reach similar conclusions and would all wait six more months, at least.

When the congratulatory e-mail announcing new promotions was distributed, Debra was caught completely off guard. Right at the top of the list was the name of her co-worker, Matthew. He was in her class, started the same month as she did, and now he was a rung ahead of her on the ladder. To be honest, Debra found Matthew somewhat pompous and self-absorbed, so initially she assumed that it was his bravado that motivated him to submit his name. Then she got word through the office grapevine that Matthew had been encouraged by a senior manager to self-nominate and had been assured that his manager would support him. Debra didn't understand. In fairness, Matthew's work was good, but it wasn't that good. Why would management select him and not her? And if not her, there were definitely several other individuals worthy of selection. Though Debra was promoted in the subsequent round six months later, she was left with a queasy feeling of inequity. She asked herself, why six months later? Was it her fault or was it a gender thing?

Similar stories from women at all levels of the corporate hierarchy point to women being promoted later and less frequently than men. Though the slight to Debra may seem to have been trivial and unintended—after all, she was promoted within six months—we believe it is the beginning of a pattern that is built up over a career, leading in the end to a glass ceiling. While the management at Debra's company would certainly disavow any gender bias, small disparities repeated multiple times over the years grow into large inequities—whether or not they are intended.

While the small slights and disparities begin early in most women's working lives and accumulate over time, they seem to accelerate at the end of women's careers. Lynn recalls an experience that literally left her speechless. The incident occurred later in her career when she was a seasoned consultant and account manager who had demonstrated her effectiveness in the marketplace for close to twenty-five years. The firm she was working for had asked her to transfer to Connecticut, and she was traveling there with Andy, her superior, the regional head of account management, to discuss the possible transfer with the local leadership. She had worked with Andy multiple times over the prior two decades and thought she had earned his respect. That was why she was taken aback when, on the way to the meeting, Andy pulled her aside to offer some advice.

"I've seen you work for many years, and I know how good you are. But don't let these guys know how much you know. It will just offend them. Low key it."

Lynn knew that Andy meant his words as kindly counsel, but he was basically telling her to mute herself. When she entered the conference room and was introduced by Andy to the local leaders—all male—she was supposed to impress the group and sell herself, but what could she say? She had just been told by one of the most senior people in the firm to sell herself short.

Lower regard for a woman with long-term experience is common in the corporate world. The graying-at-the-temples man of fifty or so who has gained valuable insight and perspective from his many years of work is an icon of American business. He is the person from whom young employees can learn, whose avuncular attention can be so beneficial to a budding career. Change the graying man of fifty or so to a graying female of fifty or so and the image just doesn't work. In business, we've found less respect for the accumulated wisdom of the veteran businesswoman than for the wisdom of the veteran businessman. And even worse, as Andy pointed out to Lynn, the businesswoman who is confident, accomplished, and knowledgeable can actually be viewed as irritating.

The personal anecdotes of women provide a glimpse of life for a female in corporate America and reveal a business world in which most women struggle more than men. We've listened to these women and consequently were not surprised by the findings of a November 2008 survey of registered voters in the United States. "More than two-thirds of women said they were being treated unfairly in the workplace (68 percent)."[3] Many of the affronts are subtle, sometimes so hard to put a finger on that they leave one questioning whether they were real or imagined. But the stories abound, each unique in its own way. Taken individually, each story can be interpreted as reflective of personal circumstances, rather than as an example of a systemic bias. But when the stories are combined, certain common threads start to appear. When woven together, the threads create a tapestry in which women have a more difficult time than their male peers. They struggle with issues surrounding mistakes, weaknesses, successes, promotions, commitment, and work experience. While no woman is perfect, and women may cause their own problems just as often as men do, we begin to see a compelling case for believing that the business world is just plain harder for women than for men.

CRACKED BUT NOT BROKEN

The image is powerful: an invisible barrier through which women can see the positions of power but cannot pass to attain them. The glass ceiling metaphor is readily recognized as representing the limitations placed by the working world on women but not men. Though "it's got about 18 million cracks in it,"[4] according to Hillary Clinton, the glass ceiling continues to be perceived by many women as a mostly impermeable impediment. Yet many businessmen see the ceiling as shattered. A look at hard data replaces some of the rhetoric with fact.

Information collected by Catalyst, a leading nonprofit organization focusing on women in business, gives a more nuanced picture of the gender divide at the top of the corporate hierarchy. The Catalyst Pyramids presented in exhibit 1.1 show that in 1998 less than 1/2 of 1 percent of Fortune 500 CEOs were female, two CEOs out of five hundred. Ten years later there was an almost eight-fold increase, to fifteen women CEOs, representing 3 percent of Fortune 500 companies. The growth in the number of

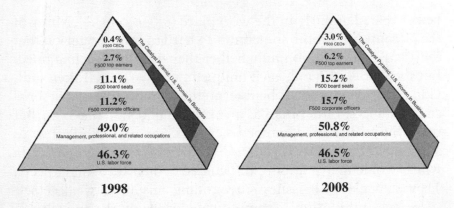

1998   **2008**

Exhibit 1.1: The Catalyst Pyramids[5]

Founded in 1962, Catalyst is the leading nonprofit membership organization working globally with businesses and the professions to build inclusive workplaces and expand opportunities for women and business. © Catalyst, October 1998 and June 2009

women in the highest echelons of the corporate hierarchy was not just at the pinnacle of the pyramid, either. Even among the top earners, the four or five most highly paid executives in each Fortune 500 company, the percentage of females more than doubled, rising from 2.7 percent to 6.2 percent, by 2008.

But then, let's look a little more closely at how things stack up. While women represented 3 percent of CEOs in 2008, they comprised 46.5 percent of the workforce, a rather large variance between top and bottom. A more distressing comparison is that women comprised more than half (50.8 percent) of the management, professional, and related occupations but only 6.2 percent of the top earners. Side by side, a comparison of the figures for 1998 and those of 2008 tells a strikingly positive story. The men sitting with Howard at the lunch table were right: women have made great progress. But within the pyramid, the differences still remain stark. Marilyn and the women in the diversity session were right: we still have far to go.

The height of today's glass ceiling can be measured more precisely, however, not at the top of the pyramid but in the middle, by looking at the number of corporate officers who are women. Corporate officers are those holding the power positions in a company—the heads of operating divisions, the chiefs of the finance functions, the top managers of the administrative departments. In 2008, only 15.7 percent of Fortune 500 corporate officers were women, even though the management pool from which they were drawn, the tier below them, was evenly populated, with females comprising 50.8 percent of its members.

Tracking the number of women who jumped from manager to corporate officer over time tells a truer, if more troubling story. Exhibit 1.2 shows the growth pattern of women corporate officers over a fourteen-year period for the years in which Catalyst collected data. (Catalyst did not tabulate data for 2001, 2003, and 2004, but commented that the results for those years were consistent with those for the years immediately before them.) In 1995, a meager 8.7 percent of corporate officers were women. This number increased gradually for the next ten years, almost doubling, to a peak of 16.4 percent in 2005. Then, something surprising happened. The percentage of female corporate officers actually decreased in 2006 and 2007 and leveled off in 2008. After a decade of progress, it's almost as if someone said, "Yeah, 15 percent, or one out of seven corporate officers, can be female. We can handle that. But that's all. That's enough."

Sue Ellen was one of the 15 percent. A star in the finance department of a high-profile beverage company, she was armed with an MBA from Columbia University and rose quickly up the corporate ladder to become the company's treasurer. She caught the eye of the enlightened CEO—a cool, suave man who was committed to gender diversity. Wanting to place a woman on his executive committee, the CEO promoted Sue Ellen to a corporate officer position, but not the one her training and prior work experience would have led her to expect. Sue Ellen was named senior vice president of human resources. While becoming chief financial officer would have been the logical

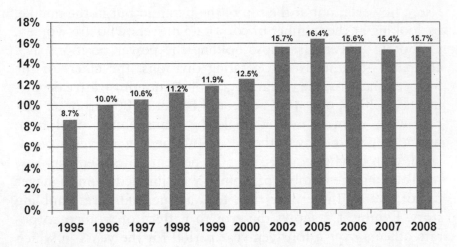

Exhibit 1.2: Percentage of Fortune 500 Corporate Officers
Who Are Women[6]

© Catalyst, June 2009

next step in her career path, Sue Ellen accepted the HR job,
thinking that "a seat at the table is a seat at the table, regardless
of what the place card says." Unfortunately, Sue Ellen's lack of
human resources experience proved her wrong. Her staff questioned her at every turn, and the CEO began to wonder about
her competence. Rather than advancing her career, her appointment undermined her once stellar reputation and weakened her
relationships with the other officers. Sue Ellen struggled in her
officer-level role for two years and then became so frustrated
that she left the corporate world altogether.

Too often, promotions such as Sue Ellen's are touted as
"breaking the glass ceiling" when in reality they are often examples of tokenism—the appointment of one woman, almost any
up-and-coming woman, to a senior-level position for which she
may be either not ready or not well suited. Catalyst tries to measure tokenism by tracking the number of Fortune 500 companies that have no more than one female corporate officer. By this
yardstick, 193 organizations, or 39 percent of the Fortune 500

companies, had only token representation in their officer ranks as recently as 2008.

But the pattern of token female officer representation over time is even more revealing, as shown in exhibit 1.3. Since 2000, the number of Fortune 500 companies with no women officers or only one such officer has not fallen below 164. That is to say that a stubborn 1/3 of Fortune 500 companies have no more than one female officer. While this is markedly better than pre-1998, when more than 50 percent of the Fortune 500 companies had at most one female officer, it still suggests that tokenism has been, and continues to be, a reality among major companies. Also haunting is the déjà vu pattern of conspicuous improvement in the late 1990s and early 2000s, followed by a leveling off and even some deterioration in subsequent years.

For women to be other than tokens, they must bring to the table experience and talents that are highly valued by the business. But even capable women who legitimately break into the corporate officer ranks are too often relegated to the less powerful and less influential positions. Rather than being

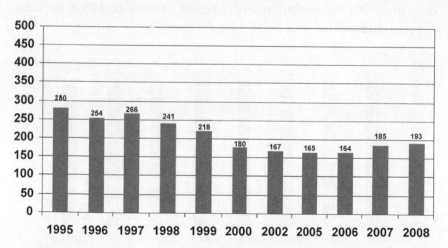

Exhibit 1.3: Number of Fortune 500 Companies with No Women Corporate Officers or Only One Woman Corporate Officer[7]

© Catalyst, June 2009

empowered by assuming "line" responsibilities—positions that typically have direct accountability for profit-and-loss or direct client service, women who make it to the top tier are too often steered into staff positions. Like Sue Ellen, they become the chief human resources officer, or the chief communications officer, or the head of some other function that is generally deemed support rather than part of the core business. Line versus staff is an important distinction because, as everyone in corporate knows, the power and prestige of a company lie in the line functions. Heads of operating companies, heads of divisions, heads of sales, heads of manufacturing—these are line positions. Line people are credited with "knowing the business."

The low numbers of women in corporate line positions attest to the tendency of even high-ranking women to be marginalized. In 2007, women comprised 15.4 percent of all officers, but they represented only 8.9 percent of the officers in line positions. In other words, 91.1 percent of line officers were men. And the progress women have made in populating line officer positions presents a now familiar pattern, as seen in exhibit 1.4. Women gained ground from 1997 (5.3 percent) to 2005 (10.6 percent), but, in 2006, the percentage of women line officers (9.8 percent) slipped downward and hasn't yet recovered.

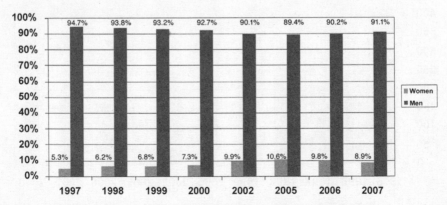

Exhibit 1.4: Percentage of Fortune 500 Corporate Officers in Line Positions by Gender[8]

© Catalyst, June 2009

Since line positions are more highly valued, those occupying them tend to be more highly paid. Therefore, it should come as no surprise that women are underrepresented among the top earners in companies. While there may be between fifteen and twenty corporate officers in each Fortune 500 company, the top earners form a more exclusive group of only four or five. In 2008, 15.7 percent of corporate officers were women, but only 6.2 percent of the top earners were women. Looked at another way, in total, the 2008 Fortune 500 companies had a little over 2,000 employees who were considered top earners. Of the 2,000, only 130 were women. On a per company basis, that was about 1/4 of a woman per company. Exhibit 1.5 compares the percentage of corporate officers who were women with the percentage of top earners who were women over the last fourteen years, and again we see a picture of marked improvement and a recent leveling off.

Some believe that the glass ceiling is the last obstacle to achieving equality of the sexes and that once women have broken into higher office, gender parity will prevail. We shall no longer need to worry because women will have made it. But the

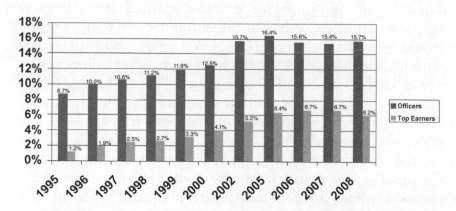

Exhibit 1.5: Percentage of Women Corporate Officers versus Women Top Earners in Fortune 500 Companies[9]

© Catalyst, June 2009

data indicate that a more complex phenomenon is in play. First, the numbers clearly show that women are not reaching the upper echelons of the business world in parity with men. Though progress has been made relative to ten or more years ago, we in corporate America are miles from achieving the equal representation of women in senior roles. Second, while the world of business may be growing more comfortable with having some women at the top, progress has stalled and by some measures has actually been reversed in recent years. Lately, the glass ceiling phenomenon has looked like a quota system. Finally, patterns of tokenism and redirection of women to staff and less influential support positions undermine whatever statistical progress can be claimed.

Men and women have been hacking away at the glass ceiling since before 1979, when the term was first coined. We believe the fact that substantive limitations still exist is symptomatic of deeper problems with issues more complicated than a simple reluctance to appoint women to high positions.

UNDER THE GLASS CEILING

The glass ceiling symbolizes gender disparities at the apex of corporate America. But many men, and even some women, would say that below the top levels, men and women are working shoulder to shoulder, climbing the steep, slippery corporate ladder side by side. Some even believe that being female can give a woman an edge in the rough and competitive corporate jungle. Though this vision of tough-but-true gender equity under the glass ceiling is one we would love to share, our impression is that in many companies, women at these levels are systemically and regularly undervalued relative to men. How men and women are paid in comparison to each other substantiates our perception.

The Bureau of Labor Statistics tracks earnings across all industries for the entire country. The aggregate data, when sorted by gender, give a bird's-eye view of the relative earnings of men and women. In 2008, the median weekly earnings for full-time employees in the United States were $722. Broken down by gender, though, the median man made $798, while the median woman made $638—a $160-a-week difference, or $8,320 a year. Looked at another way, for every dollar the median full-time working man made, the full-time working woman made 80 cents.

The male/female worker pay gap was worse thirty years ago. Exhibit 1.6 shows that, when adjusted for inflation, women earned $503 in weekly earnings in 1979 while men earned $807. Then, women were making only 62 cents for every dollar made by a man. By 2000, the gap had narrowed, to the point at which women made 77 cents for every dollar made by a man, but after that, the relative difference slowed, and women's earnings settled at around 80 cents for every dollar made by a man. Interestingly, the pattern of the pay gap is one of steady improvement through the 1990s, then a leveling off—just as we saw with the glass ceiling data.

Of the cornucopia of employment data collected and sorted each year by the Bureau of Labor Statistics, one of the most intriguing summaries is that giving data for full-time wage earners by sex and occupation. In this summary, jobs are grouped by "Standard Occupational Classification," which covers over 820 occupations grouped into 449 broad occupational classes. These broad classes are actually fairly specific, including groupings such as those of physicians, public relations managers, secretaries, and payroll clerks. Remarkably, in almost every job category, the median 2008 weekly earnings of men exceeded the median weekly earnings of women, in many cases by large amounts. The full-time male lawyer earned about 24 percent more than the full-time female lawyer. The male lab technician took home roughly 26 percent more than his female counterpart. Even male elementary and middle school teachers earned about 14 percent more than female teachers at the same grade level.

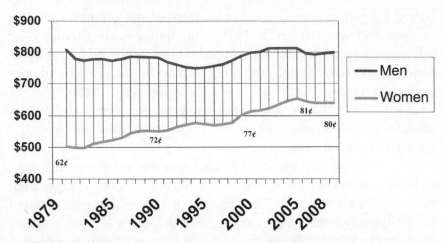

Exhibit 1.6: Median Weekly Earnings of Full-Time Employees
in the United States, in Constant (2008) Dollars[10]

Bureau of Labor Statistics, Report 1017, July 2009

When we focus on the occupations associated with the business world, the differences become egregious. Though slightly more women than men were categorized as working in management, professional, and related occupations, the men in this grouping earned at the median almost 40 percent more than the women—$1,238 a week versus $892. Men and women working in business and financial operations showed a gap of over 30 percent, with men earning $1,167 and women $885. Male customer service representatives earned $607; females earned $568. Even male secretaries and administrative assistants earned almost 20 percent more than their female co-workers, $736 versus $614. Keep in mind, these were all full-time workers.

Certainly, pay reflects many variables. For example, education and training will have a large impact on what an employee is paid, as will years on the job. Salary studies consistently show that those with a college degree average more than those with only a high school diploma. The competitive landscape and the size of the workforce are also factors. A high demand for computer engineers, combined with relatively small numbers in the market, will result in higher pay for computer engineers. The amount of responsibility a job entails will also have a big influence. Managing a product line of $10 million in sales generally garners a higher salary than managing a product line of $5 million. All these factors affect pay and may explain some of the persistent pay gaps between men and women.

Nevertheless, the year-after-year pattern of women earning less than men, regardless of occupation, makes one wonder. The American Association of University Women (AAUW) Educational Foundation went beyond wondering and commissioned an in-depth research project to explore the difference in compensation between men and women. The foundation's 2007 study, *Behind the Pay Gap*,[11] authored by Judy Goldberg Dey and Catherine Hill, attempts to answer the following question: if men and women with the same credentials and experience are doing the same job, will they be paid the same?

Drawing on data from the Department of Education *2000–2001 Baccalaureate and Beyond Longitudinal Study* and the *2003 Baccalaureate and Beyond Longitudinal Study*, the AAUW study analyzed the pay of men and women college graduates. First, it measured pay at two points in a career: one year after graduation and ten years after graduation. The findings: male graduates made more than female graduates—at both points. One year out of college, the women working full-time earned 80 cents for every dollar earned by their male former classmates (about $590 versus $740). For part-timers, it was 73 cents for every dollar. The situation became even worse with time, as shown in exhibit 1.7.[12] Ten years out of college, women graduates working full-time made 69 cents for every dollar the men made (roughly $950 versus $1375), and women working part-time made 56 cents for every dollar made by male part-timers.

But the striking revelation in the AAUW analysis is that even within the category of college majors, a substantive pay gap between men and women materialized surprisingly fast. Just one year out of college, women with degrees in mathematics earned only 76 cents for every dollar that men with mathematics degrees earned. The situation was the same in the humanities and biology, as seen in exhibit 1.8. Even in education, a field in which there were significantly more women than men, the gender pay gap was evident.

In its quest to dissect the pay gap between men and women, the AAUW study went an important and novel step further. The researchers identified five distinct areas that have a major impact on pay—education, choice of occupation, job sector, hours worked, and division of labor—and then measured how much of the pay gap between men and women was due to these factors. For example, in terms of education, the degree level as well as the selectivity of the college attended will affect pay. The choice of major will have an impact, in that male-dominated

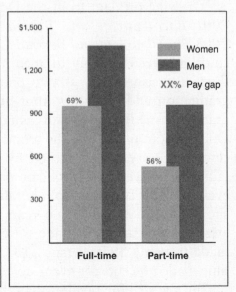

One year after college   **Ten years after college**

Exhibit 1.7: Average Weekly Wages[13]

By permission of AAUW Educational Foundation

majors (such as engineering, mathematics, and the physical sciences) pay more than female-dominated majors (such as education, health, and psychology). One's occupational choice can also influence salary, as when a mathematics major chooses to teach versus entering the business world. Men are more likely to work in the higher-paying, for-profit, and federal government sectors; whereas women are more likely to seek work in the lower-paying, nonprofit, and local government sectors. The total numbers of hours worked also need to be accounted for, since in both full-time and part-time jobs, men work more hours per week on average than women.

Controlling for all these factors, the AAUW study found that college-educated women earned 5 percent less than college-educated men one year out of school—and 12 percent less after ten years. Stated in another way, if men and women make identical career choices, the men will be paid more than the women. Even more disturbing, the study found that as more and more women choose a specific occupation—teacher, technician, phar-

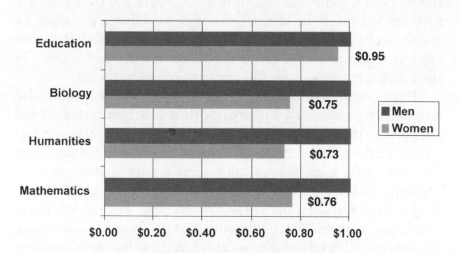

Exhibit 1.8: Relative Average Earnings within Majors, One Year after College Graduation[14]

By permission of AAUW Educational Foundation

macist—earnings in that occupation drop. In the concluding words of the study, "The gender pay gap has become a fixture of the U.S. workplace and is so ubiquitous that many simply view it as normal."[15]

On one level, pay is the people cost of running a business. Corporate compensation systems use a variety of statistical tools that take into account competitive practice, internal equity, and performance evaluations—all used to determine how much to pay employees. Companies spend large amounts of time managing the expense of employee compensation in an attempt to get it right—to make sure they're spending enough to get the people they need, but not so much that they will be at a disadvantage relative to their competitors. On an organizational level, pay is important.

Pay is important on an individual level as well. Ultimately, pay indicates the worth of a job and the value of an individual to the company. When a manager takes a new position, one of the first things he does is scrutinize pay levels for all the employees in his purview. Current base salaries, bonuses, and the ways in which these amounts have progressed over time are primary indicators to him of how much a company values an employee. With rare exceptions, managers believe that higher compensation is an indication of higher quality and ability. In the corporate world, pay and respect go hand in hand.

If pay is a barometer of value to the organization and women are consistently underpaid, then it is hard to avoid the conclusion that work done by women is systemically undervalued in the corporate world. Extensive government data and comprehensive foundation studies clearly show that women are regularly and inexplicably paid less than men. The problem lies deeper than the question of the glass ceiling. Beyond the anecdotal, the analysis of reliable data clearly shows a continuing inequity at all levels of the workforce. In a business environment where pay reflects the worth of the individual, women don't seem to be worth as much as men.

WHERE WE ARE TODAY

According to a November 2008 poll of U.S. voters, "only 20 percent of women are willing to use the word 'feminist' about themselves. Only 17 percent of all voters said they would welcome their daughters using that label."[16] Too often and for too many, the concept of feminist activism conjures up images of angry confrontations with men. We are at a point where both men and women are weary of the battle of the sexes in the workplace and want to avoid not only inflammatory language but also incendiary situations.

Some people point to the real progress that has been made since the modern-day women's movement began in the early 1960s. From their perspective, the seeds of gender equality have been sown, but they are slow growing, like a cactus plant. Give it more time, they say, and parity between men and women will become the norm. They are stalwart in their faith that as one generation replaces another, old patterns of bias will be replaced with new standards of equity. We wish we could concur, but we cannot. Evidence attests to the fact that women in business are still on an unlevel playing field. The progress achieved during the past forty years of fighting for women's rights in the workplace has stalled. And the place where we are stuck is far from providing parity between men and women at work.

When Lynn graduated from college in the early 1970s, she took her degree in mathematics and sought a job in the business world that would build on her capabilities and knowledge. She looked primarily at the insurance and financial industries, figuring that her mathematical background would be most valued there. Fearing that she would be directed to dead-end jobs in the typing pool or secretarial ranks, she made it clear on every job application that she did not type. In truth, she was all thumbs, and typing was the one course she failed in high school. Her reluctance to be assigned to a support staff occupation made her first job search more taxing, but eventually she was hired as the assistant to a sales manager at an insurance company. Her excitement and expectations were dampened, though, when on her first day of work, within an hour of her arrival at her desk, someone rolled a typewriter up to her and said, "This is for you." Not surprisingly, none of the male math majors of that time recall being automatically given an IBM Selectric.

Fast forward thirty years to when our daughter completed her college education. She graduated from a top-tier university among an impressive group of young men and women. As she and her friends dispersed through the streets of New York City looking for work, we felt we were in a time warp. Repeatedly, her female friends were steered toward jobs as administrative assistants, and a couple were actually tested on their word-processing skills. Not one of her male friends reported anything similar to this.

The experiences of our daughter and her friends in searching for work do not negate the progress that has been made by women in the business world. Certainly, doors have been opened; today, women can be found in almost every job category. In fact, women are represented throughout the corporate hierarchy. We have female CEOs, not just at "women's companies" such as Avon, but at Xerox and PepsiCo. But despite the gains, overall, positive change for women has come to a standstill.

The playing field is not level. We still have a problem, and we're stuck.

Chapter 2

SOLVING THE WRONG PROBLEM

BEFUDDLED MEN

Jim, a fit and trim fifty-three-year-old, was more successful at this stage of his life than he had ever dreamed. Yes, he went to an Ivy League college, but his hair almost reached his waist the day before his first corporate interview. He cut his hair, and corporate America more than repaid him for that first, painful, personal sacrifice. Now, some thirty years later, he headed a division of a Fortune 500 organization with over $500 million in annual revenues.

Jim's freshman class was the first at his college to fully integrate men and women, and he enthusiastically supported the coed movement. Personally, he enjoyed sharing the classroom with bright, articulate female students. He respected women of substance and ambition. His mother was strong, his wife stronger, and he liked it that way. He was perhaps excessively proud that his daughter was both an accomplished athlete and a stellar student.

Jim looked around the conference room table at his leadership group. These twenty executives, handpicked by him, were the people he relied on to get things done. He knew he wouldn't be where he was without them. They were a quality group and his successor would most likely come from among them. He had just one problem with them—eighteen men and two women. So disproportionately male. When Jim first entered the workforce, his peer group was pretty much fifty-fifty by gender, but as he moved up, the women thinned out. They seemed to disappear into the fog, to evaporate. It bothered him. He often found himself thinking, "How did this happen?"

Jim, like many corporate men, is genuinely befuddled. Jim and people like him are men who see themselves as supporters of women. They have looked into their souls and truly believe no prejudice exists there. Okay, when they first reported to a female boss it was a little rough, but they got over it. They actually learned to accept women not only as peers but as superiors in the corporate hierarchy. Their experience is firsthand and their consciences are clear. They view the world as having a multitude of qualified women, but, for some reason, most don't make it to the highest levels of the corporate ladder.

The smartest and most sincere of these men will take it to the next level and try to figure out why. Ironically, it is these well-intentioned men, as opposed to their blatantly prejudiced counterparts, who often get caught in the eye of the storm. Business titan Jack Welch and economist Lawrence H. Summers are prime examples.

Jack Welch and his wife, Suzy Welch, a former editor-in-chief of the *Harvard Business Review*, write a regular Q&A column in *BusinessWeek* magazine. In one issue, they tackled the question of why there aren't more women in senior executive positions in corporate America. While they acknowledge that there are still some "Neanderthals" who believe women don't belong in business, they explicitly state that "there is a second answer that isn't so easy. We say that because every time we mention it in speeches, the audience groans with discomfort. That answer is 'biology.' There are few women CEOs and a disproportionately small number of women executives because women have babies. And despite what some earnest but misguided social pundits might tell you, that matters."[1]

Not just the audience but the world groans when someone of Jack Welch's stature says things like this. (The fact that his talented wife was his coauthor is viewed, perhaps unfairly, as a stamp of approval.) Those who disagree with Welch go red with rage. Hard-working mothers in the business world can barely speak except to say, "Jack, *you* are the Neanderthal." Those who think there is some truth in what Welch is saying can't believe he is stirring up this ruckus again. Better to let sleeping dogs lie. Lawrence H. Summers's conjectures on this topic in January 2005 left even more people flabbergasted.

Summers, then president of Harvard University, had opined that one of the factors contributing to the relative lack of success of women in the sciences and math is "innate differences."[2] His comments were made at a small academic conference in Cambridge, but the furor they created led to a front-page *New York Times* headline: "At 2 Ivy Campuses, Conflict Is Thriving."[3] The story was covered by the *Times* for over a week, with one article declaring that there was "No Break in the Storm over Harvard President's Words."[4] Summers took a hard personal hit for openly expressing his thinking on why women's success is limited. Within two months, he suffered a no-confidence vote from the Harvard faculty and, within thirteen months, he was deposed as Harvard's president.

Lawrence Summers is not only a respected academician but also a former secretary of the Treasury under President Clinton and the current head of the National Economic Council for President Obama. You don't achieve that level of success without possessing some political savvy. How could someone of his intelligence and background make such a blunder? Yet Summers only seemed to dig himself in deeper when he refused to apologize and tried to clarify his comments: "My aim at the conference was to underscore that the situation is likely the product of a variety of factors and that further research can help us better understand their interplay. I do not presume to have confident answers, only the conviction that the harder we work to research and understand the situation, the better the prospects for long-term success."[5]

Jack Welch, Lawrence Summers, Jim, our Fortune 500 executive, and other men like them seem sincere in their desire to understand why so few women rise to the top. Their internal logic seems to go something like this: I and most of my male colleagues are not prejudiced against women, but there is no denying that there are few women in the senior ranks of my organization. Therefore, it must be something else. Something intrinsic to being female, something in a woman's biological makeup. For Welch, the answer is maternal physiology. For Summers, it's neurological wiring.

While it's intriguing that so many men are vulnerable to this line of reasoning, we think that there is value in recognizing, without cynicism, their heartfelt belief that they are not prejudiced. Time and again, we find men in business who sincerely see themselves as not biased against women and who wholeheartedly support the equality of men and women at work—in theory. Thinking they are not individually to blame for the disparities that persist, men understandably continue to look for something innately female that explains the inequities.

EXASPERATED WOMEN

Well-intentioned, intelligent women have been trying to figure out the reason for the inequities for some time as well. While most women will profess that they are not treated comparably to men in the corporate world, there is no consensus on why. Certainly, they feel the subtle inequities on a personal level. They've seen women crash into the glass ceiling. They have an instinctive as well as statistical awareness of the pay gap between men and women. But the underlying cause of the inequities is elusive. Like most men, most women just can't seem to put their finger on the root cause of the problem.

In seeking to understand the challenges confronting them, women's thinking tends to coalesce around two opposing perspectives. One perspective points outward, away from themselves, claiming the trouble is fundamentally with men. The other perspective points inward, focusing on personal inadequacies in their ability to compete with men in the business world. Frustrated, women either blame men or blame themselves.

The outward-looking point of view is the one most often associated, rightly or wrongly, with modern-day feminist activists. To those who look through this lens, the business world is a perpetual battleground pitting men against women. Women are blocked from achieving parity because of men's oppressive bias toward women. Therefore, women must band together to gain and maintain equal power. As Gloria Steinem warns, "Any woman who chooses to behave like a full human being should be warned that the armies of the status quo will treat her as something of a dirty joke. That's their natural and first weapon. She will need her sisterhood."[6] Though most feminists will claim that the ultimate goal is equality, some, though by no means all, would prefer more of a power-sharing détente with men rather than a harmonious integration of the sexes.

In the early 1990s, Pulitzer prize–winning journalist Susan Faludi went so far as to claim that the subjugation of women in the culture at large was a recurring historical phenomenon. In *Backlash: The Undeclared War against American Women*, Faludi contends that "if we retrace the course of women's rights back to the Victorian era, we wind up with a spiral that has made four revolutions. A struggle for women's rights gained force in the mid-nineteenth century, the early 1900s, the early 1940s and the early 1970s. In each case, the struggle yielded to backlash."[7] To some contemporary businesswomen, Faludi's déjà vu thesis rings true, as they recall the sexual discrimination tales told by their great-grandmothers, grandmothers, and mothers. How the highest corporate job an ambitious woman of the Depression era would ever be considered for was executive secretary; how young, college-educated women working for the phone company in the 1950s had to hide their engagement rings for fear of being fired; how working mothers in the 1980s found their careers downgraded to the mommy track as soon as they had a child. And now, with the force and regularity of Halley's Comet, the spiral is hurtling toward them for another strike. To Faludi's supporters, men's desire to oppress women seems perpetual, insatiable, and inescapable. Deep-rooted cultural misogyny can be the only explanation for such an egregious, repetitive pattern.

Yet most women we have worked with in the business world find a misogynistic premise paralyzingly depressing and too extreme to be consistent with their own personal experiences of work. They don't despise or distrust men and have no desire to constantly fight them. Rather, these women look inward and assume the roots of the disparities at work are due to some shortcoming in themselves. Perhaps if they could learn the rules of business better, understand the tactics more thoroughly, and find greater strength to persevere, then they could be as successful as men. To them, the issue is not one of men keeping women down, it's one of women not picking themselves up.

This line of thinking is pervasive in the multitude of self-help books targeted at women pursuing careers in business. "Women are the ones holding themselves back from top-level career success,"[8] claims Rebecca Shambaugh, author of *It's Not a Glass Ceiling, It's a Sticky Floor: Free Yourself from the Hidden Behaviors Sabotaging Your Career Success*. Or, as the synopsis of Gail Evans's bestseller *Play like a Man, Win like a Woman* puts it, "Men know these rules because they wrote them, but women often feel shut out of the process because they don't know when to speak up, when to ask for responsibility, what to say at an interview, and a lot of other key moves that can make or break a career."[9] These books proclaim that the path to success can be learned. The implicit message is that women, like Dorothy and her ruby slippers, have had the power and opportunity all along. The smart ones have figured this out, while the rest of the members of the female working population just need to open their eyes, take responsibility for themselves, and do what's necessary to succeed in the business world.

Sandy was a businesswoman who bought books that conveyed this viewpoint. By the middle of her career, she had already achieved some success, but she had ambitions for much more. Recently, she had been reading about communication styles—specifically, the differences between how men and women talk at work. She'd learned that men have a tendency to interrupt to make sure their points are heard, while women tend to wait until it's their turn to talk and then speak with less definitiveness and authority.

What Sandy read was consistent with her own frustrations at work. At internal meetings, she often felt unheard, not given the chance to express her ideas. Many times, the men seemed to talk right over her as if she wasn't even there. Now, after reading the book on communication styles, she could see with newfound clarity how many times men would say "just let me finish" to other men who interrupted them. The men's voices seemed to insist on being recognized.

So, armed with fresh insight and supported by the advice of her bestseller, Sandy decided to be more forceful and outspoken at internal meetings. She spoke up more often, spoke over some people a few times, and once even dared to ask her colleague Sam to let her finish what she had to say before he offered his own input.

After a month of Sandy's feeling empowered by her new approach, Sandy's boss stopped by to see her. "Are you okay?" he inquired. "Lately, you seem agitated and somewhat aggressive. You even snapped at Sam the other day at our meeting. A couple of people have asked me if you are having some problems at home. Is something wrong?"

Yes, something is wrong. Despite all their efforts to fit in, many women such as Sandy still feel on the outs. They never seem to get it quite right. What's worse is the self-punishing subliminal message that comes with this inward personal assessment—it's really your own fault. If women would just get it right, all these problems with women in the workplace would disappear.

The outward-looking perspective points to men as the primary culprit. The inward-looking perspective lays the fault at the feet of women. Ironically, the two points of view do share a common thread. Looking outward, one concludes that men need to behave differently. They need to reject their misogynistic tendencies and take the moral high ground. In essence, they need to be better men. Looking inward, the conclusion focuses on women's behavior. Women need to learn the ways and skills of the business world that they wish to enter, which is a man's world. In short, women think they, too, need to be better men.

Women are left with two approaches for dealing with men at work: fight them or become them. Women can choose to believe that men constitute a perpetual opposing force that impedes women's drive to succeed. Or women can believe that men have figured out the business world, and women just need to identify what men do and do the same thing. But these two strategies are often deeply at odds with how women relate to the men in their private lives. Most will say they generally get along well with their fathers, brothers, and husbands, as well as the men they work with day in, day out. These relationships are not based on mistrust or conflict or aping men. Yet their positive personal experiences with the individual men in their daily lives rarely seem to translate into parity in the workplace. Regardless of how well women feel they get along with men, or how well they perform in comparison to men, they just don't seem to be treated as well as men at work.

We see many men and women earnestly attempting to maintain a work environment where the sexes have equal opportunities and receive comparable treatment. Though progress has been made, significant inequalities persist. The continuing inequities and the stalled progress, despite sincere and plentiful efforts, strongly suggest that the problem is not primarily a matter of individual behavior. Neither the biases of men nor the inadequacies of women seem to be the main source of the disparity between them. Rather, we suspect it is the obstacles themselves that are the impediment—not men's efforts to preserve them nor women's ability to get around them.

LOOKING BACK TO MOVE FORWARD

In our own journey of discovery, we too struggled with finding the root cause of today's gender inequity in the workplace. While we clearly saw the lack of parity between men and women at work during our three decades in corporate life, we were challenged in understanding why. We thought that gaining a historical perspective might advance our thinking. To move forward, we needed first to look backward.

No one will dispute that well into the 1960s, business was truly a man's world. Corporate power, prestige, and pecuniary benefits were all structured to attract, retain, and motivate men. Women's numbers in certain white-collar industries such as insurance and banking may have been plentiful, but they were limited to secondary support roles, to the invisible jobs. They typed, they filed, they brought coffee. One need only review the business writings of the time to understand how completely the culture of business revolved around men.

A perfect example is *The New Industrial State* by John Kenneth Galbraith, the noted economist and prolific author of the era.[10] First published in 1967, *New Industrial State* was the definitive text on contemporary economic life and evolving trends. It accurately predicted the growth and influence of the corporate entity and the shift from industrial to service economies. What is striking when one reads through the first edition of *The New Industrial State* is how casually and consistently Galbraith spoke as if there were no women in the business environment. We are not just talking about pronouns here. We are talking about page after page of explanation and illustration that were written as if women did not exist. "A good man is committed to the common professional, artistic and scientific goals; he seeks to alter these in accordance with his instinct, taste or knowledge"[11] or "Men are, in fact, either sustained by organization or they sustain organization"[12] or "An individual comes to think of himself as an IBM man, a Corning Glass man or a Sears man."[13] In those times, the company man was the model of success, embodying the values and predominance of American business. There was no comparable concept of the company woman.

While the conservative business world may have been catering to men in the 1960s, the sociopolitical world was heralding the birth of the modern-day women's movement. Betty Friedan's groundbreaking *The Feminine Mystique*,[14] first published in 1963, challenged the secondary, supportive roles women had traditionally occupied in American society and led to a vociferous discourse on the state of women in the country. Friedan put into words the dissatisfaction of many suburban wives as "The Problem That Has No Name,"[15] and her solution took aim straight at women and work: "The amateur or dilettante whose own work is not good enough for anyone to want to pay to hear or see or read does not gain real status by it in society, or real personal identity. These are reserved for those who have made the effort, acquired the knowledge and expertise to become professionals."[16] *The Feminine Mystique* challenged women to get out of the house and into the paid workforce. With American women on the march and corporate men oblivious to their existence, a battle was in the making.

The debate sparked by *The Feminine Mystique* exploded into profound political activity in the early 1970s, when three landmark events occurred in quick succession within ten months of each other: the passage by the U.S. Congress of the Equal Rights Amendment (ERA) on March 22, 1972; the adoption of Title IX of the Education Amendments of 1972 on June 23, 1972; and the decision of the U.S. Supreme Court in *Roe v. Wade* on January 22, 1973. Each on its own was powerful ammunition in the battle of the sexes, but, taken together, they fueled an explosion of change and conflict.

Only fifty-five words long, the Equal Rights Amendment (ERA) stated:

> Section 1. Equality of rights under the law shall not be denied or abridged by the United States or by any state on account of sex.
>
> Section 2. The Congress shall have the power to enforce, by appropriate legislation, the provisions of this article.
>
> Section 3. This amendment shall take effect two years after the date of ratification.[17]

The adoption by the U.S. Congress of these succinct words delivered a potent popular message: equal rights under the law would be explicitly and unequivocally guaranteed for women by the U.S. Constitution. In the minds of many women entering the workforce at that time, the passage of the ERA represented definitive evidence that the country had come to its senses and was putting into law what was only fair and obvious. Optimistically, many young men and women had little doubt that the amendment would be ratified by the requisite 2/3 of the states. From their perspective, society had deemed women entitled not only to equal rights under the law but also to equal economic opportunity. One naturally flowed from the other. With the passage of the ERA, most of our generation thought the battle of the sexes was over and women had won.

Title IX, adopted three months after the ERA, created less of a stir at the time but probably delivered more of a long-term punch, especially since the ERA was never ratified and therefore never became law. Simple in concept, Title IX prohibited educational institutions that received federal money from discriminating by sex. The most direct impact of the legislation was on school athletic programs. Today, we sometimes forget that many schools excluded girls and young women from serious athletics, regarding their participation as inappropriate and unladylike. While women's athletic programs were greatly expanded as a result of Title IX, the opportunities given to young women to learn the rules of participation in sports, particularly team sports, proved to be the lasting reverberations of the legislation. The lessons of team play, strategic thinking, winning and losing graciously, and performing under intense competitive pressure were no longer to be solely the province of boys. Title IX allowed girls to obtain the character-building education that comes with playing serious athletics, to learn the lessons so crucial to postacademic life, particularly in the business world.

Six months after Title IX was passed, the Supreme Court issued its decision in the case of *Roe v. Wade*. The legalization of abortion, still a major subject of controversy today, gave women ultimate control over whether and when to have children. In combination with the growing array of other readily available forms of reliable contraception, the landmark decision meant that women had command of not only their bodies but their destinies. The choice of family or career did not have to be an either/or matter anymore. Babies could come after professional training. Children could wait until couples could afford good childcare. With more power over their reproductive physiology, women could assume more of the financial responsibility of providing for their families and raising their standard of living.

Taken together, the ERA, Title IX, and *Roe v. Wade* provided a clarion call to the business world to wake up to a new day. But most of the corporate world was initially tone deaf. Emerging from college in the early 1970s, we and our friends firmly believed that equality of the sexes was the inevitable future. Our career ambitions were high and many of our marriages were initially predicated on a greater extent of financial sharing, certainly more than among our parents' generation. While we felt empowered by all the political activity of the 1970s, our day-to-day work reality was that jobs still seemed to be assigned by gender. Men monopolized the management roles, the professional occupations, and anything that had a career track associated with it. Women were relegated to the support positions such as those of secretaries and research assistants. Men gave direction; women took direction. Women had typewriters on their desks; men had calculators. There was no question that men had the better jobs. Not only did their work have higher status in the corporate community, but they were paid more—a lot more.

One story from a human resources consultancy we're familiar with is emblematic of the mind-set. It was 1975, and Barbara, a sharp young woman who had initially been assigned to the research department, was now the right-hand "man" of the firm's top East Coast account manager, who resided in New York. Maria worked in the Chicago office and had also been assigned to the account management group as an assistant. The way Barbara told it, she and Maria had deduced that they were performing the same functions as the young men who had been hired as account managers in training. But neither Barbara nor Maria had the prestigious title or the higher pay. The inequity came to the fore at an annual meeting when Ned, the national head of the group, announced that Maria would be going to California and "doing what Barbie is doing in New York." Barbara approached Ned during a break and questioned why she and Maria had been singled out. "It sounds like we're going to be doing the same things that the men are doing."

"You aren't going to be doing the same things," Ned casually replied. "They are going to be account managers and you and Maria aren't."

"But I am doing exactly what the men are doing, and I've been doing it longer than most of them."

Ned's response to Barbara was classic: "But Barbie, girls can't be account managers."

It's interesting to note that in all 427 pages of Galbraith's *The New Industrial State*, the seminal business text of the time, there is not one disparaging word about women in the workplace. Rather, women seem to be irrelevant to the business world. We must say that this is consistent with what we found in our first work environments. Men had their work roles and women had theirs. The system of job assignments by gender was clear and accepted. There was no antipathy and very little ambiguity.

But eventually, companies were forced to change. Even though the ERA never became the twenty-seventh amendment to the U.S. Constitution, a number of states adopted some form of equal rights legislation, and it soon became illegal to define jobs by gender. Consciousness had been raised. Business began to respond, and work that had traditionally belonged to men started to become available to women. Suddenly, women could be doctors, lawyers, accountants, even account managers. Policemen became police officers; firemen became firefighters. At an unprecedented rate, doors that had been locked for years were opened. In the course of it all, an implicit deal was brokered: if women obtained the education and training necessary for a job, they would not be denied access to that job due to their gender.

It was not an easy transition, though. Sexual harassment and job discrimination were initially rampant. Women on the front lines recall being brought to tears by the egregious behavior of some of their male co-workers. While making a formal presentation to a predominantly male group, one woman remembers innocently saying, "I have two points—," when she was rudely interrupted by a voice from the back corner, sniping, "And we can see both of them." Her mortification deepened when all the other members of the group roared with laughter. Another woman recalls a fellow salesperson, an unassuming married man with whom she was friendly, quietly coming into her office, closing the door as if he wanted to tell her something confidential, and forcing himself on her. She was able to wriggle her way out of his grasp, but when she told her manager about the incident, his advice was, "Hey, you're a big girl, you can handle yourself." Women wanted the better jobs that had been reserved for men in the past, but the price could seem exorbitant at times. Men's reluctance to concede their exclusive possession of these jobs and to accept women in these roles was turning the once orderly workplace into a war zone.

Women's historical fight to obtain equal access to traditionally male jobs has been well chronicled in the popular press, aggressively pursued in the country's courtrooms, and romantically celebrated in the movies. In most stock representations of the early conflicts, the corporate world is the villain—the stalwart, conservative organization that will go to extremes to continue the repression of women. This depiction of the business world belies the significant time and money expended by many corporations to assure that women had the right to any and all of the corporate jobs for which they were qualified. From the corporate perspective, job access was the big problem. To rectify it, business had to proactively and aggressively address sex-based job discrimination and hostile work environments. Though some companies resisted, most addressed the problem aggressively. Policies were rewritten, value statements were changed, and administrative rules were revised. Virtually every major company explicitly proclaimed nondiscrimination as the new standard and decried sexual harassment toward women.

A crucial component of the antidiscrimination effort was mandatory, company-wide diversity training. Most major corporations invested in a one- or two-day session that denounced sexual harassment and reinforced the company's policy of equal opportunity employment. The classes taught managers what to do, or more often what not to do, to accommodate women in their ranks. Employee communiqués announced that harassment was cause for termination, and that any woman who was sexually harassed had a right to speak up. Hiring initiatives made it clear that women as well as men were to be recruited for management and professional positions. The messages were unambiguous and direct, but interestingly, different by gender. Men were told to be tolerant of women and to avoid inappropriate and offensive behavior. In other words, don't be a jerk. Women were told to learn the rules, fit in, put in your time like any good corporate citizen, and you will be treated fairly.

The corporate energy devoted over the past thirty years to getting women into jobs that were traditionally reserved for men has resulted in enormous success. Today, roughly 50 percent of managers, professionals, and those in related occupations are women. Classes in medical and law schools are composed of equal numbers of men and women. Over 30 percent of the students at graduate-level business schools are women. Women have reached the top rungs of the corporate ladder and can be found on all the other rungs as well. The Bureau of Labor Statistics data on Standard Occupational Classes confirm that women are represented in virtually every single job category, from chemical engineer to bus driver, from chief executive to janitor. The sexual harassment that intimidated and abused so many women in the past has become legally, politically, and socially repugnant.

Today, corporate jobs are not considered either male or female, and no woman is barred from a job solely because of her sex. Our review of corporate history has led us to conclude that it is time to declare the once formidable access issue for women in business solved. This is not to say that gender discrimination at work is over. We certainly proved in chapter 1 that we are far from gender equality. Rather, we believe that business's continued focus on getting women into the corporate system, though successful in addressing the job access problems of the past, cannot and will not resolve the issues women face today. In fact, business's persistence in some efforts may actually exacerbate today's difficulties.

DIFFERENCES AND HEADCOUNTS

Amanda felt bad. Recently promoted to manager, she had just completed a day and a half of diversity training. Though she had started the sessions feeling good about herself and her colleagues, she definitely felt bad now. The audience for the training consisted of all the managers in her department, about twenty employees. During the first day, the leader of the session went around the room and asked men and women to talk about their roots, their upbringing, their values, themselves. The men pretty much outranked the women of the group, but in this setting the women were encouraged to speak as equals—and share.

Maybe Amanda's discomfort came from sharing too much. She told of always being competitive in nature, loving to play games, and hating to lose. Growing up she had found an outlet in sports, but these juices would now flow in competitive business situations. She then listened to others speak of their backgrounds and characterize themselves. Though she interacted with these people every day, she had never connected with them this way before. The training was like group therapy.

Everyone was so accepting—until the leader started lecturing about the innate differences between men and women. "Women are naturally nurturing; men are competitive. Women are more understanding; men are more driven." The list went on and on. The leader then counseled, "Take your underlying nature into consideration when you are dealing with the opposite sex at work. Don't deny it."

Amanda wanted to sink into the floor. She had just told everyone how competitive she was, how driven and ambitious. Being nurturing and being understanding were not her strong points. Now she felt so exposed, so unattractive, so unfeminine. That's when she started to feel bad.

With the power of corporate America predominantly in male hands, the diversity message to the power brokers has been and generally continues to be "let the women in and learn to live with them." As if these women were aliens landing from Mars—or maybe Venus—most diversity training attempts to educate participants on what is inherently different about the sexes, and then preaches tolerance.

Men are competitive; women are collaborative. Men interrupt; women acquiesce. Men are succinct and direct in their communications; women are verbose and indirect. Men are self-promoting; women are self-effacing. Men are analytical; women are creative. Men are rational; women are intuitive. Men are stoical; women are expressive. One diversity training seminar we attended displayed six separate sketches of a woman's face, her eyes widening or her mouth frowning to reflect the various emotions she was experiencing. Whether it was expressing joy, fear, or anger, the female face was easy to read. This was followed by another six slides showing a man's face meant to express the same set of emotions. Each picture of the man's face was exactly the same. Fear looked like joy, which looked like anger. It wasn't a mistake. The six different emotions the man was feeling were clearly labeled on the bottom of each slide.

The well-intentioned purpose of this type of training is to promote understanding and tolerance, but many women we speak with tell us that this common approach actually tends to make matters worse for them. First, the training creates a conundrum for a businesswoman: What is she supposed to do with this information? Her personality may or may not conform to these female stereotypes. If most of the "feminine" characteristics apply to particular women, delineating them in front of men makes these women feel like misfits. The subliminal message is this: whereas male workers are naturally endowed with the appropriate traits for business success, women are born different and always will be. They can try to adapt, but they will be fighting their God-given nature. Real women will never fit into the business world.

Or perhaps a particular woman's style is naturally more taciturn or intensely competitive, exhibiting characteristics the trainers have attributed to men. Theoretically, this should improve the woman's chances of success, but having these "masculine" traits is likely to result in her being shunned by both men and women as abnormal or unappealing. And frankly, it usually doesn't make the woman feel so great about herself. What woman wants to be seen as masculine? Just as bad is the predicament of the poor sensitive man who is stereotyped as "feminine" because he has been known to blush or shed a tear or two.

A further spurious premise of most diversity training is that male and female traits are inborn and static. The truth is that most of the characteristics labeled "masculine" and "feminine" are transient cultural concepts, as seen through the prism of the diversity trainer's personal perspective. Different cultures and different generations have had different models of masculinity and femininity at different times. Even within one generation, concepts may change over time. Take the American perception of the female athlete. Women athletes, especially those who played team sports, had a limited appeal to our parents' generation. Their competitive drive and aggressiveness were considered distastefully masculine. The beautiful, acquiescent femininity of Jackie Kennedy was their ideal. The prevailing attitude is best summarized by Lynn's mother's regular admonition to her: "Ladies don't sweat; they perspire." But today, young female athletes are considered to be appealing and admirably sweaty, as evinced by images of the Williams sisters' muscled, moist, taut bodies plastered on billboards. Perceptions change. Even our parents now sincerely admire their granddaughter's athletic prowess.

Affinity groups, a relatively recent means of promoting a diverse workforce, can have some of the same inadvertent drawbacks as the classic approach to diversity. The idea behind these groups is to create support networks for employees who share a common bond and face similar challenges of discrimination in the workplace. The common feature is generally race, ethnicity, gender, or sexual orientation. Theoretically, employees in an affinity group can rely on their fellow members for advice on how to handle difficult situations, for a perspective on the environment in which they work, for release from daily tensions, and for affiliations to counter loneliness. For women and members of other minority groups, affinity groups can be very effective in providing comfort. But they can also be an impediment to achieving the equality that is their core goal. Bonding over what you have in common, ethnically or physiologically, with some people emphasizes what you don't have in common with others. This easily degenerates into the creation of divisive camps within a company. Like affirmative action, affinity groups can be effective in helping to break down barriers. But once a group has broken into the system, maintaining formal affiliations exclusively based on race, color, creed, or sex can actually discourage egalitarian integration.

If focusing on gender differences is an ineffective tactic for creating an environment of gender equality, female headcounts may be an equally misguided measure of success. Too often it has been assumed that if there are equal numbers of males and females in a job—as engineers, for example—then it's reasonable to assume that there are no gender-related problems for women in that profession. But an equal headcount does not mean equality. We've seen the pay gap that exists between men and women across virtually all job classifications. We've enumerated the daily inequities that women endure at work solely due to their gender. Even if the headcount numbers are level, the playing field may not be. Certainly, a low female headcount can be indicative of a problem. But the headcount is a symptom, not a solution. The glass ceiling is a perfect case in point. Merely increasing the number of women in the upper echelons of business will not bring about equality of the sexes throughout an organization. The issues women face today are too complex for a headcount to be treated as a cure-all.

Finally, if we consider the amount of attention companies have given to providing women access to any job for which they're qualified, it is not surprising that some men feel that the scales have tilted too far to the benefit of women. They look around and see women everywhere. So why is it necessary to continue all the initiatives and training that were intended to get women into the system? These men begin to feel that business has overshot the mark, and women have become a favored class rather than second class. Men's resentment grows, creating another workplace problem for women.

The methods used by business to bring women into the corporate system were based on a recognition and acceptance of the differences between men and women. But emphasizing differences between people may perpetuate discriminatory values, and any student of human nature knows that undue favoritism breeds ill will. The intent was pure, and the result regarding women's access to jobs has been positive. But continuing down the same path will most likely not yield further progress and may actually fuel disharmony. Business needs to realize that the methods used to solve the problem of getting women into the corporate system—diversity training based on acceptance of differences, headcount management by gender, the use of affinity groups, and other current approaches—may not be effective in addressing today's issues. The problem has fundamentally changed. We must redefine the problems that women face and fashion new solutions that will lead to true equality between men and women at work.

THE RIGHT PROBLEM

"Grandpa, I need to figure out what I'm going to do in life. I only have a year and a half left in college, and then I'm out in the real world," said our daughter. She and her grandfather had always been close. "I'm a math major, so I'd like to build on that somehow. But I'm not sure what direction to go."

"You know, I remember having a conversation like this with your mother," Grandpa replied. "She was thinking about becoming an actuary when she was your age, since she also was a math major. Now, I barely knew what an actuary was back then, but we had a neighbor who lived down the street who happened to be an actuary for an insurance company. So one day I asked him how your mother could get into the field, and I still remember what he said: 'That's not a suitable job for a woman.'"

Our daughter was stunned. "You're kidding," she said.

"No, that's exactly what he said. But things are a lot different today. No job is off the table for you."

Today, no woman can be denied a position solely due to her gender. The enormity of that statement often escapes people. But, it's true—and what a huge success it represents. The progress made in opening doors for women in business is nothing short of phenomenal. Since the modern women's movement began in the 1960s, the corporate world has undergone a transformation of enormous proportions. Both men and women have done what was asked of them. Most men have overcome their prejudices and let women into the system; many, many women have obtained the education and training they needed and done their jobs well. This success is so pervasive that it is often taken for granted. Too rarely do men and women take a moment to acknowledge and celebrate this outstanding accomplishment, which has been achieved in only one generation.

Despite the triumph of getting women into the system of business, true equality between men and women has not yet been attained. Pay differences proliferate, the job satisfaction of female employees deteriorates, and progress has stalled. The highest levels in the largest companies are still bastions of male power. Rather than bemoan these problems that women face today, we suggest harnessing the energy, the sincerity, and the power that has been so successful in the past and pointing it in the right direction.

The previous problem, that of access—of certain positions in the corporate system being reserved exclusively for men—was clearly visible. It could be easily identified the moment a management meeting was convened. Progress could be measured by anyone with a personnel list and a calculator. The behaviors and obstacles that kept women from obtaining the jobs traditionally held by men were conspicuous and often egregiously offensive, not to mention illegal. Today's issues of gender inequity are more subtle and complex. The patterns of discrimination have evolved from direct aggression to passive aggression. It's not that women are excluded; they are just not included. It's not what is said to women; it's what is said about them. It's not that women don't have the good jobs; it's that they don't get ahead in their jobs. The new nature of the problem makes it more difficult to illuminate and more challenging to eradicate.

We believe that the fundamental problem facing women in business today has metamorphosed from *getting into the corporate system* to *working within the corporate system*. Today, women's experience as they work within the corporate system is simply more difficult than that of men of comparable talent and ability. Though the language of the old and new problems may contain some overlap, the distinction is huge. The old problem was attributable to personal mind-set and corporate policy. The new problem is one of group dynamics and corporate culture.

With this new perspective, the glass ceiling and pay inequity can be seen not as problems in and of themselves but rather as manifestations of the fundamental problem of women working within the corporate system. What is crucial is the concept of comparable treatment. If women are not doing as good a job as their male counterparts, they should be lower on the ladder and paid less. But more often, we find that men and women of comparable value are not treated comparably. Women have the jobs, they are in the corporate system, but they do not move through the system with the same ease, alacrity, and success as their male counterparts.

Corporate culture is at the heart of today's situation. What people do and how they act are not always reflections of what they truly believe. Sometimes behaviors reflect the cultures people live in as much as or more than personal principles. This is especially true in an environment such as the business world, where following orders and maintaining discipline are prerequisites for survival. We contend that the corporate system and the business culture it creates are plagued by remnants of the past that foment disparity between men and women today.

Corporate culture is hard to see but impossible to avoid. This is why identifying the new impediments to gender equity are so elusive. Many men and women are frustrated by today's issues at work because they don't recognize them as cultural norms. They continue to look at each other or themselves as the problem, for it's difficult to perceive the force of corporate culture and the way it creates and sustains inequities.

We believe confusion and frustration can be replaced by understanding and progress, once the right problem is brought to light. Acknowledging that a change has occurred allows us to celebrate the successes of the past and to be optimistic that more progress is possible in the future. In addition, we can let the majority of men, women, and business communities off the hook for the gender inequities that persist. For the most part, the new problem is not a result of the individual biases of men; few men profess continuing prejudice against women. Nor is it necessarily due to the inadequacies of women; multitudes of working women have proven they can perform the tasks required for a career in the business world. It's rarely even the fault of individual organizations; the vast majority of companies sincerely want to solve the gender inequities and diversity challenges in their workplace. We can eliminate the guilt, blame, and finger pointing, and move on. Framing the right problem regarding gender issues—that women's experience *working within the corporate system* is more difficult than that of men with comparable experience and worth—opens wide the door to understanding the invisible systemic and cultural forces that keep us from achieving true equality of men and women at work.

Chapter 3

CAUGHT ON A MALE PROVING GROUND

WORKING WITHIN THE SYSTEM

Michael sat at his desk, shaking his head in disbelief. His co-worker Maureen had just left his office. Michael had always thought highly of Maureen, but in this instance, he found her judgment seriously flawed.

Since they had first started working together five years earlier, Michael and Maureen had been kindred spirits. Both were MDs who, at about the same point in their medical careers, left promising private practices to join a major pharmaceutical company. Their reasons for the career shift were strikingly similar. Both felt that they could have a greater impact on the health and well-being of the population by working for a large pharmaceutical company on the development of effective drugs.

But now Michael thought Maureen might be committing career suicide. Ironically, Michael agreed with Maureen. They both thought that the new Alzheimer's drug should be brought to market immediately and did not need more clinical trials. Maureen had put together what Michael thought was a strong and compelling presentation supporting this position, and both were disappointed when their boss, Larry, didn't agree.

Michael's reaction to Larry's decision was reflexive, though. He thought to himself, "That's how it goes sometimes." Long ago, Michael had accepted that, in corporate life, you win some and you lose some.

The next day Michael was ready to move on when a clearly agitated Maureen stepped into his office asking, "Can I speak to you?" When Michael nodded, she closed the door and continued, "I think we should go to John about the Alzheimer's drug." John was the head of their division and Larry's boss.

"I'm not sure that's such a good idea, Maureen. I think this is over and we have to let it go," Michael cautioned.

"No, it's been on my mind all night, and I think this is a big mistake. Larry just doesn't get it," Maureen insisted.

"Look, I can't stop you from doing what you think you need to do, but to go around Larry? Are you sure you want to do this?"

"Yes, I'm sure. Will you come with me?"

"No, I don't think so," Michael protested. "It doesn't feel right to me."

"Okay," Maureen said. Then she stood up and walked out.

Michael was uneasy because, from where he sat, Maureen was stepping outside the bounds of her assigned role. She was subordinate to Larry. By circumventing him without his knowledge, she was violating an unwritten rule of business: you don't challenge the power structure by going around your boss. You stay within the boundaries of your responsibilities and submit to the authority of those who are more empowered than you. The business system—what protocols are followed, which behaviors are acceptable—is guided by a number of these general rules.

We have stated that the essential problem women face in business has shifted from *getting into the system* to *working within the system*—that today, women's experience in functioning within the business world is just plain harder than that of comparable men. To understand why, we must explore the nature of working within the corporate system and what is required by its general rules.

In most major companies, strong corporate cultures exert pressure on employees to conform to certain standards. Some of the requirements are specific to an organization, such as how to prepare a report or how to dress for a meeting. Others are basic working rules that are intrinsic to the entire system of business and apply across cultures. The rules set a common code of behavior that not only promotes efficiency and productivity within a company but also allows for the mobility of people between businesses. Often referred to as "just how things are done," these rules provide guidance to employees for getting along, fitting in, and relating well to others.

Although they are pervasive, the overarching rules tend to be tacit—they are sometimes called the invisible rules. Rarely are these everyday working principles documented in corporate literature or explicitly taught in company training classes. Instead, they are acquired through experience, conveyed by mentors, learned from friends and family, and reinforced by co-workers. Their origins can be found in the behaviors expected from those in the military and on athletic teams, with a sprinkling of the spirit of fraternities. Since, historically, men have had an advantage over women in being exposed to the rules early in their lives, a cadre of self-help books has emerged to help women "catch up."

Five of the more important general rules are:

- be a team player,
- find mentors and win advocates,
- demonstrate commitment,
- bond with your co-workers, and
- be prudent in challenging the power structure.

These rules are staples of corporate life that enhance a company's productive operation. They promote consistent behavior and universal purpose, which are crucial components of corporate order and organization. Respecting the power structure keeps everyone focused and toeing the line. Bonding with co-workers and being a good team player facilitate smooth daily employee interactions. Finding mentors and winning advocates encourage the transfer of knowledge and the sharing of experience from one generation to the next. The amount of emphasis that is placed on each rule may vary from company to company, but to some degree, all the rules are present in and part of every corporate culture. Demonstrating intense commitment to your job may be more valued at a high-powered financial institution than at a fast food restaurant, but it counts in both places.

Group dynamics primarily enforce the rules, and the resulting pressure to conform to cultural expectations can be both powerful and elusive. Sometimes censorious looks deliver the message that an employee is not following expected behavior. At other times, exclusion from a lunch group or an important meeting will signal disapproval. Direct confrontations are rare. Rather, subtle indications and passive intimations are the norm. Nevertheless, within a short period of time after being hired, employees are expected to pick up the signs of what is acceptable and what is not in their environment, or else leave. One senior executive of a major multinational corporation, while speaking at a leadership conference, likened the dynamic to the body's rejection of a splinter. "People don't get fired for not fitting into the culture; it's more of a throbbing organizational pressure that leads to an employee's departure."

Theoretically, women should be able to adapt as easily as men to a company's culture and comply with its rules. Yet we find it is something in the invisible rules that usually trips up women in today's business world. Women's work product is rarely the problem. Many women will say they are trying to follow the rules, but they find themselves lost on the playing field. "It's not like I haven't tried to figure this out. I've bought the books," explains one businesswoman, "but it's as if the rules don't work for me." As in the case of the metaphorical splinter, the pressure of corporate culture eventually leads to these women either being rejected by the system or being sidelined in their advancement.

That women have more trouble than their male counterparts with the business system's rules has been perplexing to us over the years. Often we've witnessed women doing or saying exactly the same things as their male peers but experiencing startlingly different outcomes. Why should women's experience of working within the corporate system and abiding by its rules be different and more difficult than that of comparable men? To find answers, we began to look more closely at corporate business culture and its rules. Clearly, business has been a man's world in the past. We began to think that cultural norms that are vestiges of that prior world might still be permeating business today and interfering with gender parity at work. Learning what behaviors are typically required of a man—and a woman—in traditional American male cultures gave us some insights.

A MAN'S WORLD

Recently, while waiting for a flight at JFK International Airport, we wandered over to a newsstand in search of some reading material. We found an extensive collection of magazines displayed in an orderly fashion and sorted by categories including "Men's Interests," "Women's Interests," and "Other." Under the heading "Men's Interests" were the expected copies of *GQ*, *Esquire*, and *Maxim*, an assortment of sports and car magazines, and, unexpectedly, all the business periodicals.

Today, saying that business is a man's world sounds archaic. Not only is this viewed as politically incorrect in most circles, but it is arithmetically inaccurate. The Bureau of Labor Statistics data clearly show that close to half of the workforce in the United States is composed of women. Studies by Catalyst have indicated that for at least the last decade, virtually half of all management, professional, and related occupations have been filled by women. Technically, the business world would seem to belong to women as much as men. Yet, for many, it doesn't feel that way. Despite the prevalence of women in the workplace, the culture and operating principles of business seem to subtly—

and sometimes not so subtly—continue to reflect its origins as an environment designed, developed, and controlled by and for men. As one sociologist commenting on the influx of women into the workplace observed, "Clearly, while some women successfully fit in, elements of work arrangements and the spirit of work still conveyed an aura of maleness even as the outright male monopoly declined."[1]

Business and the American male have forged a strong sociological bond over time that has endured in many ways despite the entrance of women. For many American men even today, who they are and what they do for a living are one and the same thing. Ubiquitous conversations starters attest to this. Just ask any man, "If you're introduced to another man you know nothing about, what is one of the first things you say?" Whether they are meeting on a golf course, on a cruise ship, or at a cocktail party, most men regularly ask, "So what kind of business are you in?" For many men, their identity as men is inextricably linked with the way they earn their living.

This is not to say that women do not gain personal identity from their work, the positions they hold, and the size of their paychecks. The majority of working women, like their male counterparts, clearly view the work they do and how well they do it as a huge component of who they are. It's more a matter of how society assesses men. Many of us are conditioned from an early age to link a man to how he earns his money. When we were growing up, we recall knowing the occupations not only of our fathers but of each of the men that lived in our immediate neighborhoods, though none of them were around during the day when we were home. In retrospect, the local fathers probably didn't even know our names, but we knew if they were doctors, lawyers, electricians, plumbers, or businessmen and often what companies they worked for. The historically tight connection between work and concepts of American masculinity is substantiated by a fascinating fact that Susan Faludi uncovered in 1989 in her research for *Backlash: The Undeclared War against American Women*. A "little-noted finding" in the Yankelovich Monitor survey, a nationwide poll that tracks social attitudes, showed that "for twenty years, the Monitor's pollsters have asked its subjects to define masculinity. And for twenty years, the leading definition, ahead by a large margin, has never changed. It isn't being a leader, athlete, lothario, decision maker, or even just being 'born male.' It is simply this: being a 'good provider for his family.'"[2]

The connection between perceptions of manliness and being a good financial provider has not been lost on the corporate world. Historically, business has not only served the purpose of providing men with occupations and financial remuneration; for many men, it has also reinforced their masculinity. In "'The Best Is Yet to Come?' The Quest for Embodiment in Managerial Work," Deborah Kerfoot and David Knights explored this link between business and masculinity and found that "corporate capitalism is both the vehicle for the expression of this masculinity and a major driving force. For in elevating competitive success . . . as *the* reason for existence, the capitalist corporation provides a legitimate outlet for masculine preoccupations with conquest and control."[3]

In a number of ways, the economic arena in America continues to serve the purpose of reinforcing masculinity even today. Like driving fast cars or excelling in sports, being successful in business is still often recognized as a hallmark of masculinity. Even though women may participate and succeed in these activities, society generally does not bestow upon them the gender identity boost that it gives to men. The men who excel in these areas are frequently viewed as more manly. Professor Robin Ely of Harvard Business School, commenting on her research on masculinity in today's workplace, explained this phenomenon as follows: "Research has documented how mainstream organizations conflate stereotypical masculine traits with effective performance in white-collar jobs, such as manager, scientist, and lawyer: Success in these jobs is often measured by how well one fits the desired masculine image. Hence, these jobs, too, are proving grounds for masculinity."[4]

The contemporary system of business is still, in many ways, a competitive proving ground for manhood. Within this context, manhood becomes a relative term. For men who compete in the everyday economy to demonstrate their masculinity, being perceived as "real men" can become a never-ending quest. Kerfoot and Knights observed that, ironically, this makes the "man's world" of business a very insecure place for men. "In short, the very pursuit of security through achievement, conquest, success and wealth generates precisely those self-same conditions of insecurity that make the pursuit compulsive and unending, thus closing the 'vicious cycle' and denying masculinity the possibility of escaping from itself."[5]

Many companies learned to exploit as a motivational force the connection between business and the pursuit of masculinity. The values, protocols, and rules of the business world were frequently designed to perpetuate an environment of competition as historically defined by men. Even today, enter just about any company, and it won't take you long to identify the more successful as against the less successful or to separate the executives from the rank and file. Such distinctions are usually vividly apparent but rarely critical to the efficient or productive operation of the organization. Rather, the perks of higher positions, from reserved parking spots to private bathrooms, are part of a system that has evolved to publicly reward those who are winning the internal competition.

For us, understanding the deep-rooted historical relationship between work and concepts of masculinity was an initial step toward gaining clarity as to why women are having more trouble working within the system of business than men. Once we recognized that many of today's corporate cultures perpetuate characteristics of the man's world of business, we began to see more of what leads to the disparity between the ways in which men and women experience work. The reasons why the obstacles are where they are became more apparent. Recognizing that the economic arena in America still retains many of the aspects of a proving ground for manhood allowed us to dig deeper in the right spot.

MEN ON A PROVING GROUND

While many sociologists have begun to explore what it has meant to be a man in American culture, Michael Kimmel's work, especially in *Manhood in America: A Cultural History*, is particularly comprehensive. In analyzing masculinity's competitive nature, Kimmel described three critical behavior patterns that men have historically exhibited on male proving grounds that struck us as especially pertinent to the corporate world. The first was the need for men to identify themselves as "not feminine"—proving manhood meant distancing oneself from being anything like a woman.[6] According to this standard, being seen as embodying feminine qualities sapped men's strength and weakened their character. This need to be separate from things feminine is what Kimmel also referred to as "the flight from the feminine."[7]

Once all this is articulated, we see behaviors in the corporate setting that are reflective of the pressure on men to follow this pattern. Howard recalls male co-workers giving him grief for having enjoyed what they considered a "chick-flick" over the weekend. Lynn remembers thinking she had built a good rapport with a male co-worker who had children about the same age as hers, frequently discussing their common trials in raising adolescents. Yet she found him extremely reluctant to talk about the topic when they ran into each other at an airport and he was with a group of men. Though today many men are growing more comfortable getting in touch with their "feminine" side, part of being masculine on a proving ground seems still to involve metaphorically creating a distance from and not identifying too much with things deemed feminine.

A second way in which men have traditionally proven their masculinity, according to Kimmel, is a bit more subtle: men have competed primarily with other men for the recognition and approval of their manhood. In other words, men have seen other men as the ultimate arbiters of manhood. Kimmel characterized this as a "homosocial enactment": "In large part, it's other men who are important to American men; American men define their masculinity, not as much in relation to women, but in relation to each other."[8]

Taken in a corporate context, Kimmel's observation gives us a possible reason why the feedback some women provide to their male co-workers is sometimes inexplicably less valued than that provided by men. Or why, when a woman praises the work of a male peer or subordinate, it often does not generate the same glow in a man as when he receives similar recognition from a comparable male in the hierarchy. If men on a male proving ground regard more highly what other men say, it's not necessarily a matter of what is being said but of who is saying it. In such cultures, women's opinions about men are not as big a part of the equation; men are primarily chasing the opinions of other men.

The third behavior Kimmel identified was exclusion as having been the typical male response to the pressures of conforming to the strictures of a male proving ground. Whether it's by excluding women or excluding minorities, men have historically felt more like men when they kept to or "bonded" with their own and kept out "the others." Furthermore, exclusionary behaviors were particularly strong whenever there was a perceived threat to traditional concepts of masculinity. "So where can men go to feel like men? This is one of the questions fueling the anger of the men's rights groups, who seek to prop up traditional definitions of masculinity in the ways that besieged men have always done: by clearing everyone else off the playing field."[9] Accordingly, one test of manhood on a male proving ground involved men not only separating their identity from anything feminine, but also physically separating themselves from women.

The pattern of businessmen banding together in unisex groups is certainly familiar in today's business world. The ruckus over admitting female members to the Augusta National Golf Club, site of the Masters Tournament, comes to mind. The stubborn resistance of the approximately three hundred male members who, according to the New York Times, were "among the country's business, financial, political and sports elite,"[10] may have had more to do with shoring up their manhood through exclusion than with blatant misogyny. (Though misogyny cannot be completely ruled out in this egregious example.) Closer to home, this banding together of men may explain the lack of success of the businesswomen we know who spent a fortune improving their golf games in the hope of connecting with their male business peers on a common footing. No matter how good their games, they were rarely invited to complete a foursome with men.

These three behaviors—being "not feminine," seeking the approval of other men, and banding together exclusively with men—are familiar to us in a corporate context. We have seen these protocols reflected in the behavior of many men throughout the business world. At the same time, we know many of these men eschew these behaviors in their private lives. Yet they feel the need to conform to them in a corporate setting. This seeming hypocrisy is somewhat perplexing, but it may be explained by pressure to conform to a corporate culture. Group dynamics make it difficult for an individual to act against the beliefs of the group, even if that individual personally disagrees with some of those beliefs. The noted authority on business cultures, Edgar H. Schein, emeritus professor of management at the Sloan School of Management, commented on the power of the group dynamic in this way: "If someone asks us to change our way of thinking or perceiving, and that way is based on what we have learned in a group that we belong to, we will resist the change because we will not want to deviate from our group even if privately we think that the group is wrong. This process of trying to be accepted by our membership and reference groups is unconscious and, by virtue of that fact, very powerful."[11]

With this understanding, the influence of today's corporate culture on the working relationships between men and women takes on an added dimension. Reflecting the historic norms of a man's world, many business cultures today continue to exert pressure on men to conform to the protocols of a male proving ground. Responses to this pressure may include the behaviors identified by Kimmel, even for men who personally might find some aspects of the behaviors objectionable. For in addition to the normal stresses of meeting deadlines, solving problems, producing quality products, staying within budgets, and pleasing their bosses, men on a male proving ground have to worry about perceptions of their manliness. Even though business has traditionally been a man's world where men have held the reins of power, the proving ground aspect of this man's world creates insecurity for them.

Though the protocols of a male proving ground exert their force primarily on male behavior, women are in many ways casualties of this behavior. "Not being feminine" focuses on differences between men and women and creates distance between them. Seeking the approval of men may result in the approval of women being regarded as less valuable. Banding exclusively with men clearly excludes women. The cultural norms to which many men feel a need to conform in the workplace are not necessarily reflective of their feelings about women. But inadvertently, and sometimes deliberately, the experience of women in business suffers as a consequence.

Seeing that many businesses today retain aspects of a male proving ground in their corporate cultures goes a long way in helping us explain the gender discrimination that persists at work. But it's only part of the sociological construct. To complete the picture, we must examine more thoroughly the gender roles that are imposed on women on a proving ground of masculinity.

THE OPPOSITE SEX

Historically, the man's world of business reflected a simple premise regarding the genders: men were men and women were women. The gender roles assigned to each sex were separate and distinct. Companies' cultural norms, as well as the behaviors promoted on the male proving ground, reinforced the concept of separation by focusing on differences. In this context, relative to men, women were the opposite sex. And on a male proving ground, having an opposite provided a necessary counterpoint.

Before the modern-day women's movement, most companies explicitly maintained distinct gender roles by setting policies and creating environments that reinforced the precepts of the proving ground. To ensure that company men were seen as the masculine driving force, jobs were assigned by gender. Certain occupations were considered appropriate only for women. Women were the support staff, the secretaries, the typists. Men need not apply. In further support of traditional masculinity precepts, women in these roles were clearly second class citizens both in pay and in status. Their secondary position meant that they had no voice in the "homosocial enactments" of men seeking the approval of other men. Women had no power, so they had no say. In addition, men and women were clearly segregated. Predominantly female departments such as typing pools and research departments were usually set up in rooms separate from those of the men (rent *Desk Set*).[12] If an executive regularly went to lunch with his secretary, it was most likely not because they were good friends. Lynn had a clerical job in her father's office one college summer, and what she particularly recalls is his excessive need to say to any and every man they saw on their way to lunch, "Meet my daughter; she's my daughter." Frankly, his tone was not consistent with parental pride. Later, he quietly whispered to Lynn, "Don't want anyone to think I'm having an affair." Business protocols clearly required the segregation of the sexes—both physically and socially. Any integration of the sexes was looked on with suspicion. No gender conflict existed as long as both men and women accepted their opposite-sex roles.

When women began to obtain access to what had traditionally been male jobs—to get into the system—corporate management faced a unique quandary. Unlike the situation in other male proving grounds, such as athletics, in the business arena, the entry of women was a direct, unrestricted assault on the status quo. Women wanted and expected to have access to every corporate position for which they were qualified. In contrast, women who

entered the military were, and technically continue to be, prohibited from combat roles. These positions are the most highly
regarded, the ones you win medals for, and they remain for the
most part the exclusive preserve of men. When Title IX required
parity in women's collegiate athletics, the teams themselves stayed
single-sex. There was no direct, head-to-head competition
between men and women. As with the original WNBA slogan, it
was more akin to "We got next," in that the women played on
the same basketball court as the men, but not with the men. In
contrast, when women advanced on the economic arena, they
rightfully wanted no-holds-barred access, complete integration
and parity with men. No more opposite sex.

The perceived loss of an opposite sex left many men on the
male proving ground without a clear counterpoint. How could
men prove they were men if they were competing one on one
with women for the same jobs? How could men dissociate
themselves from women if they had to work next to and with
women day in and day out? The exclusions and segregations of
the past were labeled unacceptable, discriminatory, and illegal.
Yet, for many men, the need to assert their masculinity on the
male proving ground of business remained.

We suggest that in many corporate cultures, the gender role
of women as the opposite sex on the male proving ground of
business didn't completely disappear when women assumed traditionally male jobs. It went underground. What has evolved is
a code of conduct in many companies wherein businesswomen
are often expected to buttress masculinity through corporate
protocols rather than through corporate regulations. Instead of
corporate management explicitly imposing strictures, it is now
corporate culture that compels women to comply. This is why
many of the slights against women have moved from direct
aggression to passive aggression.

In the culture of a male proving ground, women satisfy their
role as reinforcers of masculinity when they are considered to be
as dissimilar from men as possible. This can be seen today in
both formal and casual business situations, when the conversa-

tions between men and women are often based on their differences. Recall the corporate-approved approach to diversity training where the stereotypical opposite-sex characteristics of men and women are highlighted and stressed. Think about the side conversations between men and women before a meeting is convened or at a business conference. Often, the chatter is opposite-sex oriented, flirtatious, stilted, or segregated; rarely is it a search for what a man and woman have in common.

The expectation in some business settings that women should be segregated from men is another carryover from business as a man's world. While today, actual physical separation of the sexes is supposedly not required, you wouldn't know it from looking at the lunch tables in most corporate cafeterias. Technically, it is illegal to separate or distinguish jobs by sex, but informally and outside of work, the groupings at most organizations still tend toward men with men and women with women. Again, it is the pressure of corporate culture that is usually the dictator of this standard. Lynn remembers working with a man as his consultant, then joining his company and finding that this same man was now somewhat aloof toward her, particularly in social settings. They'd been work associates for over five years, so she felt comfortable asking him directly why there had been a change. "I'm hanging on here by a thread myself," he explained. It seemed that being seen congregating with women could only diminish his standing in the corporate culture.

The homosocial enactment of men seeking and valuing the opinions of other men can also be seen in many of today's business cultures. In some settings, the expectation is for women to understand that it is primarily the opinions of other men that count. As a result, in many companies, women are regularly expected to defer to men. This requirement is at the heart of a fairly frequently heard complaint about today's strong businesswomen: "These women don't listen." But careful examination of the accusations in context will usually reveal that these women are very good listeners. What they don't do is defer. This may explain why older, more experienced businesswomen frequently run into unanticipated problems in the corporate world in the later part of their careers. Young women, like young men, regularly bow to seniority. More experienced employees are usually revered and respected, so there is not as much need for them to be deferential—but that doesn't always hold for women.

Business has largely been successful in getting women into the system. But it has achieved neither parity between men and women nor full integration of the sexes. We see this as due to a fundamental conflict: business's goal of achieving gender equality at work inherently conflicts with business cultures that sustain the behaviors of a male proving ground. On a proving ground, men and women are anything but equal; women are expected to be the opposite sex—different and deferential. Disparity between the sexes promotes the gender roles that men and women are often expected to play. The failure to reconcile this conflict poses a challenging problem. Women are caught in the middle. They cannot simultaneously play the role of the opposite sex on a male proving ground and be equal participants in business.

PARITY PARADOXES

Maureen was walking down the hall, having just left her co-worker Michael's office. She wasn't angry with Michael for not going with her to see John, their division head—their boss Larry's boss—but she was frustrated.

"I can't believe this," Maureen thought to herself. "I know I'm right on this. And Michael does, too. This Alzheimer's drug should go to market as soon as possible."

Maureen decided to spend a few minutes in her office to cool down and think this through. Gazing out of her window at the geometric shapes of Manhattan's office towers, she gradually moved from agitation to a more analytical mode of thinking.

"The real problem is Larry," she reasoned. "He never seems to hear me. I can say something logical, even insightful, and he hardly notices. But if Michael says the same exact thing, Larry's all ears. Maybe I should have insisted that Michael do the presentation instead of me. Maybe then Larry would have responded more favorably. God knows, that's been true in the past. But I did all the work and wrote the material, so it made sense for me to be the presenter. I can't be hiding behind Michael all the time, using him to make my points."

Maureen's spirits lightened a bit when she thought of John, Larry's boss. Though she didn't work directly with John very often, she felt that they had a mutually respectful professional relationship. She was aware that it was John who had made the final decision to hire her, and she recalled having a good rapport with him during the interview process.

"John's different," thought Maureen. "He will at least listen to what I have to say. Once he hears the case I have to make, I'm sure he'll agree with the direction I'm suggesting. And, if John concurs with the analysis, then Larry is sure to get on board. It would be better if Michael was with me, if we went together, but I still think this is the right thing for me to do."

In Maureen's position, what other alternatives did she really have? She could have adopted a "win some, lose some" attitude as Michael did. But, "win some, lose some" means that you trust that you *will* win some. Maureen believed she had won very few, if any, not because she was incompetent or incapable but because she was not heard. She could have tried to convince Michael to go back to Larry, since Larry seemed to hold Michael in higher regard. But, this would have underscored Maureen's feelings of being powerless and second rate. So Maureen settled on her third option, finding someone in a position of authority who, she thought, would listen to her reasoning. But she was likely to run into trouble here as well. At best, she would win her case with the division head, but the damage to her relationship with her direct superior would probably be irreparable. At worst, she wouldn't convince the division head, or, more likely, the division head would question why she was circumventing her boss. Maureen would pay a steep price regardless of which alternative course of action she chose.

For Maureen and many women like her, the cumulative effect over time of these types of situations can be personally demoralizing and career derailing. If a woman takes the passive route, just letting issues go when she feels unfairly treated, she'll be seen as a weak, relatively insignificant player. If she takes the aggressive approach, challenging decisions when they don't go her way, then she'll be seen as a difficult employee who doesn't know how to work within the system. This puts businesswomen in a paralyzing predicament. The invisible rules of business that work for men just don't seem to work as well for women.

When women took on the roles that had historically been reserved for men, the system malfunctioned for them. Rules that worked well for men on a male proving ground didn't work as well for the opposite sex. Because women's participation as equals of men violated many of the precepts of being a man on the male proving ground of business, the rules inadvertently made parity for women in business unachievable. They created *parity paradoxes*, which put women at odds with men and the business cultures they worked in, no matter how competent they were or what they did. The parity paradoxes are the unintended consequences of rules of behavior that continue to permeate the American business world.

The parity paradoxes offer a new perspective on the plight of women in business. They debunk the arguments that women have it in their power to achieve equity in the workplace or that men's misogyny is the primary cause of the problem. Instead, the parity paradoxes clearly point to systemic and cultural issues as the major impediments—systemic because the rules are inherent in the system of business; cultural because corporate cultures perpetuate vestiges of a male proving ground and are the primary enforcers of business's rules. By understanding the parity paradoxes of which so many women find themselves victims, we can finally determine why inequality between men and women persists and begin to identify solutions that will promote true gender equity.

Chapter 4

PARADOX #1:
THE TEAM PLAYER

**If a woman is a team player, she rarely receives
recognition commensurate with her contribution.
If a woman seeks recognition for her contribution, she is seen as not being a team player.**

THE RULE OF TEAM PLAY

In our early thirties, we joined the New York office of a
highly successful midwestern human resources consulting
firm. The company had slightly over five hundred employees
when we were hired, but had grown to over three thousand by
the time we left. During our thirteen-year tenure, offices were
opened in every major U.S. city as well as in Europe and Asia. The
firm's intense corporate culture even provided a Harvard Business
School case study in how to maintain a quality service business
while growing revenue at a rate of over 20 percent a year.

Looking back on the years we worked for this iconic organization, one aspect of employee behavior particularly strikes
us: neither of us can recall one single associate who used the first

person singular pronoun, "I," when talking about his or her jobs and accomplishments. It was always "we." "We have worked for over half of the Fortune 500 companies." "We have the largest computer network in our industry." "We believe in quality service to our clients." "We will get back to you." Even our professional advice to clients was always couched as "We have an opinion," never "I think . . ." Whether a lawyer, a secretary, or the CEO, every employee talked this way. We all honored the maxim that there is no "I" in team.

Be a team player. Listen carefully, and you'll hear speech reflective of team spirit in virtually every corporate setting. At Avis, "We try harder." At GE, "We bring good things to life." As consultants, we have spoken with thousands of employees at myriad major companies and consistently found "we" to be the preferred pronoun for personal expression, regardless of accuracy or relevance. Obviously, no current employees were around at the inception of New York Life Insurance Company, but you'd think they had been, when so many repeat, "We have been in business for over 160 years." An employee of a wine and spirits company who has been recently convicted of DUI will look you in the eye and say with complete sincerity, "We have a long tradition of responsible alcohol consumption."

Team-play protocols infuse not only the language of business but also its everyday work processes. Client teams, management teams, and project teams are all standard work units in corporate America today. Rarely is a work product produced by one person alone. If a business issue is important, a team is convened to study it. Though one individual may do the drafting, the team's report is almost always attributed to a group of employees. Team meetings and team conference calls are the dominant agenda items on most work calendars. Business schools, more than other academic institutions, stress the importance of teamwork by regularly assigning their students to "learning teams." And, the higher you rise in an organization, the more likely it is that your workday will consist of jumping from one team meeting to another, in which building a consensus, facilitating a group decision, and motivating other team members are the requisite leadership skills. The 1977 bestseller *Games Mother Never Taught You* got it right when it counseled young, novice businesswomen that "the principles of team play are among the most important unwritten rules of business."[1]

The team-play metaphor is a mainstay of business because it works: it perfectly captures the concept that corporate America is founded on the principle of harnessing and directing a group effort. The Bill Gates type of entrepreneurial genius may be the spark, but the bonfire of corporate power is based on creating and managing a group to magnify individual inspiration. For companies to keep an edge in a competitive marketplace, employees must pull in the same direction. Too many employee geniuses in an organization can actually disrupt operations if the geniuses are not all focused on the same goal. In her capacity as vice president of management development, Lynn recalls working with executives in the freewheeling music business and noting that while many individuals may have been creatively gifted, only those record labels that had a cohesive management team were successful in bringing innovative artists to market. The other labels would be bogged down with infighting and stalled by conflicting efforts. The senior leadership at the successful labels not only agreed on their business direction but enthusiastically supported each other, even those who might have strongly disagreed with each other at times. All seemed to instinctively appreciate that, as tough as it can be to squelch those big egos, everyone is better off when the leadership acts as one for the good of the business.

Team-play rules reinforce these values. They communicate that nothing would be accomplished without the cooperative effort of fellow employees; that the whole is greater than the sum of its parts; that everyone is important and no one is that important. All need to coalesce around the common cause—all are on the company team. Sports metaphors proliferate in the business world and reinforce the message. If one team member hits a home run, the whole team celebrates. If one player makes an error, the whole team suffers. In business as in sports, personal star power has little value unless it advances the team's objectives. And if you are not a star but you are a good team player, you still get a Super Bowl ring. Like assists in basketball or sacrifices in baseball, employees' self-sacrificing efforts on behalf of the whole are essential to corporate triumph.

The rules of team play are ubiquitous in business—they are essential to corporate America. Everyone in business knows this. Everyone entering business learns this. Every ambitious employee must follow these rules and accept their demands. The very pervasiveness of team-play principles is what makes the team-player paradox so devastatingly detrimental to gender parity.

A SYMBIOTIC RELATIONSHIP

Arthur suspected before the July 1 fiscal year began that there would not be enough money in the budget to pay employees the bonuses they had expected. His firm had just been acquired, and he had been named the new managing director. Though the new parent company's squirrelly budgeting process was unfamiliar to him, Arthur was an accountant. He knew numbers. He knew these budget numbers just didn't add up.

"Don't worry about it," his new boss told him.

"But if we hit the target performance numbers, there will not be enough money to pay target bonuses," Arthur insisted. "The numbers don't balance."

"We'll find the money somewhere during the year. We always do," his boss answered.

These reassuring words provided Arthur with little comfort, given the hard, cold reality of the math. As the financial year wore on, Arthur regularly raised the issue but got the same dismissive, why-don't-you-back-off reply.

Come the following June 30, Arthur had to announce that despite a strong business performance, there was not enough money to pay target bonuses. He spent the next two weeks traveling around the country, addressing disappointed and angry employees. Frustrated, they hammered away at him with the facts. They had met demanding financial targets; they had expanded their client base in a declining market. How could their bonuses possibly be below target?

"I have to take responsibility for this one," Arthur repeated to each audience. "The bonus formula did not work. I apologize."

Never did Arthur say that a superior had screwed up the budget. Not once did he mention how he himself had challenged the budget, not only with his superior, but every first day of the month at the financial review meeting. Arthur never shared publicly that corporate finance eventually admitted to him that he had been right, and they had made a mistake in their calculations.

Arthur took the hit.

Taking a hit for the team is one of the many unwritten demands of team play that may seem blatantly unfair and may, at times, be personally demeaning. Counterintuitively, the requisite self-deprecation can seem at odds with the popular perception of the need to sell yourself in the business world. As with other invisible rules of business, team-play requirements are not listed in any employee handbook or classroom text. Those lucky enough to have participated in team sports have a big head start, but eventually all the employees entering the workplace must gain at least a basic understanding of what is required of a team player if they are to survive. If they are to excel, they must acquire a PhD in team play.

But the paybacks for learning the lessons of team play are proportional to the effort. Arthur's publicly humiliating ownership of the bonus calculation error was rewarded within four months when he was promoted to head one of the major divisions of his company. At the time, no one said there was a direct cause and effect relationship between Arthur's taking the hit and his sudden and surprising elevation. Rather, management characterized him generically as a good team player. For those who understand team-play dynamics, the timing was far from coincidental.

Simply put, being a team player is career enhancing. That's how the system works. A team player's self-sacrifice and subjugation of ego are acknowledged with commensurate rewards and community commendation. If, without bravado, an employee performs feats of unselfish teamwork in support of a worthwhile business contribution, the work world keeps a scorecard that will eventually show that this person is a winner and is due recognition. The sublimation of individual needs and desires for the good of the whole will result in paybacks from peers, subordinates, and especially superiors. The lead time may be long, but the outcome is assured. Along the way, team players may be humbled and lose a little of their personal identity, but in the end they gain the appreciation of their teammates and the grander, sometimes more glamorous group identity of the team. Sony Music CPAs don't consider themselves accountants; they are in the music business.

Adherence to team-play dictums are scrupulously, if subjectively, evaluated by managers and peers in annual performance reviews. Does an employee take ownership of mistakes and not blame others? Does he chip in for the benefit of the whole, even if this results in personal inconvenience and requires extra hours? Does the employee whine or complain when assigned work below his station? Does he represent the company well, promoting the company rather than promoting himself? Does the employee take pride in being part of the organization, never denigrating its name? The list of demands may be long, but the paybacks for good team play are potentially quite substantial.

Typically there is a lag, a gap period between an employee's self-sacrifice and the company's payback. The deferral of the reward is itself another test of an employee's team-play mettle. A good team player never complains during the interim, but rather displays quiet trust that the payback will come and be fair. Almost like a novice in a religious order, the employee is monitored during this time period to assess his devotion to the company and his faith in its leadership's judgment.

Corporate recognition for good team play comes in a variety

of forms. Higher salaries and generous bonuses are the most conspicuous. Rarely is the actual team-play incident that triggered the increase in pay directly connected to the financial reward. Rather, like Arthur, employees will simply be acknowledged as good team players. The corporate community has a variety of other goodies to give as well. Plum job assignments leading to job promotions are classic and often more substantial long-term career boosts granted to the good team player. Garnering co-worker respect and camaraderie is less tangible but psychologically potent. When your fellow employees treat you as "one of us," "an important part of the team," the aggravations and indignations of a bad work day can quickly dissolve. The ultimate reward is of course being considered "one of us" in the leadership group—the elevator to the executive floor is only accessible to those perceived as exceptionally strong team players. No matter the form of the payback, the rule of team play in the end must prove to be good for employees as well as good for the company. The symbiosis must eventually benefit both for the system of business to work.

While the rewards for team play can be substantial, the consequences of behavior antithetical to team play can be catastrophic. Being a loner, a sole contributor, or a complainer are all at odds with being a good team player. But of all the violations of team-play rules, self-promotion is the most egregious. We would occasionally witness the self-destructive self-promotion cycle in action. It was hard to watch. An employee felt undervalued and began to talk himself up to his peers and superiors. They responded with indifference. The employee then talked up his accomplishments even more loudly, which resulted in a resounding silence from his manager and his co-workers. The employee ratcheted up his campaign to incessant self-promotion, which led to his being ostracized.

One brilliant executive compensation consultant we worked with was particularly vulnerable to this cycle. We can't say whether the problem started with his unabashed self-promotion, or whether the company consistently undervalued his contribution, but the cycle was well underway by the time we met him. As in a long, dysfunctional marriage, neither party could retrace its steps. Even though this ten-year employee was highly regarded by his clients and totally committed to the company and his work, he and the organization had to divorce. Being labeled a self-promoter, "not a team player," is like having a red flag next to your name, saying, "Beware! This person primarily thinks of himself and won't work well with others." It's a career-limiting epithet.

The system demands that employees be team players, and in return it delivers potent paybacks that recognize and reward employees' contributions. The company receives all the benefits of the employees working together as one. And the employee gets the monetary, psychological, and emotional benefits of being part of a team. Any loss of personal identity is counter-balanced by the acquisition of a strong group affiliation. This is how the system works—mostly for men.

LESS RECOGNITION

Louise was explaining to Lynn why she was retiring at age forty-five. "I've been working since I graduated from college, almost twenty-five years. I'm tired."

Lynn had worked with Louise for twelve of those twenty-five years and had sat in the office next to her for eight of them. She had seen Louise take the hits.

First, there was the time-recording incident when she was initially hired. Employees were supposed to record not only the time they billed to clients but all their nonbillable time spent working for the business, either in the office or elsewhere. This was used as a measure of an employee's dedication to the job. Louise had worked for a nonprofit organization before entering consulting and thought the nonbillable time was just filler, what you wrote in to make your time add up to an eight-hour day. For almost two years, she worked overtime, evenings, and weekends, and no one noticed that her timesheet didn't reflect her efforts. "They thought I was a dilettante" is how she explained it. "What I did was invisible to them." Yet she never blamed her manager for not explaining the system to her or complained that her efforts had been undervalued for two years.

The clients assigned to Louise were also an irritant to her. Ben was six years her junior and hired two years after her, but the moment he walked in the door, he was assigned the big accounts. "Nothing personal," Louise would say, "but it was annoying when Ben got the major financial corporations, while I had to work with all those low-budget, second-tier companies."

But Louise was a trouper, a team player. She was old enough and tough enough to stay focused. "They want a worker bee, I'll give them a worker bee." Raised in Minnesota farm country, she was naturally hardworking, nonconfrontational, and self-effacing. A great listener and keen observer, she would compliment her co-workers on what they were really good at, not providing that superficial fluff that passes as support. Full of specifics, she would say, "You really make a good, clear presentation," or "This report states the crux of the issue so well."

Eventually Louise was assigned two big-name clients. Though the assignments were small, she built up a working rapport that expanded into larger streams of business. The big clients loved her. In her own quiet way, she was direct, honest, and reliable. One client even starred her in an employee video as a pension expert. Competitors would say it was impossible to steal a client away from her. Her business relationships were loyal and long-term, and the firm seemed to be finally recognizing her talents and efforts when they made her a partner.

But her feelings of career success turned out to be short lived when, a few years later, the company decided to open a suburban office near her home. Based on her tenure and experience, everyone, including Louise, assumed she would be named the local office manager. When the regional manager wanted to meet with Louise on a Friday afternoon, this was the news she thought he had come to deliver.

Lynn had only to look at Louise's face when she came out of her meeting to know things had not gone as expected. "It took him an excruciating hour and a half, but this is essentially what he said," she recounted. "When we open a new office, we like to choose as the office manager the person with the strongest track record, the most local knowledge, and the highest seniority. However, in your case, we are going to make an exception."

No wonder Louise was "retiring."

Being part of the team is a 360-degree rewarding experience. Superiors provide career-enhancing paybacks. Subordinates respect you. Peers consider you "one of their own." People buy into the team-play rules and subjugate their personal egos, partly because it feels good to belong, but mostly because they believe that their individual contributions will be recognized fairly over time. But for too many women like Louise, the system doesn't work. It's not that women don't eventually get some payback; rather, their rewards tend to be smaller and deferred much longer. While it is difficult to prove a negative, we have regularly observed that women who are strong team players rarely receive timely recognition commensurate with their contribution. The glass ceiling reveals the inequity on a large scale. So does the pay gap between men and women doing the same jobs. Lower pay and rank may not result solely from ignoring women's team-play contributions, but pay and rank are certainly the most visible and measurable paybacks for good team play.

Let's begin with money, the most obvious payback. The U.S. Department of Labor data clearly demonstrate that women, as a group, are paid less than their male co-workers in the great majority of job categories. From corporate lawyers to administrative assistants, women doing the same job make less than men, on average.[2] But Labor Department data are merely a snapshot at one moment in time. When the image is changed to time-lapse video and the perspective to a single career, it becomes clear that relatively small differences in pay grow into ever-larger pay gaps the longer one stays in the workforce. This is because annual salaries are not subject to zero-balance budgeting; pay increases are generally calculated as percentages of current salary. Consequently, although the dollar difference between a 3 percent and 3.5 percent annual pay increase on a $70,000 salary may be only $350 in one year, the cumulative effect after ten years is that the employee who regularly receives 3.5 percent increases will be earning close to $4,700 more than his counterpart who receives 3 percent raises. If the more highly rewarded co-worker had received a full 4 percent increase, the difference after ten years would be closer to $9,500. It adds up. And this is what we see happening to women in the workforce. Relatively small differences in pay increases add up to significant disparities over time.

Our experience working within the system is that the corporate practice of annual increases as a percentage of base pay both masks and exacerbates the problem, and that the performance evaluation processes relied upon to provide objective evaluations can actually obscure and rationalize the bias. Larger pay increases for men are justified by either a higher performance score or a well-documented personal assessment by a manager. We've read these appraisals and they tend to go something like the following: this person (who happens to be a woman) is good, but this other person (who happens to be a man) is better—he contributes more, fits in better, feels more part of the team. Since the manager's assessment is ultimately subjective, and the differential is small, a 3 percent versus a 3.5 percent increase, the festering gender pay discrepancy slips through the system.

Howard remembers the day when the subtlety of this bias became vividly apparent to him. As the manager of an office with a 125 employees, he was responsible for reviewing every annual salary increase to ensure that, in aggregate, they did not exceed the total budgeted amount of 4 percent. Some employees might get an 8 percent raise, a few would get zero, but they all had to average out. Howard had reserved a full day to talk to all the managers about their salary recommendations for their staff. Typical of these talks was a discussion he had with the head of sales.

"These look good, except for maybe Nicholas," Howard began. "He looks a little high to me. He really hasn't won much this year. Let's knock him down from 5 percent to 4 percent."

The head of sales defended his initial suggestion. "Nicholas has worked hard, but he's had a run of bad luck. Besides, I don't want Nicholas to leave for a competitor. He's good. I think he has great potential." Eventually, Howard and the head of sales compromised at 4.5 percent for Nicholas.

"Also, Laurie looks a little low to me," Howard added. "She's a good team player. Wasn't she key in bringing in some big accounts this year? I know she's young, but let's pick her up from 3.5 percent to 4 percent."

"I can live with that," the head of sales concurred.

And so the day went on. At 7:00 p.m., Howard looked over the final numbers scrawled over the original recommendations. He was stunned. Every employee whose raise he thought was overstated by the manager was male; every employee whose raise he questioned as understated was female.

Similarly opaque is the difference in career-enhancing opportunities offered to men and women. The disparity would hobble any climber of the corporate ladder. Every corporate citizen knows that a career is built on the opportunities made available to you. In consumer goods, you have to be given responsibility for a product with a large market; in advertising, it's the big-budget account; in consulting, it's the Fortune 100 client. Of course, no one starts out being the lead on Coke. You work your way up. You are either assigned a lower-level role on a big account or a big role on a lower-level account. Often your training includes both of these experiences. Eventually, you pay your dues as a good team player and are deemed ready for a big one.

Many women, though, experience a disproportionate delay in being assigned the big ones, if they ever get them at all. They are only given opportunities with smaller clients, or they are assigned as the perpetual number two on a larger account. One firm had an annual benchmark, which was that every account manager had to carry a minimum of one million dollars of business. Fairly regularly the major clients with recurring business such as annual pension plan requirements would go to the men. Sara, a seasoned account manager, would lament, "Every year I start with a big, fat zero, while Don begins with $800,000!" The firm claimed the assignment was justified because Don was professionally designated as an actuary, while Sara was not. But, a few years later, the first female actuary to work in the office ran into the same client assignment pattern despite having exactly the same professional designation as Don. To her credit, Sara continued to be a good team player and found her million by selling enough new business each year. In the ten years she worked in that office, though, she was never assigned accounts with recurring business that was even close to her quota.

While lower pay and fewer opportunities can be discouraging, perhaps the most disheartening team-play inequity derives from a sense of not belonging. Normally, that sense of belonging is a reward for being a good team player, but too often, women feel like outsiders in the corporate world. They don't get the same slaps on the back, they don't sit at the same lunch tables, and they are left in the office during the golf outings. In essence, they don't feel part of the group. While many women will support other women at work, all of us, regardless of our gender, want the broader camaraderie that comes with being part of the greater whole. Being on the team means feeling that you belong, regardless of your gender. Occasionally, we've heard men who've worked for predominantly female companies or departments lament the void they perceive and their feelings of exclusion. "Too much estrogen," one man said. But women, more often than men, experience this same feeling of being peripheral to or estranged from a male-dominated world of business.

A few years ago, Brian Lehrer of WNYC radio explored the different camaraderie experiences of men and women when he did a radio segment on "work across gender lines."[3] Listeners were asked to call in if they had ever worked in jobs that had traditionally been populated by the opposite sex. Men called in about having been secretaries and teachers of preschoolers. Women spoke of being bus drivers and construction workers. All the men said they had been welcomed into the female work environments. The male secretary said it was "wonderful"; the male teacher said it was "great." But the sentiments of the women workers couldn't have been more different. The female construction worker used the word "scary" as she feared being set up for injury. A utility worker said she experienced discrimination, especially by the union. A young woman bus driver said that both the general public and her co-workers were more critical of her driving than of the driving of males. All the women said doing the work wasn't the problem; it was the aggravation and isolation.[4]

For years, Lynn tried to explain to Howard her similar, periodic, depressing sense at work that she didn't belong, was not welcome, didn't fit in. Howard thought Lynn was being hypersensitive, until he heard how she was treated when she became a partner at a major consulting firm.

At the beginning of the selection process, Lynn clearly had the requisite track record to be a partner. Her client billings were in the millions; her billable time was well over the partnership threshold; her length of service with the company was exactly that of others with comparable account management responsibilities when they made partner. Her peer feedback and work performance reviews had all been strong. So her expectations and spirits were high. After all, becoming a partner would be a crowning achievement in her career.

A year earlier, Howard had been invited to join the partnership at the same firm, and the occasion was almost a love fest. One executive was all smiles, pumping Howard's hand and saying how delighted he was to have him as a co-owner of the business.

"We couldn't be happier, Howard," he exuded. "You are exactly the sort of person we want. We see great things for you in your future here."

Howard was beaming for a month. Like Sally Fields at the Oscars, he could feel that "They like me. They really like me."

Lynn was made a partner in the year she expected, but the message was muted. The man who had embraced Howard now looked a little cranky when he opened the conference room door and told Lynn to take a seat. No handshake. No congratulations. "The firm would like to make you an offer of partnership," he began.

Lynn assumed his demeanor was nothing personal, perhaps due to acid indigestion, so she enthusiastically responded, "Thank you. I am thrilled!"

Somberly, he continued, "Well, in offering you partnership, the executive committee made a business decision."

The meeting was short and perfunctory. No "welcome aboard" or "glad to have you with us." Later, when Lynn recounted the meeting to Howard, he was incredulous. "A business decision? Are you sure that's what he said?"

"I'm sure," Lynn replied. "Very sure. It's not something you forget."

All in all, we have witnessed inequity in both the psychological and the material paybacks provided to excellent female team players in American companies. Their pay has been less, their opportunities fewer, and their feelings of alienation higher. Women who had faith that their adherence to the team-play rules—their personal efforts and self-sacrifice—would be fairly and equitably recognized over time felt duped and betrayed. They had kept their part of the bargain, but still did not feel part of the club. For so many women, the team-play rules simply are still not working.

MARGINALIZED

If the recognition and rewards for team play are smaller for women than for men, could it simply be because men are better team players than women? Some say that women are more naturally individual contributors, figure skaters, while men are more attracted to teams, hockey players. Others argue that team play is really learned through athletics, and since more boys and men are involved in sports, they're better team players. Truth be told, many men will hint at this difference to each other when women are not around. "This woman talks too much" or "That woman doesn't know how to work well with others" are euphemistic ways of saying women are not good team players.

Understanding what it means for you to be a good team player and how you learn the rules leads us to a different conclusion. First, the athletic field justification for assuming that men are better team players than women is seriously specious. Since Title IX was adopted in 1972, young women have been exposed to sports en masse. According to a National Collegiate Athletic Association Gender Equity Report, close to half of student athletes are female.[5] More significantly, teamwork principles are inculcated in classrooms as well as on sports fields. From science to history, most educational institutions incorporate team projects into their curricula. The myth that girls are not taught to be team players is just that. Today, we have a generation of women who understand and practice teamwork thoroughly. Their years on the soccer fields, the basketball courts, and the softball fields, and their hours behind the desks and in the halls of corporate America have taught them well. Women's lack of exposure to or ineptitude in team play is not the cause of the inequity in their rewards.

Nor do we think women's lesser recognition is solely attributable to the mind-set of individual men. Interestingly, the managers Howard spoke to in reviewing employee pay increases comprised both men and women. None of those managers would advocate paying men more than women merely because of gender. There was nothing in either their background or their demeanor to indicate such invidious intentions. Yet their aggregate behavior produced a biased result. Somehow, individual actions—when taken as a whole—morphed into a biased pattern of rewards.

When our son was seventeen years old, he played on a varsity basketball team at a school that he had attended since kindergarten. We knew most of the boys on his team and had watched them grow up over the years. At one point during the season, we commented to our son on how unexpectedly macho the boys had become as they had grown older. Our son replied, "They aren't macho guys. They're just a bunch of guys acting macho."

Our son's observation reflects what we see in the business world. The influence of a group, in this case a "macho" group, often produces consequences beyond what individuals personally believe, intend, or, at times, even control. This is why the whole can be greater than the sum of its parts, and why a group of upright citizens can turn into an angry mob. In corporate America, it's the system of business and its group dynamics that can drive the way men and women perceive and treat each other. The pressure to conform to the group tends to perpetuate patterns of the past and results in women often failing to get their due.

Many companies are still haunted by cultures in which employees are most comfortable when women are quietly supportive. Though we talk about women first entering the workforce after the women's movement, in reality large numbers of women were working well before that time and were firmly entrenched in invisible jobs. The historic Metropolitan Life Insurance building in New York City, built in 1909, attests to their numbers—the company had to install extra large elevators to accommodate the wide skirts of its many female employees. Women were the secretaries, the file clerks, the assistants— working in the helper jobs that were ubiquitous and uniformly taken for granted. As the doors to traditionally male jobs began to open for women, the pattern of undervaluing women's work was often carried forward. In most work cultures today, women are pressured to continue the tradition of being quietly supportive and "nice" in performing thankless jobs—characteristics consistent with good team play. These quietly supportive women are generally considered likable in a business culture, but they are rarely regarded as deserving of team-play paybacks commensurate with those of men.

The team-play problem for women is exacerbated by a second cultural perception: female ambition can be threatening on a male proving ground. In a competitive setting, it's one thing to be beaten by a man but quite another to be surpassed by a woman. Historically, this was explicitly compensated for in corporate policy. Lynn's Aunt Lillian was a young female attorney at a national insurance company in the 1950s when she was told that she would never be promoted to manager because it would "insult the men." Today, such corporate policies are illegal, so the men who feel insecure must fend for themselves. One effective tactic for them is to marginalize women's accomplishments. Consistent with the fact that manhood is defined primarily by other men on a male proving ground, we've found that many corporate men are most sensitive to being bested by a woman when other men are around. One on one it doesn't seem to be as big a deal. But in a group, we have heard men minimize a woman's accomplishments almost out of courtesy to the beaten man. Quips run along the lines of "Her sales numbers are high because she got the easy accounts." Or "Yeah, her presentation was good, but it wasn't anything special." Personally, Lynn recalls a national contest in one firm in which she worked, where individuals were asked to submit creative business ideas. The ten judged most innovative were to be presented in person to the executive committee. One of Lynn's made the cut, but she recalls that when she arrived to present it, the committee was clearly surprised to see her. They thought the idea had originated with someone else, a man from her office. But the strangest part was the dampened enthusiasm for her suggestion once her identity was revealed. The unspoken message seemed to be: "We thought your idea was good, but now that we see who came up with it, it's not so hot."

The team-player paradox derives from a business world that historically undervalued women's work and consequently tended to undervalue the contributions of individual women.

We've seen the remnants of this throughout our careers, and we've noted it not only in the experiences of those we work with but in our own experiences. Recently, we came across a 1986 letter documenting our pay when we were applying for a mortgage. Though we both had the same title at the time and we were working for the same firm with roughly the same level of responsibility and experience, Lynn was paid $77,000 and Howard, $98,000, a difference of over 25 percent. Finding this scrap of paper got us thinking—Lynn always made less than Howard. Not a lot less; just enough to give us both a sense of unease, a feeling that it might not be fair. While our education, professional credentials, and job experiences have been very similar, the starting salaries, annual pay increases, and bonuses have always tilted a bit toward Howard. Every year, though we were employed at a number of different companies, Howard's pay increases were always a little more than we expected and Lynn's a little less. You'd expect some differential over time—sometimes Howard getting more than expected, sometimes Lynn. But that never happened.

The American Association of University Women's study, *Behind the Pay Gap*, shows that professions that draw on male-dominated majors (e.g., engineering, mathematics, physical sciences) are associated with higher pay than those that draw on female-dominated majors (e.g., education, health, psychology). But its more disturbing observation with respect to women's career choices is that "if 'too many' women make the same choice, earnings in that occupation can be expected to decline overall."[6] A compensation consultant we knew gave empirical confirmation of the study's conclusions when she candidly shared what she had seen: "As soon as women dominate a department, or a profession, you begin to see the rates of pay increases slow down and the average pay level drop." Public relations and employee communications were two examples she used. Pay levels in human resources departments, which have become primarily female, and finance departments, which are predominantly male, also illustrate the phenomenon. The system of business in America seems to continue to have an embedded bias that undervalues the work of women, even if their work was previously performed only by men.

The deeply entrenched rule of team play clashes with the deep-rooted subordination of women and their work in the business world. This is why the rule of team play works well for men, but usually not for women. For the recognition and rewards to be equitable, the rule requires that teammates be treated fairly relative to each other. If a subset of teammates is considered inherently second class, then the paybacks cannot be uniformly commensurate with the contributions. The second class citizens will always receive less, no matter what they do. Today, the secondary group—women—receives less than the primary group—men. The conflict is so ingrained in our business culture that employees tend not to see it. But it's there. This is why if a woman is a team player, she rarely receives recognition commensurate with her contribution.

SEEKING RECOGNITION

Jane was eager to become a division head as early as possible. In her mid-thirties, she had an MBA from the University of Chicago and a history of stellar job performance. A 24/7 worker, she had more successful turnarounds under her belt than many who had been in the business twice as long. After only four years, her manager nominated her for promotion to division head, even though only a handful of exceptional men had ever achieved that status so early in their careers. Nevertheless, her manager felt that Jane's contributions to date plus her future potential warranted the exceptional consideration.

Jane was not promoted that year. She was told that it was too early, that she needed to put in more time and be patient. Ever the go-getter, Jane's reaction was direct and forceful: "These people must not be aware of all I've done and what I'm capable of doing. I can fix that."

So Jane started to talk herself up. She noted her accomplishments to managers and co-workers. She was more assertive in internal meetings. She sought out special assignments that would show how talented she was. She even developed a sophisticated spreadsheet that tallied all of her sales statistics and shared it with peers and managers alike. The next year, she was put up for promotion once more.

Again, she was denied. This time the feedback was more harsh and disapproving. "Jane comes on too strong. She's not considerate of others. She dominates meetings. She's not as good as she thinks she is. She's just not a good team player."

Jane was frustrated and crushed. She continued to be productive and do good work, but she started to feel isolated and distant from her co-workers. No one seemed to be supporting her anymore. Jane could almost hear people saying, "Who does she think she is, anyway?"

In the next round of promotions, Jane's story was pretty much over. Labeled an egotist, not-a-team-player, her reputation had deteriorated to the point where her name wasn't even submitted for division head. Fed up, Jane quit.

When you are not getting the recognition you feel you deserve, the natural human reaction is to speak up, to do something that draws attention to you and your accomplishments. Almost as if there has been a big misunderstanding, you begin by talking to peers and superiors about the fact that your work contributions are not being recognized. Or you attempt to raise your profile and demonstrate your talents by taking on high-visibility projects or particularly challenging opportunities. But for women, these are risky moves. In a business world that has historically kept women in subservient roles and often continues to reflect this bias, self-promotion by women can be more of an irritant than an eye-opener. Many corporations want women to be satisfied with the gains they have made, rather than dissatisfied with the recognition they receive in comparison with men. When Lynn was made a partner and it was described as a "business decision," she was disappointed by the cool response, but she dared not complain. Lynn knew the organizational response would be "We made you a partner; what more do you want?" Certainly, she was treated better than the women who had come before her. So she should be satisfied, happy. The way she was treated in comparison with her male peers was irrelevant.

Team players focus on what's good for the team, not on what's good for them, for they have faith that they will eventually be rewarded fairly and equitably. But women have been relegated to second-tier roles for so many years that their willingness to sublimate their egos for the good of the team often goes unnoticed. Yet women who speak up for themselves in an attempt to gain the recognition they feel they deserve are violating the fundamental rule of team play. By drawing attention to themselves and their plight, they are proving that they don't know how to play the game. They run smack into part two of the paradox: if a woman seeks recognition for her contribution, she is seen as not being a team player.

Ironically, from what we've witnessed, the largest contingent to suffer the consequences of the team-player paradox is that of working women who appear to be fairly well established in their careers. These women seem to have paid their dues, patiently waited their turn, and earned their positions. No longer at entry levels, they think they are secure enough to say they are not getting a fair shake. Right at the point where they should be breaking through that glass ceiling, team-play protocols trip them up, and they lose their footing on the corporate ladder.

The pattern is almost spooky. Women who have worked well for a company for ten years, sometimes twenty, all of a sudden become a problem. Management is often befuddled, not understanding how these "good team players" could become so discontented so suddenly. But the backstory is often that these women have been enduring the slights for so long that they feel they must speak up. They do it for themselves; they do it for the younger women; they say something because the pressure builds up over time. But to promote yourself is to violate the code of conduct demanded of team players. And the higher the position you aspire to in the corporate hierarchy, the more unforgiving are the team-play rules.

But what about men? After all, the slots at the top are few and the competition to get them is tight for men as well. Don't many corporate men sometimes feel taken for granted and undervalued? Howard had such an experience during his career. At one company, no matter what he did or said, management never saw him as a big contributor. Lynn could relate to that. But there was a big difference in their experiences. Howard eventually left that company, sought a new job, and went on to be quite successful. Howard felt his new employer recognized him fairly, and he was no longer tempted to promote himself. Everything was back in balance. Couldn't women do the same thing?

Not really. What we have seen is that men may feel taken for granted at some isolated point in their career, but women run into the sense of being undervalued at company after company. It's rare that women feel appropriately recognized and equitably treated. For women, the problem is systemic. The bias comes from the business world, not from any one manager or organization. Faced with the lack of delivery on the promise that comes with team play, women have no place to go. They can't speak up, lest they be labeled as not team players; it's difficult for them to find a new company where the bias doesn't exist; and they can't tolerate the continuing inequity. They are boxed in. This is the team-player paradox.

Chapter 5

PARADOX #2:
MENTORS AND ADVOCATES

Hard work and talent attract mentors and advocates.

Talented women who work hard rarely attract highly regarded mentors or win influential, loyal advocates.

THE POWER OF MENTORS AND ADVOCATES

What do Warren Bennis, George Debelle, and Freddie Laker have in common? Certainly they are not household names, yet each has been publicly acknowledged by a renowned international business executive as a major contributor to his success. Howard Schultz, CEO of Starbucks, thanks Warren Bennis for giving him a key piece of advice early in his career. Bennis counseled Schultz, "Recognize the skills and traits you don't possess, and hire the people who have them."[1] George Debelle discovered Gerry McCaughey working in a meat-packing plant and introduced him to the world of finance and real estate. McCaughey was twenty-three years old at the time and eventually went on to be CEO of CIBC—the Canadian Imperial Bank of Commerce, a global financial institution. Richard Branson, founder of Virgin Atlantic Airways, asserts that Freddie Laker gave him the strategic foundation for starting his own airline and taking on the behemoth British Airways. Bennis, Debelle, and Laker were mentors of these powerful men.

Business is a world of empirical learning where mentors and advocates are the professors. Under their tutelage, employees decipher how the system of business works. The keen students advance up the ladder of success. The practice is akin to those of olden days, when acquiring a craft meant talented apprentices learning firsthand from the masters. Knowledge, skills, and power are transferred from the older to the younger, thereby opening doors and creating opportunities. Ask almost anyone who has advanced within the system of business, and he will point to one or two specific individuals who were instrumental in his own personal story. Whether it's through the intervention of a father or a father figure, for the powerful and successful, gaining their power and success is rarely an independent venture.

While companies may run structured training programs and employees may attend formal business school courses, most elementary learning in the business world is through doing—what's known as on-the-job training. By working with co-workers, subordinates, managers, and customers, employees learn what they have to do and how to do it properly. But once an employee is ready to move beyond the basics, mentors and advocates step in. An employee's manager may become his mentor or advocate, or he may not. Managers are responsible for the training and development of all the employees under their charge and are consequently expected to be balanced in the attention and appraisals they give to all of these employees. Mentors and advocates, on the other hand, feel justifiably biased in favor of an employee. They have made a determination that this individual is worth investing in and supporting. Once committed, they're on the employee's side, giving the employee an advantage relative to others.

Good mentors/advocates teach the more sophisticated workings of the corporate system, acting as personal coaches to advise, counsel, and even forewarn their protégés. One mentor will take a young employee under his wing and explain the vagaries of corporate politics that can unwittingly derail a career. "The Bronfmans own the candy store" were the wise words of warning of one Seagram executive in counseling an employee on why he should never challenge or agitate the family owners of the business. Another mentor will introduce a person he considers a high-potential employee to key contacts and clients, transferring confidence in his protégé's abilities. "I'd like you to meet William here. If I'm not around, feel free to call on him." Sometimes, a mentor may just periodically drop in on a younger employee, providing guidance and perspective on how to play the game. "Well, you could confront him right now, but you might want to let it sit for a day or two. Let things settle. I've found that this guy is better when he has had time to cool down." It is particularly powerful when an advocate puts in a good word for an employee to influential senior executives when the employee is not even in the room. "Brett's been working with me lately, doing an excellent job. We think very highly of him." Regardless of the approach, the value of mentors and advocates is immeasurable. They not only teach; they make careers.

Every corporate entity employs mentors and advocates. The designation may not be printed on their business cards or show up on organizational charts, but they're there. Some companies try to counter the informality of the system by establishing formal mentorship programs or by fostering a strict meritocracy through rigorous performance management and comprehensive feedback. While these attempts to make career ladders more structured and dispassionate may help spread some of the advantages of having a mentor or advocate, they don't blunt the power or compete with the chemistry of the informal approach. An effective mentor or advocate tutors you one-on-one on the ins and outs of the business based on lessons he's learned from years of experience. He is watching out for you personally from a lofty position. His mere selection of you, his taking an interest in you, builds your self-esteem. The benefit to a career is inestimable.

Howard knows well both the advantages and the randomness of the mentor system. At the age of thirty-two, he was "selected," and the resulting experience reverberated through the rest of his career. Howard's mentorship story began on Thursday, June 14. We remember the date well because Lynn had given birth to our daughter, our firstborn, the day before. We were both consultants with the same company at that time, and on that particular Thursday, Pete, the CEO of our firm, was coming to the New York office where we worked. Ours was a relatively small office—with twenty or so employees—of an up-and-coming midwestern consultancy, and this was Pete's first visit since we had been hired. Given the rarity of such a close encounter with the CEO, Howard took a couple of hours away from the hospital to attend the afternoon employee meeting that Pete was conducting.

Tingling with the excitement of becoming a new father, Howard was in rare form that day. Though he still can't remember the particulars, he believes he was more assured, articulate, participative, commanding, and downright charming than he had ever been before, or has ever been since. The CEO took note. Seven months later, Howard found himself on a special three-month assignment as Pete's assistant. Every minute of every day, Howard shadowed Pete in all he did. Whether it was joining Pete in testing new desk chairs or accompanying him to a lecture he was giving at Harvard Business School, Howard got to see and experience all that being CEO entailed. Howard sat by Pete's side in high-level executive conferences as well as at broad-level employee meetings. He assisted Pete in creating long-term company policies and monitoring short-term corporate financial results. He addressed minor personnel issues and acted as a sounding board on major client and market challenges. Normally, someone of Howard's rank would not even be exposed to discussions at this level, much less have any input on the decisions. But from the trivial to the pivotal, Howard was part of it all.

Undoubtedly, the most far-reaching lesson of Howard's intense experience with mentorship was the chance to observe Pete up close and discuss with him personally his effective management style. The value of this osmosis learning cannot be overstated. Howard saw how Pete constantly weighed long-term benefits against short-term gains; how he made decisions in a crisis; when he communicated broadly with employees and owners, and when he didn't. Throughout Howard's career, when confronted with a difficult situation, he would think back on the decisions Pete had made and their results. Howard had seen it done, so he had acquired more confidence that he knew what to do.

Harboring no false modesty, we still sometimes marvel at how Howard was handpicked for such a unique opportunity. While Howard was a promising employee and a strong consultant, he is the first to admit that there were many others in the firm who were arguably just as deserving, maybe more so. He cannot help but acknowledge that the euphoria and optimism that suffuse almost every parent after the birth of a child, especially a first-born, presented him in his best possible light that day, the only day the CEO happened to be visiting the office. Frankly, if it had been a day later, Howard might have appeared listless and exhausted from lack of sleep. Or, if it had been the day before, he might have missed the meeting altogether. But the stars were aligned in precisely the right way to give this opportunity to him at a crucial, early juncture in his career. Such are the happenstances that contribute to many a mentor relationship.

All the corporate training and business courses in the world could not have done for Howard what Pete did. Howard profited from the distinct advantage of a strong mentor relationship: one-on-one, targeted attention. A senior person is singling you out as someone noteworthy. He is devoting his valuable time to your special needs and investing in your future potential. Along with the tremendous boost to personal confidence, it shouts to the system that you warrant attention. Not only does it enhance your résumé, but it enhances your reputation. Beyond just giving you a worthwhile learning experience, it gives you an advantage in the competitive world of business. People notice, doors open, opportunities materialize. Your name is on the short list of high-potential candidates for a long time.

This strong testament to the power of mentoring will come as no surprise to most employees in the corporate world. They are aware of the immeasurable importance of influential, loyal, and highly regarded mentors and advocates. While hard work, intelligence, perseverance, and initiative all contribute to career success, those attributes without the help of mentors and advocates are rarely enough. Like the tree falling in the proverbial forest, an employee's efforts will often go unheard and unheralded without the attention and support of a well-placed mentor/advocate. For the talented employee who works hard, an effective mentor and advocate can make the difference between an astounding career and a mediocre one.

PASSING THE BATON

The value of attracting highly regarded mentors and winning influential advocates is usually considered from the perspective of the younger, less-experienced employee. He seeks to leverage the knowledge and position of a more senior person, thereby advancing his own burgeoning career. And, as we've said, all ambitious employees quickly learn how much an effective mentor or advocate can do for them. Less frequently discussed is mentorship and advocacy as critical to the survival of the corporate entity. Companies are managed and organized to promote the longevity and stability of the institution as a whole. Mentoring and advocacy are two of the more crucial processes that support these goals. By passing along knowledge to future generations of employees and developing the best and the brightest as its future leaders, corporations are improving their odds of enduring. Seeing the benefits of mentoring and advocating from a corporate perspective provides insight into why this often haphazard approach helps today's businesses to thrive.

First and foremost among the benefits of mentoring and advocacy to a company is the cultivation of key talent. Mentors connect with employees who, they believe, have potential, and then teach their mentees what they can't learn anywhere else. Advocates select employees who, they believe, warrant special treatment, then sponsor them for positions of pivotal responsibility. Through their efforts, mentors and advocates identify the critical talent that will position the company competitively into the future. In Lynn's role as vice president of management development, she found that one of the more pressing desires of business leaders was simply to meet the people that were deemed to have high potential. "If we don't find these people and develop them, we may not be around in ten years," was a commonly expressed sentiment. Formal programs to train the "hi-pos" were less important than identifying and individually mentoring these people. Instinctively, senior management knew that the unique one-on-one development opportunities honed by informal mentoring and advocating were time-honored ways to ensure that the next generation's leaders would reach their full potential and bring the organization along with them.

An American Express business executive once remarked to Howard, "The institutional memory of a corporation is surprisingly long." Over the years, we have found this to be stunningly true. Regardless of how high or low the employee turnover, companies have an uncanny ability to retain their past. Mentors and advocates are integral to this process. Mentors divulge the unwritten rules of the culture to their mentees, making sure the rules travel from one generation of employees to the next. They share the folktales that are so often undocumented but that make a company's history so rich. The mentor will illustrate his lessons with stories of founding fathers pulling all-nighters to deliver their first big proposal on time, or teams testing a breakthrough product ad nauseam, never quitting until they got it right. Advocates promote those employees they feel fit well in the culture. They look for employees who respect the traditions of the organization and personally embody the values that underlie the company's way of operating. By passing the baton from older to younger employees, mentors and advocates contribute to the stability and continuity of the corporate entity and instill pride in their company's corporate traditions.

Looking at corporate financial statements, you will rarely see an expense item for the time and energy expended through informal mentorship or advocacy. From a financial perspective, the system is wonderfully cost-effective. The informal and arbitrary nature of the processes makes any identification of specific cost virtually impossible. Some would even argue that effective mentoring and advocacy save a company money. By reducing the turnover of key talent, by enhancing the continuity and stability of business operations, by transferring critical knowledge without the cost of formal training programs, mentors and advocates make an organization more efficient.

Because of the many benefits mentoring and advocacy offer, most companies encourage their senior leaders to participate in the process. Two of the standard questions regularly posed to managers by senior executives are: "Who are your most talented employees?" and "What are you doing to develop and retain the talent?" The expectation at most corporations, whether explicit or implied, is for senior people to share their knowledge with junior people. Building the talent base and developing your successor are simply part of being a good manager.

In addition to the protégés and the corporate entity, mentors and advocates themselves gain from the practice of free-form mentoring and advocating. Almost as a perquisite of seniority, they receive the ego feed associated with wielding power in an organization. They can make or break careers. Acknowledged as having the acuity to select those employees who deserve special attention, they can frequently groom their own successor and shape their personal legacy, typically in their own image. On the softer side, it can just plain feel good. Not only do mentors and advocates receive respect and gratification from junior employees, but also they have the moral satisfaction of having done something good for another person. In the course of our careers, we have extended ourselves to several individuals as mentors and found that years later, though we have all left the company, we are still exchanging holiday cards and visiting when in the vicinity. While the pecuniary rewards of being a mentor or advocate are usually nil, the psychic rewards are plentiful.

The invisible rule that employees should find mentors and win advocates is mutually beneficial to junior employees, senior employees, and employers. It advances employees' careers and advances companies' business interests. It boosts senior employees' egos while passing on invaluable knowledge to junior employees. From a distance, it looks as if everyone wins. However, a closer examination of the informal and arbitrary nature of most approaches reveals some unintended consequences that put women at a disadvantage relative to comparable men in the workplace. For not so obvious reasons, the rules of mentoring and advocating just don't work as well for women as they do for most men.

THE MENTOR PROBLEM

When Lynn's brother was growing up, their father would periodically relate little parables to him in preparation for his entry into the world of business someday. In thinking about mentoring, one particular tale comes to mind—what came to be known in Lynn's family as "The Red Sweater Story." It goes like this:

> Once there was an ambitious young man who worked in the mailroom of a big company. One day he noticed that the head of the company started work earlier than anyone else, arriving most mornings at 7:00 a.m. So this young man bought himself a bright red sweater and started coming to work at 6:30 a.m., and the first thing he would do was wheel his mail cart

to the executive floor and deliver the CEO's mail. It didn't take long for the CEO to notice the young man—since they were the only two in the building—and he started chatting with him. Well, one thing led to another and the young man went on to be wildly successful, eventually becoming CEO himself.

When he finished the tale, Lynn's father wanted to make sure that his son was absorbing the life lesson. "Do you understand what I'm trying to tell you here?" he asked. To which Lynn's irreverent adolescent brother supposedly replied, "Sure, Dad. To be successful in life, I need to buy a red sweater."

The truth is that the role of the employee in the mentoring process at most companies is not too far from that of the employee in Lynn's father's story. A capable junior employee works very hard, produces high-quality output, and demonstrates talent. With continued effort and a little luck—and maybe a red sweater—the junior employee is identified by a seasoned senior employee as one who has potential. They connect. The senior employee shares his knowledge, wisdom, and experience with the junior employee through personal attention and one-on-one learning opportunities, thereby "teaching him the ropes." As we've seen, the practice benefits all involved— mentor, mentee, company. Throughout the history of business, this highly personalized, subjective approach has worked well for men in developing successful careers and creating many a great leader. But our direct experience, combined with what we've heard from many women, leads us to conclude that the traditional, informal practice of mentoring tends to be significantly more beneficial for men in the workplace than for their female counterparts.

The problem starts at the very beginning with being selected. A woman must be chosen in order to benefit from a mentorship connection. It's a top-down system. While employees may do things to try to be noticed or to increase their appeal, ultimately mentors select mentees, not the other way around. Just as if they are standing at a mixer waiting to be asked, women often don't get the chance to dance unless they're invited. They can be just as talented and work just as hard as their male peers, but unless a potential mentor takes notice, they are neglected. Too often this is exactly what happens. Working women simply don't attract their fair share of the choice, respected mentors. On the corporate dance floor of mentoring, men are doing most of the asking, and the ones they ask are mostly men.

"Frankly, I don't get it. I never get the opportunity to work directly with Ted," is how Emily expressed her frustration with the mentoring process. "And now that I think about it, neither do most of the other women in the office. But guys who came in ahead of me and after me have all had their time with him." In Emily's office, the standard operating procedure was that the more experienced executives would select from a pool of new hires the people they wanted to assist them on a project. Ted was the most senior person in her office and also one of the most highly regarded people in her field. Having the opportunity to work with him was a primary reason why she joined his department. Emily was trying to be patient, but it was almost a year now and she was still waiting to be asked. In the meantime, Emily had been trained mostly by senior women, and she had learned a lot from them. But Ted had something special to offer—not because he was a man, but because he had an extraordinary talent and working with him was akin to apprenticing with a master. Emily lamented, "Ted's nice enough when I see him around the office; he just seems uncomfortable working with women. Or maybe it's that he is more comfortable working with men."

Since personal chemistry is a major component in successful mentoring, relationships are rarely imposed. Ergo, Emily's frustrations. Rather, these relationships are allowed to develop informally and spontaneously within the system of business. Just as when Howard was asked to spend time with Pete, circumstances align in special ways that create a spark of interest. As a result, mentors gravitate toward mentees whom they like and with whom they feel most comfortable. In a business setting, that degree of comfort tends to occur too often among and between men.

Beyond the problem of being selected, the nature of the advice handed down from a mentor to a mentee can pose idiosyncratic challenges to women. Mentoring is highly personal. Most of the counsel that is proffered by mentors is drawn from their own work experience. Through years of personal effort, observation, and learning from others, mentors have developed their view of what works and what doesn't—their own version of "the way things are done around here." This is what is passed on to the mentee.

But even when women are fortunate enough to attract a noted male mentor, they often suffer an unanticipated consequence—what has worked for their mentor doesn't always work well for them. Probably the most common example is that of a woman seeking a pay increase. The standard advice when asking for a raise is to be assertive, to take control of the situation, to make a clear case for pay that fairly reflects one's work contribution and competitive practice. The traditional counsel to women, as well as men, is that they need to rationally lay out why they feel they deserve an increase and support their case with specifics. Fathers and husbands, often the most supportive and sincere of male mentors to their female family members, will reiterate this advice, telling of how, over the course of their careers, they have won substantial raises by using this tried and true approach. "Just talk to your boss. Be firm and direct. Be as objective as you can, and don't be emotional. Show how confident you are in your ability, your performance, and your value. Your boss will respect you for it." Yet woman after woman will tell how these wise, well-intentioned words frequently fall flat. More often than not, her manager's body language, if not his explicit words, will express disappointment in her for merely asking for more money. The unspoken sentiment is "You want more? After all I've done for you, after all the company has given you, you're asking for more? I thought you were such a nice, good person, but now you seem greedy." Even if the woman does get the raise, far from earning her manager's respect, she frequently feels as if the relationship has taken a hit.

Quite often, it comes as a surprise to men that what works for them doesn't necessarily work for women. Many men rarely recognize the impact their gender has on a situation, for they are conditioned to see *their* world as *the* world. This makes it particularly hard for them to foresee the peculiar obstacles that women deal with regularly at work. Not only do male mentors often fail to anticipate these obstacles, but also they may have trouble identifying with their female mentees' experience. Some even express skepticism and discomfort when women share the hurdles they face. In our personal experience, Howard was incredulous many times when Lynn would speak to the same manager he had spoken to, sometimes using exactly the same words, and receive an entirely different reaction. No matter the intent, men can't help with problems they either doubt or don't see. Their counsel can be dangerously blind to some of the real issues women confront. As a result, the female mentee can be left adrift, even though she's been given what appears to be time-tested advice.

Now, one might think that if women are mentored by successful senior women, this issue would be solved. But frequently, the blind spot is replaced by new quandaries when women seek female mentors. As we've shown statistically, not as many women in business reach the highest levels of the corporate hierarchy as men do. Too many either hit a glass ceiling, go to a different company, or leave the work world altogether. As a result, the pool of senior women available to mentor other women starts off smaller. Then there are issues of chemistry and quality. Some businesswomen are conflicted about supporting younger women in the workplace. Whether they are motivated to prove to their male peers that they are corporate friendly, that they are not feminist militants, or whether they feel threatened by the possibility of no longer being viewed as exceptional female achievers, some senior businesswomen shy away from mentoring younger women. Or, sometimes, successful career women have made enormous personal sacrifices for the sake of their careers—no husband, no children—rendering them less attractive role models to the next female generation. Taken together, young women either have difficulty finding women willing to mentor them, or they may not want to make the sacrifices that some of these senior women have made.

Perhaps the most frustrating problem women encounter with regard to the current mentoring system is sexual politics. Here is where mentoring can become messy, since any intense, exclusive relationship between an older man and a younger woman is too often assumed to have a sexual component. We once witnessed a male senior executive from a Fortune 500 consumer products company working in a close mentoring relationship with a young female employee, in an arrangement much like the one Howard had with Pete. Moving from one important meeting to another, invariably in tandem, these two were a particularly stunning-looking pair. She was tall, dark-haired, and willowy; he was a graying-at-the-temples Brit. Whenever they entered a room together, others' eyes would roll. Most unfairly assumed that her primary appeal to the senior executive was sexual, and few gave her much leeway. If she sat quietly by his side during a meeting, she was said to be a lightweight; if she spoke up, she was called callow. No matter what her credentials were, her elite position was assumed to be based on her appearance, not her hard work and talent. Rather than offering the chance of a lifetime, the attention of the senior executive derailed her career. After a few months, the young woman disappeared from the company. Interestingly, about a year later at the same company, a different male senior executive was similarly shadowed by a young man. Despite the closeness of their relationship, no one assumed there was a sexual bond between them. Within five years, that young man was named president of a major division.

While a younger, male protégé can be viewed as an aide-de-camp whose future looks bright, the value of a younger female protégé is frequently unfairly invalidated by the assumption of motivations that are either lascivious or opportunistic. And to be honest, attraction and intimacy are components of strong mentor relationships, regardless of the genders of the mentor and mentee. Something about the younger person triggers a reaction in the mentor, a belief that this person is someone special. The appeal of the younger person to the more senior one is part of the reason why the younger person is selected. Once the younger person is chosen, the mentor shares personal experiences and private insights. The relationship is naturally close. While mutual attraction is characteristic of all mentoring relationships, when an older man and younger woman are involved, the presumptions of the business community can often undermine the relationship.

Nor is a woman immunized from sexual politics if she has a female mentor, though sexual innuendo is rarely the problem here. Rather, the relationship is too often undermined by the presumption of feminist activist motivation. The older woman may be suspected of recruiting impressionable young women into the feminist fold for political reasons, and therefore, the fact that the young women were born female becomes their predominant qualification. This was so widely assumed to be true at one company that when a man was transferred into an all-female department, the prominent woman department head announced that he would arrive "as soon as he has recovered from his sex-change operation." Gender, rather than the distinguishing talents of the younger person, becomes the key factor in the mentor/mentee relationship.

Young men seeking the benefits of a mentor can run into problems analogous to those that women face. They too can be passed over in the selection process, or be selected by an unimpressive mentor, or receive advice that doesn't work for them, or fall prey to sexual politics. But the current informal system of mentoring tends to work far better for men than for women. The odds are much more in men's favor. Women face a parity paradox. They understand that hard work and talent are required to attract mentors. But, despite all their hard work and talent, women don't attract the highest-level mentors as often as their male peers do. And when they do, the reason behind their selection too often becomes suspect.

THE ADVOCATE PROBLEM

Discussions involving advocacy take place thousands of times a day throughout the business world. Though many of these discussions are informal and of short duration, they can have a long-term effect on a career, as in this situation: Eric's office was asked to bid on an opportunity that, if the bid was successful, would likely be that fiscal year's most prestigious piece of new business. They had only two weeks to pull it all together. On a blustery winter Monday morning, Eric, the head of sales, sat in his office with three managers, Jeffrey, Jessica, and Brian, strategizing on how to craft a successful proposal.

"The lead on our client team will be key," noted Jeffrey. "From what I know of this company, they value long-term, professional relationships. Chemistry between us and them will be important."

"Who are you thinking of?" inquired Eric.

"I was thinking of Alan. He has good experience, he knows the industry, and he's on a bit of a roll in new business situations."

"Or how about Peter?" interjected Jessica. "He's got time available, and he connects very well with large clients."

"No, I wouldn't go with Peter. His work has been a little weak lately," countered Brian. "But I would give thought to Caroline. Didn't we get some positive feedback on her recently from a client in this industry?"

"Yeah, she's okay. She writes a good proposal," said Jeffrey, tapping his pen on the table. Then he added more forcefully, "But I'm keen on Alan. I'm always impressed with his work, and he gets so energized in front of clients. I think he's our best candidate."

"Alan's good, too," nodded Jessica and Brian.

Eric closed it out. "Okay, everyone seems to feel good about Alan. This is a big one. Let's go with him."

Fast-paced, instinctive decisions are constantly being made in today's business world about who will be the lead person assigned to a large client, or who will run a promising new product line, or who will be on the team for an exciting new opportunity. After all, not only do companies compete with other companies, but employees compete with each other for the choice opportunities. It is the nature of the competitive marketplace to foster efforts where many try but only a few win. In deciding who wins, there is often someone like Jeffrey present, advocating for his favorite candidate and trying to shift the odds. Personal advocacy is a standard business practice that has helped make the free market work so well. But, like mentoring, advocacy in today's business world tends to work better for men than for women.

Advocates perform a different function than mentors. Advocates don't teach; they champion. Though the same person may be both mentor and advocate for an employee, the main role of the advocate is to lobby on another's behalf, creating opportunity as opposed to providing education. Advocates are strongly on your side, willing to go to bat for you. They not only think you can do the job; they want you to be the one doing the job. Their focus tends to be more immediate than a mentor's, giving consideration to recently demonstrated ability over future potential and talent. As in the example of Jeffrey advocating for Alan, they are impressed by the hard work already done and the results already produced. While mentoring can open doors and provide unique opportunities for learning, effective advocacy delivers the goods. The distinction was made clear to Lynn when she needed to ask senior executives to participate in a formal corporate mentoring program for minorities and women. "Sure, I'll work with someone, share what I've learned," most said unhesitatingly. But then, the executives would add, "But don't ask me to advocate for them."

In comparison with mentoring, advocacy is both more private

and more public. Because advocating typically takes place behind closed doors, employees often don't know who, if anyone, is advocating for them. Most likely, Alan has no idea that Jeffery is giving him such vigorous support. At the same time, Jeffrey's advocacy for Alan is clearly visible to the people gathered around the conference table. For an advocate to be effective, he must speak up and promote his person of choice to others. Anonymous advocacy is an oxymoron. Whereas mentorship is often a private, one-on-one relationship between the mentor and mentee, advocacy always involves at least one other party.

Because of the confidential, informal nature of advocacy, women cannot say definitively whether or not the system is working for them. They do know, however, that women are not advancing in the corporate world at the same rate as men and that working within the corporate system seems more difficult for them. So, it's fair to infer that today's advocacy practices tend to benefit men more than women. But our experience is more than just a matter of inference. We've been in the rooms where these conversations take place. We've seen advocacy in action. Sitting in countless meetings like the one between Eric, the head of sales, and the three managers has given us a window into the subtle disparities between the fates of men and women in the advocacy process. We've seen that highly talented, hardworking women don't win the influential, loyal advocates as frequently as comparable men do.

The first way in which advocacy breaks down is that qualified women are not mentioned as frequently in discussions of employees who should be tracked for special opportunities. Howard recalls attending an after-hours office party one spring evening when he was visiting a local office in his division. Talking to one of his subordinate managers while looking over a room full of young employees, he asked who in the group were the strong performers. The manager identified four or five employees—all male. Howard had to follow up with, "Any women?" in order to elicit a few female names. All too often in the discussion of qualified up-and-comers, women are overlooked. In this case, we don't believe this was a conscious omission—it's unlikely that the manager was even thinking of gender in his response to Howard's question. More likely, though we can't be certain, it was a mental oversight—the notable women simply did not come to mind.

Even when women's names are raised for consideration, we've seen that they are more likely to be easily dismissed or quickly passed over than comparably capable men. We hear interesting little catch phrases that are used to undermine and stereotype qualified women. "She's a bit polarizing," "She's too difficult to work with," "She's overly emotional," and "She's not ready" all mask a generalized discomfort with a woman in a crucial position or a lead role. In the discussion reported above, when Brian mentioned Caroline for the key role, the odds are that at least one of the meeting participants wondered if the client would have a problem with a woman leading such an important team. We say this from experience, knowing that one of Lynn's clients confessed to her that a partner from her own firm, without Lynn's knowledge, asked this question directly of him: "Are you okay with a woman as your account manager?" It's doubtful that any such question was ever asked of any client about her male colleagues.

A more common and insidious way of eliminating women from consideration is damning them with faint praise. "She really puts in the effort." "She's trying hard to improve her writing skills." Jeffrey's acknowledgment of Caroline's ability to put together proposals was lackluster compared to his support for Alan. However, after this discussion and decision took place, the participants likely felt that they were quite egalitarian in their deliberations. "Of course we considered Caroline, but she just didn't have the same level of support as Alan" might have been said following the meeting. Regardless of whether women are overlooked, dismissed, or tepidly supported, the outcome is the same. Capable women are not championed as frequently or as forcefully as comparably capable men.

In the advocacy process, women often don't know who is

on their side and who is not. They may think they're attracting influential, loyal advocates and are often caught by surprise when the promotion or opportunity doesn't go their way. What can especially blindside a woman is a friendly, even mildly flirtatious rapport with a male executive. In many of those cases, the personal dynamics of the relationship belie the business reality. Time and again, we've seen a man being attentive and flattering to a woman in his direct dealings with her and then questioning her competence in a private conference at which she's not present. This tends not to be as true for work relationships between less experienced and more experienced men. Men usually know when other men don't think highly of them or just don't like them. In general in the business world, we've seen that alliances between men tend to be stronger and more transparent than those between men and women.

Sexual politics can also infect advocacy practices with regard to women in much the same way as they affect mentor relationships. When a male employee advocates for a woman, his support can be compromised by the presumption that sexual attraction is a primary motivator. Men have been known to rib each other about hidden intentions. "You must think she's good looking" or "Of course you'd pick her" might be said in a meeting in a jovial manner, at the same time undercutting the prospects of the woman being considered. Also, as with mentoring, the support of a female executive for another woman can be hypocritically impaired by suspicions of bias—of feminist zeal. Though the undermining may be slight, its effect is magnified because the audience tends to be at a higher level in the corporate structure. That's why advocacy can be so potent—it focuses on where the power lies.

The paradox that women face regarding advocacy is to some extent hidden, almost subterranean. Women in business know just as well as men that influential, loyal advocates are critical to their careers. They also know that they must compete to attract these advocates by working hard and producing good results. But they are literally out of the room when the practices of advocacy work better for their male peers than for them. From our perspective, having been in that room, we see qualified men being championed more frequently and more strongly than equally qualified women. We see advocacy for capable women more easily dismissed by gender stereotypes, or undermined by sexual politics, than for comparable men. The disparity exists, and the paradox is discomfiting.

THE PARADOX

Hard work and talent attract mentors and advocates. Young men and women learn this quickly upon entering the business world. They try their best to gain the attention of more senior employees who can teach them the tricks of the trade, open doors of opportunity, and champion their abilities. Yet the current mentoring and advocacy practices in business don't work as well for women as they do for men. Talented women who work hard rarely attract highly regarded mentors or win influential, loyal advocates to the same degree. This parity paradox confronts many women and contributes to the challenges women face in working within the system of business.

In analyzing how mentorship and advocacy practices fail women, we see again that corporate cultural forces are a major contributing factor. Vestiges of a male proving ground can foster behaviors among men and between men and women that inadvertently create the mentorship/advocacy paradox. When male senior employees more frequently select young men to mentor than women, we see the gender segregation aspects of the proving ground at play. When women are passed over by advocates, or advocated for less vehemently than men, we see the continued undervaluation of women's contributions in the workplace. When men rib each other about advocating for a woman, we see the competition among men for the approval of other men, at the expense of women. Though they are perhaps not consciously prejudiced against women, men perpetuating these behaviors have an adverse effect on women seeking to attract mentors and win advocates. They tilt the playing field by presenting women's male peers as more appealing candidates to respected mentors and influential advocates.

But in addition to the cultural vestiges of a male proving ground, we suggest that other, personal factors may be at play here as well. As we've noted, mentorship and advocacy are top-down processes in which senior employees take the active role of "selecting," and junior employees have the primarily passive role of "being chosen." From the junior employees' perspective, there's only so much they can do to attract mentors and win advocates. They can work hard and demonstrate their talent; they can try to be in the right spot at the right time; they can wear a red sweater. But at the end of the day, the process relies on senior employees proactively choosing to mentor or advocate for the employee of their choice. Examining the subtle elements that sway senior employees' selections can provide insight into why women are regularly disadvantaged in today's corporate mentoring and advocacy practices.

Risk to the individual and personal identification are important additional influences that can often lead senior employees to choose men rather than women. At a glance, the risks associated with mentorship and advocacy seem to lie with the junior employees. Will they be selected? Will someone champion them effectively over others? Will their mentor's advice be helpful? Can they live up to expectations? But the senior employee who chooses to act as a mentor or advocate also takes a risk. That's because, in the corporate community, a senior person's choice of whom to mentor, and even more importantly, whom to advocate for, is clearly indicative of the judgment of the senior person. The hackneyed phrase in the corporate community is "Our employees are our most important asset." But distinguishing between these human assets is one factor that defines an effective business leader—picking good people. Therefore, the higher-ups value not only the up-and-comers, but also the people who find the up-and-comers. The risk can be great for advocates because they visibly champion, to their peers and superiors, individuals they deem worthy. They say to this elite audience: "In my judgment, this one can do the job better than anyone else." Advocates and mentors truly stick their necks out for their protégés. Regularly choosing losers can reduce their clout and even flatten their career curve. Consequently, mentors and advocates are judicious in their choices. Not only are they investing time and energy, but they are risking their reputation among peers, superiors, and even subordinates.

In terms of risk to mentors and advocates, men are generally safer choices than women. Selecting a male employee to mentor or advocate for is the conservative choice, in what tends to be a conservative environment. Mentoring a young man continues the practices that prevailed in the past and rarely breaks new ground. In contrast, selecting a woman often draws attention to the choice—though it shouldn't. If it were done more often, it wouldn't draw such attention. But for now, it puts the mentor or advocate "out there" in a way that selecting a male doesn't. Choosing a female introduces gender into the equation, whereas a male choice appears to be genderless.

While we've noted that sexual connotations can undermine the female employee who is chosen by a mentor or advocate, such innuendos can also be risky for the mentor/advocate. Even when suspicions are unfounded, which they usually are, they can provide powerful ammunition to a man's co-workers in the never-ending competition on the male proving ground. Female mentors and advocates don't necessarily escape vulnerability by selecting women either, since suspicions of activist intent and gender favoritism are often aroused. As a result, in today's business world, many men and women see it as simply safer to mentor or advocate for a man. While we believe relatively few senior employees and executives consciously say to themselves "I don't want to mentor a woman," the best managers—who are usually the best mentors and advocates—have a keen intuitive awareness of risks that can jeopardize their own careers, and, therefore, they gravitate toward male protégés.

The intimate nature of mentoring may present an additional risk to the individual. The attraction that initially brings a mentor and mentee together may blossom into a romantic liaison. We have occasionally seen mentor relationships between senior males and junior females go in this direction. While some who act on a mutual attraction achieve a happy personal outcome, for many others, such a relationship may pose a threat to their reputation, marriage, and family. On a more sinister level, an initially exciting fling can turn into a sordid reality. Even if no physical intimacy takes place, the possibility of being accused of sexual harassment, rightly or wrongly, is real. Although false accusations of sexual harassment are rare, a male attorney who worked in a human resources department was so conscious of this risk that he remarked, "It's just better if I stay away from any close one-on-one working relationships with women." Whether he doesn't trust working women or doesn't trust himself, the result is the same. This tends to be an issue primarily for male mentors. While sexual liaisons occur between senior women and junior men, as well as between mentors and mentees of the same gender, they are less prevalent than among senior males and junior females.

While the desire to avoid what they view as unnecessary risk is one factor influencing men to avoid female protégés, another is personal identification. Senior employees and executives tend to choose employees with whom they identify. They are often naturally attracted to young, talented employees in whom they see something of themselves. The pattern is so prevalent that it's parodied in popular culture as "mini-me." In our experience, mentors and mentees actually do tend to look alike. This identification component can put women at a strong disadvantage because in a historically male culture such as business, men are discouraged from identifying with women. The "flight from the feminine"[2] imperative pushes a number of men to dissociate themselves from their female co-workers. This makes a connection between a male senior employee and a female junior employee less likely. Most corporate men are simply conditioned not to see much of themselves in women.

Senior employees know that when they play the mentorship/advocacy game, their choice of protégé may put them at risk. They want to make choices that play to their advantage by minimizing their risks and maximizing their reputations. In addition, in such an informal system, mentors and advocates are often drawn to those employees with whom they personally identify. Unfortunately, the too frequent consequence is that mentors/advocates focus on men more than women. When mentors and advocates choose to support women, the risks at times seem sufficiently real to them that we have seen well-intentioned, high-placed men drop their female protégés at the first sign of trouble. The loyalty and vehement support that mentors and advocates give to younger men is, sadly, rarely given to younger women to the same degree.

So, what's a woman to do? Given the informal, passive, traditional processes that we have discussed, women have little control, and their careers are hindered by the mentor/advocate paradox. Regardless of how hard women work or how talented they are, they often fail to attract highly regarded mentors or win influential, loyal advocates as successfully as do their male peers.

Chapter 6

PARADOX #3: COMMITMENT TO THE JOB

A woman who is committed to her job and career is often presumed to have a deficient personal life. A woman with a fulfilling personal life is frequently seen as not seriously committed to her job and career.

THE VALUE OF COMMITMENT

A mathematics professor once told Howard, "I'd rather have a B student in my class who's committed to his work than a prodigy who's there only because he has to be." The workplace mirrors this preference to an extreme degree. Employers and managers relish the employee who is committed to his job and his company. Such an employee can be trusted, can be counted on to be there when needed, and can be called upon to go "above and beyond." Like the soldier willing to give his life for his country, the employee willing to devote his life to his job is cherished by the corporate world. In contrast, those employees perceived as lacking commitment are seen as clock watchers who work only because they have to. They are the drones who are passed over for promotion and denied career-enhancing assignments. In the corporate system, the uncommitted are easily replaced, while committed employees are considered priceless gems.

A committed workforce can accomplish astounding feats. As with a sports team of mediocre talent but great heart, the energy can be inspiring and contagious. As a result, the achievements of a committed group can reach heights that no gifted but apathetic group of contributors can approach. The 1980 U.S. Olympic hockey team—a group of amateur and collegiate players who routed the seemingly invincible Russian contenders—is still hailed as the "Miracle on Ice." Similarly, the meteoric rise of Microsoft, Apple, and Google is in no small part attributable to the youthful exuberance and unwavering dedication of their early staff members. The authors of the classic *In Search of Excellence,* Thomas J. Peters and Robert H. Waterman, captured the power of employee commitment when they articulated what a company needs in order to excel. "The basics, in our opinion: quick action, service to customers, practical innovation, and the fact that you can't get any of these without virtually everyone's commitment."[1] Based on Peters and Waterman's research, a committed employee population is a cornerstone of excellence.

Great companies cultivate commitment. They begin by looking for employees who share a common passion for their business and their values. The zeal may be for something concrete that the company produces—cars, video games, haute couture—or it may be for something intangible, something the company does—publishing books, building skyscrapers, exploring solar energy. When Lynn worked for a music company, virtually every employee, from the administrative assistants to the presidents of record labels, lived a life of music. All had some music-generating device in their work area, and at the end of the day, these employees donned their headphones as others would reflexively put on their overcoats. Whether it was rock, country, or opera, music was their passion. In the less exciting business arenas, employees may be committed to the values that the company represents or to the way the company conducts its business. Metropolitan Life employees are serious about their company's stability and longevity. Avis employees parade their efficiency and frugality. Though insurance contracts and car rentals are more mundane than rock bands, the corporate headquarters of MetLife and Avis teem with employees who are proud of what they do and committed to their companies—and the higher up the corporate ladder they are, the more intense their commitment.

To underscore the value of commitment, corporate cultures honor their heroes of commitment. Valiant and sometimes humorous anecdotes of personal sacrifice and extraordinary effort are recounted. In the early days of IBM, employees would say that the company's initials stood for "I've been moved." At another company, tales are told of Tim, who had been traveling on business for so long that at one point he lost track and had to call his secretary from a distant airport to find out why he was there. "Sally, I'm in Denver. Why am I in Denver?" (He was supposed to catch a connecting flight.) Or there is the story of Harry, who had not taken a single vacation day in two years. Then, when he did, because his family firmly insisted, he sent e-mails from his BlackBerry every half hour while he was on the beach. His staff swore that the sea air cleared his mind and his week off was one of his most productive.

Companies not only sing the praises of their committed employees; they also amply reward them. Committed employees' work ethic is touted in performance reviews. Their above-and-beyond effort is used to justify higher salaries. Their future prospects are defined as promising. But one of the more intriguing benefits that accrues to these employees is that their failures are minimized. Two employees can make exactly the same error of judgment, but managers will say of the one perceived as totally committed to his work, "That's not like him," "It was a mistake anyone could make," or, our personal favorite, "A momentary lapse because he works so hard." In essence, high-ranking managers tend to personally identify with the committed employee and forgive his mistakes as anomalies.

Business puts a high value on committed employees. Management knows that a loyal and dedicated workforce gives a company a huge competitive edge over its rivals. But commitment to a company has become complicated lately. Cradle-to-grave employment with one organization is rare on a résumé and viewed almost as showing a lack of personal initiative. Also, companies have created an additional challenge for themselves by practicing a commitment double standard. That is, while most companies expect a high level of loyalty and dedication from their employees, they are rarely willing to return the same level of commitment. The lack of mutuality was glaringly exemplified when a major technology firm preached at an annual meeting of its top 500 managers the blind-loyalty principles extolled in "A Message to Garcia."[2] This century-old Elbert Hubbard parable is popular with many large companies, as it tells the story of a soldier during the Spanish-American War who endures wrenching trials and harrowing hardships in his relentless efforts to follow his orders, never questioning his mission or doubting his purpose. Layoffs and downsizing coupled with paltry severance benefits were a perpetual reality at this highly profitable technology firm, yet managers were told, "This soldier is the model of loyalty and dedication to an organization to which you should aspire." Then, within two weeks, in the company's never-ending quest for more profits, these same managers were ordered to plan for their third round of layoffs that year, which included some of the managers themselves.

Despite the hypocrisy, companies continue to crave committed employees. The financial and competitive advantages are too great for them not to distinguish between those who are totally dedicated to their jobs and those who are not. Lifelong loyalty to a company may no longer be the standard, but expectations of unwavering commitment while on the payroll may actually have increased. Perhaps it is precisely because it is so difficult for organizations to create a deep level of loyalty today that employee commitment is so highly valued in the business world of the new millennium.

PROXIES OF COMMITMENT

While the corporate world values and seeks committed employees, its ability to discern commitment can be somewhat inconsistent and its criteria ill defined. This is understandable. After all, no manager can see into an employee's soul to determine how he truly feels about his job and employer. Nor is it appropriate that an employee's zeal for his employer should be the sole yardstick. Employee commitment needs to be weighed against employee contribution to the business. As a result, the whole exercise of assessing employee commitment tends unavoidably to be more subjective than objective. It varies with a manager's personal perceptions and a company's values and ideals. Nevertheless, there are certain common markers that are used fairly consistently in the corporate world to identify the committed employee.

By far the most common measure of commitment is time spent working on the job. Time shouts commitment. From overtime to late-night hours to weekend work, the amount of time an employee puts into his work outside the nine-to-five is considered a prime indicator of the importance of his work in his life. New college graduates may find this reality overwhelming at first, when their new co-workers boast and brag about how late they left the office last night, or how many hours they put in over the weekend. They quickly learn, though, that this is not about the time it takes to do the job; this is about what it takes to be seen as a committed employee. "He's here all hours" or "He really puts in the time" are descriptions of dedication, not dimwittedness.

Time as a measure of commitment also has the advantage of being visible and quantifiable. Managers can readily identify those employees who arrive at work early and stay late. Companies can compute hours worked and include them in performance reviews. The benchmark is rarely just time spent doing productive and profitable work. Face time—time spent seeing and being seen by the powers that be—counts, as does research time, down time, co-worker social time, prospect-development time, and company-softball-team time. Just being there has traditionally been viewed as enhancing esprit de corps and reflecting dedication. One employee was incredulous when he was denied a promotion because his "total time," represented by a number that was spit out by his company's HR system on performance reviews, was considered inadequate. "Your work is excellent. Your billable time is above target and your clients love you. But your total time is a problem." This employee had missed the fact that in his organization, the hard number for total time was a soft proxy for employee commitment.

Odd as this is going to sound, we have found that in the corporate world, quality of work product typically takes a backseat to time as a measure of commitment. That's not to say that the employee who produces excellent work in a forty-hour workweek isn't valued. He is just not seen as deeply dedicated and is therefore not entitled to the perquisites of the committed—plum assignments, promotions, bonuses, forgiveness, high esteem. Despite his quality work, the nine-to-fiver is rarely the corporate ideal. While the company may be satisfied with the job he is doing, there is a sense that he cannot be pushed. He will only give so much. Looked at in another way, business is looking for maximum production from its employees. By the time you take into account salary, benefits, cost of office space, payroll taxes, even overtime, it is significantly more efficient for one employee to make twenty widgets than for two to make ten each. This is why companies prefer to get more work out of fewer people. Consequently, if the work product is good enough, the employee who is seen as putting in more time is often assumed to be more productive and therefore a more valuable commodity.

But time as a measure of commitment may reward the slow

and inefficient, a clear flaw in the measurement. And the measurement may have other limitations, as well. As anyone who has been waylaid by the office gadfly will tell you, the extra time some people spend in the office can actually be counterproductive. Employees who stay in the office just to be seen there are often wasting not only their own time but that of their fellow employees. They distract and irritate rather than build morale. These are all reasons why managers need to insert their personal perceptions into this most black and white of measures. Despite its popularity, time as an indicator of commitment can be an imperfect measure.

Boundless energy and positive attitude are also viewed as strong indicators of commitment. Employees highly enthused about their work are often assumed to be completely dedicated to their jobs. These employees run from meeting to meeting, ever ebullient about whatever task is placed before them. One such employee gushed to us, "Every morning I wake up excited about going into the office." To which, an acquaintance of ours dryly responded, "*Every* morning?" While our friend was a bit cynical, we have had people like this work for us, and it can be a pleasure. No job is too big or too small for them. They never whine or complain. They are always moving and always focused on what you want to get done. Unfortunately, that doesn't always mean that they actually get done what you want them to get done. Lynn recalls a highly energized employee working for her once, and, she has to confess, it took Lynn a little too long to realize that while the woman was a whirlwind, nothing was being accomplished. Lynn found herself blinded by the zeal and blindsided by the woman's lack of productivity. Enormous energy doesn't always translate into fruitful work.

A quieter indicator of commitment is the personal identity an employee takes from his work. Identity entails your ownership of your work, making the link between who you are and what you do. By this measure, committed employees see their work as a reflection of themselves and can't fall asleep at night unless a job is done well. The depth and simplicity of the sentiment struck

Howard when he called an employee in the human resources department to thank her for the way she had handled a particularly sensitive issue concerning the dismissal of an employee. Her brief but eloquent response was, "That's okay. It's just what I do." To this human resource professional, what she does and how well she does it are part and parcel of who she is.

Now one might think that the quieter and more dignified characteristic of personal identity is a solid barometer of true commitment. But like the others, it can go awry when an employee's concept of self is so singularly consumed by his job that he loses all perspective. Myopic managers from hell can fall into this category. These are the people who go through a secretary a month since they presume that, regardless of pay grade, all others should be as devoted to their job as they are. They may demoralize all those around them and are the quintessential target for their co-workers' muttered complaint, "Get a life."

Finally, personal sacrifice is a popular proxy for commitment. When a deadline looms, when a customer needs immediate assistance, when the meeting date has been changed from next week to tomorrow, when the senior executive wants the revenue projections first thing in the morning, self-sacrificing employees are the first responders. For these employees, all other obligations are set aside, no questions asked. Because work takes precedence, they will miss dinner engagements, forfeit play-off tickets, or postpone vacation plans almost as a point of pride, an honor badge of commitment. The inconvenience suffered by them, and sometimes their families, is seen as reflective of their work as the highest priority in their life. They will move themselves and their families from New York to Omaha—or from Omaha to New York—to take a position that the company is having trouble filling. Both large and small sacrifices are tracked. For example, many managers will hold in high regard an employee who sends an email with a 5:00 a.m. time-stamp even though its content may be trivial. More than putting in the time, personal sacrifice is about the employees' relinquishing control of their time. One ambitious employee summed it up this way:

"From 6:00 a.m. to 8:00 p.m., they own me." But being inconvenienced doesn't always translate into the production of good, valuable work. The potential flaw with personal sacrifice as a proxy for commitment is that pain is seen as substance.

Time, energized attitude, identity, and personal sacrifice are the salient standards of commitment. Each has its yin and yang, which is why there needs to be an element of management discretion in any ultimate assessment of an employee's dedication level. In making their judgments, managers generally view the means of demonstrating commitment as gender neutral. Business seeks commitment from all of its employees but acknowledges that the degree of commitment may vary from employee to employee for a range of reasons, many of them personal. But by talking to women across a variety of industries and examining our own experiences, we began to see a pattern that is quite disturbing—a systemic bias in the area of commitment that puts women at a disheartening disadvantage relative to men. Within the corporate world, today's concepts of commitment combined with gender roles derived from the past create an unintended paradox that can have particularly cruel and hurtful consequences for many women in business.

COMMITTED BUT DEFICIENT

Leslie and Maggie were on a train heading home from Boston to New York. As the northeast corridor flew by outside the Amtrak window, they started to unwind. It had been a long day. For six hours they had met with Donna to hash out all the problems they were having with one of the company's larger accounts. These three professional women, the senior members of the client team, were accountable for the client, and they had been having trouble getting it right. So they had spent the whole day painstakingly going through every detail. Why was the client dissatisfied? What did the client need and expect? Who on the client team was working well, and who wasn't? What should their strategy be going forward? How should responsibilities and team composition be realigned? It was arduous and at times combative work, but they had emerged with a feeling of accomplishment.

As the conductor punched and returned their tickets, both Leslie and Maggie felt some of the tensions of the day abating.

"Boy, that was tough, but I think we got done what was needed," Leslie said.

"Yeah, I agree," concurred Maggie. Then she added, "I haven't worked that much with Donna, but she certainly lives up to her reputation. Hard-working, focused, no nonsense. She can be intense."

Leslie knew that some people reacted strongly, and sometimes negatively, to Donna's style, so she wanted to share her perspective with Maggie. "No question she's intense. But she's good and gets things done. I've worked with her quite a bit and have always found her to be reasonable and effective. I know she pushes people hard, but she pushes herself just as hard."

"Do you know much about her? Is she married?" inquired Maggie.

"Yes, she's married and has two young kids. A boy and a girl, I think," Leslie responded.

"Wow, I would never have guessed," Maggie said. Then, almost under her breath, she added, "Poor kids. Imagine having Donna for a mother."

Leslie didn't know how to respond.

Though a bit catty, Maggie was expressing a sentiment that runs rampant through the business world and today's culture in general. The popular perception is that there's probably something wrong on a personal level with a woman who is committed to her job and good at it. If a man dedicated as many hours to his job as Donna did, and with the same intensity, hardly anyone would question his dedication to his children. In contrast, even though business loves and lauds commitment, a woman who is committed to her career is often presumed to have a deficient personal life. This is a particularly mean-spirited and disturbing assertion—one that is often met with denial and incredulity. But, unfortunately, we have found the belief to be quite commonplace.

Whether on television or in films, popular culture is replete with examples of competent, hard-working women who have troubled personal lives. This image of the successful woman hasn't changed much in over forty years. Have you ever seen Sally in the original *Dick Van Dyke Show*?[3] In this popular American television series, which aired from October 1961 to June 1966, Sally Rogers (Rose Marie) is a witty, dedicated member of a three-person comedy writing team with Rob (Dick Van Dyke) and Buddy (Morey Amsterdam). A running theme of the show is Sally's perpetual search for a man and her inability to attract any serious prospects. *The Mary Tyler Moore Show*[4] in the 1970s was more progressive in portraying a working woman in a positive light, but even after seven seasons, the show ended with Mary still searching for Mr. Right. Fast forward to 1988 and the film *Working Girl*,[5] in which a young, intelligent, hard-working secretary (Melanie Griffith) outwits her highly driven, ambitious boss (Sigourney Weaver). Weaver's role is that of the classic, successful businesswoman bitch—very smart, professionally accomplished, irritatingly condescending, shamelessly manipulative, and totally incompetent romantically. Of course, at the end of the story, the sweet and talented secretary gets the sexy, rich businessman (Harrison Ford), and Weaver's businesswoman gets no one. Jump forward another eighteen years to 2006, when Meryl Streep portrays Amanda Priestly, the epitome of female success, in *The Devil Wears Prada*.[6] The managing editor of a top fashion magazine, Priestly has power, wealth, and beauty. She not only runs the magazine; she is the magazine. At the same time, she's a distant spouse whose husband wants to divorce her and a flawed mother whose twin daughters are spoiled and bratty.

These images do more than just entertain. They tell us the way many people in society view the woman who is committed to her job and career. And, as far back as most of us can remember, from Sally Rogers to Amanda Priestly, the message has been the same: the successful, committed businesswoman cannot expect to have a successful, committed personal life. And she is probably not a very nice person, either. In the real world, the damning of the dedicated businesswoman takes many forms. Often it's a petty aside on the woman's ability to be a good wife or mother, like the comment Maggie made about Donna. Or it's a negative predisposition toward women seen as proficient and committed to their work. Even Lynn's secretary confessed, after they had been working together successfully for years, that when she first saw Lynn when she was applying for the job, her initial reaction to Lynn's professional style and demeanor was "Oh please, don't let that be the person I'm supposed to work for." Or, disguised as caring, the belittling frequently takes the form of pity. One senior executive, explaining why he gave a particular woman an opportunity to become a manager, said that "After all, work is all she has in her life." The commentary can cut to the core of the woman's character, as did a statement by one experienced, highly successful salesman about a female fellow executive: "I admit that I respect her work, but I certainly don't like her or admire her." Regardless of the form of the put-down, the opinions tend toward the personal and pejorative.

The deleterious effects of being perceived as committed to one's career seem to be borne primarily by women. The man who demonstrates commitment is generally lauded as a valuable, reputable employee—a "good man." Barring any conspicuous marital infidelities, his personal life is presumed to be blandly blissful. Even if there are marital or family problems, they rarely earn him much negative attention at work. In contrast, the woman who meets the commitment threshold is not necessarily considered a "good woman." While she may be hailed within the business community for her dedication to her work, she often carries an aura of being something less than likable personally and being flawed on the domestic front. She must be an unloving spouse, a poor mother, a one-dimensional personality, or just a distasteful human being.

The disparity in the perception of committed businessmen versus committed businesswomen does not seem to derive directly from the measures of commitment themselves. Putting in time, maintaining a positive and energetic attitude, identifying with your work, or sacrificing yourself for the job does not automatically make you a disagreeable character. So where does the unflattering stereotype of the committed businesswoman come from? We see the presumptions about committed working women and their deficient personal lives as rooted in the gender roles inherent in the culture at large and deeply embedded in the work culture in particular. As the modern business world developed in the postindustrial age, men's responsibilities in their work and personal lives were well aligned. Being a man meant being a good provider. At work, where men competed with other men on the male proving ground, commitment and hard work translated into greater success and greater financial rewards. Since the male's primary role at home was that of breadwinner, his business success was a domestic success. Far from a conflict, there was an easy symbiosis between a man's work life and his personal life.

This was not the case for postindustrial-age women. As the opposite sex, women were expected to play supportive roles. Being a "good woman" had nothing to do with being a financial provider. If anything, members of the opposite sex were not supposed to work outside the home—they were supposed to be committed to caring for their families and supporting men in the ongoing competition among men. As the workplace changed and women began taking positions traditionally reserved for men, women were, in fact, committing themselves to work as much as their male colleagues were. But this contravened the cultural expectations carried forward in the business world of women as the opposite sex. By those standards, not only were women not fulfilling their opposite-sex obligations of being supportive of men and family, but they were adding to the competition, making men's jobs even more difficult. A conflict arose: a woman couldn't fulfill her obligations as a member of the opposite sex and be committed to her work at the same time. Something had to give. Thus there evolved the popular perception that the woman who is committed to her work must have serious deficiencies in her personal life. Or, in other words, "How would you like to have her as your mother?"

Recently in business, this issue of women and work has been viewed as a work/family conflict. But we think there is more going on here. The traditional work/family conflict is a challenge employees must deal with in achieving balance and juggling priorities. It is a logistics problem, not a character flaw. In contrast, the commitment paradox is based on the perception of women by others. When colleagues—superiors, peers, and subordinates—make negative judgments about women who are committed to their jobs and careers, their verdicts are usually mere opinions reached with little factual knowledge. In our earlier example, Maggie knew nothing of the quality of Donna's parenting, but she assumed Donna was a poor mother. Worse, once these assumptions are made, people seek validation by seeing what they want to see, inferring what they want to infer. Lynn recalls feeling that her parenting skills were constantly being scrutinized, especially when our children were younger. In what seems almost ridiculous now, she remembers a one-on-one discussion with a company's conservative CEO in which she felt compelled to defend her parenting style. At a gathering of executives and their families, he had seen her with our very tall four-year-old son on her hip. Later, the CEO intimated to her that our son seemed a bit old to be carried around by his mother.

The news media perpetuate the disparagement when their reporting on prominent women routinely informs on their marital and parenthood status, especially if that status is problematic. A recent interview by *60 Minutes* television journalist Morley Safer of Anna Wintour, the renowned editor of *Vogue,* is a case in point.[7] Within the first five sentences of the story, we know that Ms. Wintour is a divorced mother of two. Less than thirty seconds later we learn that behind Ms. Wintour's back, many who work with her call her "Darth Vader in a frock" and "Nuclear Wintour," the latter name being characterized as less harsh. The subtext clearly seems to be "Look at the personal price Anna Wintour has had to pay for her enduring success." Rarely do we see prominent men subjected to the same punishing personality analysis.

One might ask, "So what?" Does it really matter that people perceive women such as Anna Wintour as unpleasant and deficient in their personal lives? Is Anna Wintour any less successful because of this? We think it does matter, on two levels. First, it's psychologically demoralizing. Hillary Clinton got it right when she was asked during the January 5, 2008, presidential primary debate to respond to surveys that showed that she was less likable than the other candidates. "Well, that hurts my feelings"[8] was her memorable rejoinder. And to make matters worse, there is really no good way to deal with the defamation, as Mrs. Clinton learned when she felt the need to follow up her initial debate response with the awkwardly defensive, slightly self-pitying "I don't think I'm that bad."[9] Nobody, male or female, wants to be seen as fundamentally unlikable, yet this is the presumption too many women are forced to contend with in today's business environment.

But besides hurt feelings, there is a professional consequence to being perceived negatively. In the competitive world of business, negative impressions take a toll. No one is immune to the way he or she is perceived. The presumption of driven women having deficient personal lives simply puts women at a disadvantage relative to men. Such women are frequently viewed as unhappy individuals, not good to work with, not nice people. It is one of the elements that makes the playing field unlevel and makes the experience of work more difficult for women than for comparable male co-workers.

PERCEPTION VERSUS REALITY

"I love my job," Angela declared. "I get to fly around the world and meet big, important institutional investors. The research and problem solving are intellectually stimulating. The pay is great. And I'm good at it!"

Angela had the bravado and self-confidence typically associated with Wall Street types. But instead of projecting the standard dark-suited visual image, she was tall and blond, dressed in stylish violet with diamonds adorning her fingers and earlobes. She looked a good decade younger than her fifty years, due to daily workouts at 5:30 a.m. and a lifetime of fastidiously avoiding the sun.

"What about Robbie and the boys? Do you think that your commitment to your job has negatively affected them?" we asked.

"Ah, the boys, the boys. They're teenagers now, and who doesn't have trouble with adolescent boys? But they're good kids. Are their grades as good as I'd like? No, but what parents do you know would say their kids' grades are? They'll both go to college, good colleges. Robbie's been great with them. They're good kids."

"And Robbie? Do you think that your career has taken a toll on your marriage?"

"Robbie knew who I was when we got together. And I knew who he was. He has his own passion; he has his own business. Robbie and I are going on twenty-five years together. Not too bad for nowadays. We've worked it out." Angela sighed, then leaned forward and continued in a tête-à-tête tone, "Frankly, I actually think our marriage is better than some of these mom's-responsible-for-the-home couples. I know our sex life is better." She laughed.

Angela always laughs. She is not an unhappy person. Yes, she has seen that the business world is tougher on women than men, and that women have yet to reach parity in many ways. Like most of the working women we have spoken with, she has good days and bad at her job and at home. But she is deeply committed to both.

A lifetime of working with committed businesswomen has firmly convinced us that the business world's perception of them does not fit the reality. The presumption that the personal lives of most committed businesswomen are deficient is just plain untrue. Rather than being grounded in fact, it's a supposition that is carried forward reflecting archaic gender roles, not contemporary realities.

Talking with today's accomplished women reveals them to be dedicating themselves to their jobs and careers just as much as their male peers and still living fulfilling, bountiful personal lives. For most of them, their work is integral to a rich and productive adult life of contributing to the world. In addition, being financially productive builds their sense of self-reliance and self-esteem. These are the daughters of the women's movement, and they live what their mothers and grandmothers were striving for—the opportunity to experience the independence and rewards associated with doing good work. Contrary to the negative propaganda, most of these women have found that being committed to their work enhances their personal lives.

That's not to say that work and personal lives don't often compete for time. Such conflicts occur regularly and can be stressful in anyone's life, regardless of gender. But a hectic life of balancing the demands of work and family can be exceptionally rewarding. Lessons learned in one forum may apply to the other. An office manager once tutored us on how to handle conflicting client priorities. "Try to catch things on the first bounce" was his memorable juggling metaphor. His centering business principle of "don't panic—get the important things right" was especially applicable as a life lesson one crisp winter morning when Lynn was walking up Fifth Avenue on her way to work. We had just dropped off our three-year-old daughter at nursery school and our six-month-old son was at home with our caregiver. The night before, Lynn had been on the local New York news as a human resources expert, and several parents at the school had seen her and complimented her on the interview. That evening we were hosting a holiday party in our apartment for forty people from our office. It felt good. We were in control. Our children were healthy and happy. Lynn was a mini-celebrity for a moment. Then, Lynn glanced down at her low-heeled pumps and saw, in the bright sunlight, that one was navy blue and the other black. A small thing in the big picture.

Professor Faye J. Crosby of Smith College validates the experience that Lynn and so many other women share. The research presented in her book, *Juggling: The Unexpected Advantages of Balancing Career and Home for Women and Their Families*, debunks many of the myths about working mothers and counters the negative presumptions about women who commit to their jobs and careers. "The evidence . . . is that women who combine significant life roles are better off emotionally than are women with fewer life roles." In this context, "life roles" are considered to be those of wife, mother, professional, business-woman, volunteer, and so forth. "Even as they acknowledge stress and time pressure, jugglers demonstrate less depression, higher self-esteem, and greater satisfaction with life generally and with different aspects of life than do women who play fewer roles."[10] Professor Crosby's sociological studies validated Betty Friedan's conjectures. Working outside the home enhances a woman's total life experience, just as it does for a man.

Today, the vast majority of women work outside the home. According to the Bureau of Labor Statistics, 61.1 percent of all women age twenty and older participated in the labor force as of May 2009. This compares closely to the 75.4 percent of all men who participated in the labor force at the same date.[11] More noteworthy is data collected in 2008 showing that 71.4 percent of mothers with children under eighteen were in the labor force.[12] What's more difficult to document is how most of these women make it work. While traditionalists believe that women are still responsible for the home and family, we think this view is outdated and out of sync with the way couples actually live today. In the majority of dual-adult households in America, the responsibilities for generating income and handling domestic obligations are shared. In the past, women's salaries may have been considered pin money, and men's work may have been finished when they brought home the paycheck, but today it's hard to find a household in which domestic, financial, and parenting duties aren't shared to some significant degree. Yet men who are committed to their work are rarely denigrated for having deficient personal lives due to their additional home-front obligations. Rather, it seems the modern man can have it all. He's Brad Pitt with a brood of toddlers around his knees; he's Matthew McConaughey walking down the beach with an infant on his hip. He's President Obama cheering on his daughter's soccer team from the sidelines. The reality is that both men and women are "having it all" and "doing it all" today; it's just that women are more likely to be scorned for it or subjected to negative perceptions.

Anecdotally, we do hear about one area of disparity between working men and working women with families: parental guilt. Among men and women who are committed to their jobs and careers, we see more women than men who are troubled about potentially neglecting their familial responsibilities. This is most apparent when young children are involved. Gary Trudeau humorously captured the sentiment in an old Doonesbury cartoon: "J.J. asks her husband Rick: 'I know you love Jeff [their young son] as much as I do. So why don't you seem as torn up about not being able to spend time with him?' Rick's response: 'Well, it may be because I'm spending a whole lot more time on family than my father did. And you're spending less time than your mother did. Consequently, you feel guilty while I naturally feel pretty proud of myself.'"[13]

While there is likely some psychological truth in Trudeau's perspective, traditional expectations of motherhood are also major contributors to the guilt disparity. Many of today's corporate cultures presume that mothers have a greater responsibility than fathers for the health and well-being of children and family. The women who buy into this expectation assume more guilt as a result. Not that all working women do buy into the expectation, though. With a humor they may share only among themselves, working mothers will laugh at how much their young children love their daycare arrangements: "Johnny doesn't cry when I drop him off in the mornings. He cries when I pick him up and he has to go home!" Though the women are self-deprecating, this childcare experience is more common than popular culture would lead one to believe, and it brings many a working mother great pleasure, comfort, and relief. It can also leave a working mother feeling guilty about not feeling guilty.

Other than the difference in parental guilt, we have found no correlation between commitment to one's job and career and the quality of one's personal life—for either men or women. Men who are fully committed to their work are just as likely as women to have deficient personal lives. Similarly, most women who commit to their careers have fulfilling personal lives comparable to the lives of their male peers. The presumption that committed women are somehow personally deficient *because* they are committed to their jobs is both cruel and unfounded. Yet when women refute this presumption and share their priorities and their contentment, they frequently find themselves in the middle of a paradox.

HOBSON'S CHOICE

Lynn was sitting at her desk when she overheard what started as an innocent conversation outside her office door.

"Yes, my wife is pregnant. She's due in April," beamed Wesley, a tall, patrician, young salesman with a Harvard degree and a square jaw.

"That's so exciting! Congratulations!" offered Tess. "What is she planning to do about her job?"

"Well, she'll stop working about a month before she's due, as long as she's feeling well," Wesley replied. "Then, after the baby arrives, she may come back to work part-time, or not at all. We think it's best for the baby if she stays home as much as possible."

"Makes sense," Tess said. "You know, I've seen so many women try to work full-time at a demanding career and have children, too, but it's always a problem. I just don't think a woman can do both well at the same time. One or the other suffers."

Lynn could hardly believe her ears. Tess was an experienced, highly regarded businesswoman—like Lynn, a partner in the firm—and far from holding Lynn up as a role model, she had just invalidated Lynn's existence.

Although it is rarely expressed this openly, the opinion voiced by Tess persists. There is an enduring perception in the world of business that being a good mother, a good caregiver, or a good wife is incompatible with being a fully committed employee. Consequently, a woman with a fulfilling personal life is often seen as not seriously committed to her job and career. The rationale seems to be that the woman with a rich family life must be placing her domestic obligations on a higher plane than her work responsibilities. Consequently, her commitment to her work must be compromised. Unlike the working man, who is lauded for being a dedicated father and an enlightened, modern man, the working woman who visibly puts her family first may be seen as suspect. To some, her personal priorities preclude her being as dedicated to her job and career as her male peers. Many managers and co-workers see women with satisfying private lives as having made a choice—maybe an admirable choice—the inevitable outcome of which is that they contribute less at work and should be compensated accordingly. The irony, of course, is that most men and women will say that family is the most important thing in their lives. But when a woman openly acknowledges the priority of her family in her life, her commitment to her work is often called into question.

The dilemma is in some ways a by-product of the broader cultural belief that women have choices. They choose to work outside the home or inside the home; they choose to have children or not to have children; they choose when and whether to come back to work after giving birth; they choose to work part-time or full-time. This either/or proposition is women's prerogative, and all their options are socially, culturally, and politically acceptable today. But making a choice communicates one's priorities. It tells the world what is important to you. In contrast, traditionally, men's priorities are less visible, since men are not seen as having to make similar choices. They don't have to publicly declare their priorities to the world. Women are more "out there," more subject to scrutiny, and therefore often more subject to business bias.

When our son turned eleven, we celebrated his birthday with a Sunday afternoon bowling party. Unfortunately, Lynn was working on a challenging client project that was due the following Monday. She had spent Saturday in the office, working furiously with her client team, but they still weren't done. So they started again Sunday morning, determined to complete the project on time. Lynn gave Howard periodic updates from the office. "I might be done by noon." Then, "It's taking longer than we thought. Why don't I meet you and the kids at the bowling alley?" Later, "I'm still at the office. I'll try to get there for the pizza and cake." She missed the party and didn't get out of the office until late that night. The next day, Lynn recounted this tale to one of her male colleagues. He grimaced and said, "Please don't tell me that. I have this image of you as such a good mother."

The truth is that conflicts such as this do occur. Over the course of raising two children, each of us has had occasion to miss a family event we wanted to attend. But a missed party doesn't define a parent as poor or deficient. At least, not in Howard's case. The sacrifices he's made in his personal life—missed parties, delayed or interrupted vacations—have been seen as signs that he is a good provider for his family. Yet, to Lynn's male colleague, the issue was an either/or matter—Lynn had to be either a good mother or a dedicated worker; she could not be both. This sentiment is at the core of the commitment paradox that many women face. In a business environment with vestiges of a male proving ground, women's traditional gender role of the opposite sex—good mother, supportive wife—conflicts with women being competent competitors with men. For a woman to be living a fulfilling family life and excelling as a businessperson can be incongruous in such an environment. Often, the first reaction is to say that if a woman is seen as committed to her work, her personal life must be suffering. The mirror image of this reaction is equally powerful. If a woman has what is traditionally seen as a fulfilling personal life, she can't also be fully committed to her job and career. On a male proving ground, she just can't have both at the same time.

The proxies of commitment, applied in an environment that tends to keep women a step behind men, often reflect this historical conflict. When applied in a corporate world that retains vestiges of "a man's world," the proxies can fail to accurately indicate the strength of a woman's commitment. That's because the proxies can rely on appearance and impression more than substance. The woman who takes two hours off in the afternoon to attend a parent/teacher conference appears less committed to her work than the male employee who takes two hours off to meet with his financial advisor. The woman who leaves the office every day at 5:00 because the caregiver tending to her elderly father leaves at 6:00 appears less committed to her job than the male employee who sticks around the office every evening until 6:00, socializing. The woman who leaves early may work additional hours at home, but they're not as visible. Time as a measure, especially total time in the office, can obfuscate true employee dedication as well as quality and quantity of work. As one woman told us, "I think I'm more efficient than most, and I'm being penalized for it."

Each of the subjective measures of commitment—time, energized attitude, personal identity, and self-sacrifice—may belie the commitment of a woman who openly says she puts her family first. All too often she will be judged as unprofessional and not dedicated to her position. Some women know this and fib. They know that less-than-committed employees suffer monetarily, receive less recognition, and have fewer opportunities for advancement. So they try to counter the cultural bias by concealing their dedication to their personal lives. When women first entered the professional workforce, they would not display photos of their families in their offices. Many would hide their pregnancies for as long as possible, never sharing their physical discomfort or morning sickness episodes. Many still enter fake meetings or conference calls on their calendars to reserve time for parent-teacher sessions or children's sports games. They devise special codes for personal time that they share with only a trusted administrative assistant. While the cover-up can be tiring, the alternative is worse. As one woman noted, "The day I came out of the closet and started being honest about how I had been juggling my work and my family obligations was the day my career started to go south."

Most galling might be the gender double standard that can often be seen in today's world of business, as in the case of one company that tried to humanize its top five executives by having them share their life stories at a meeting with managers. When the chief financial officer (CFO) stepped up to the podium, he was a bit stiff and uncomfortable, being unaccustomed to speaking to large audiences unless he was talking about numbers. Following the CFO's presentation, the CEO took the microphone to add a few comments. "You should see his calendar," marveled the CEO. "He's reserved time for all of his son's soccer games for the whole season. I don't know anyone who works harder than him, yet he gets to every one of his son's games." The women in the audience blanched, one whispering to another, "I do the same thing. But I wouldn't dare let anyone know."

The differing perceptions of working men and working women with regard to their decisions about marriage and children are also jarring. When a young woman announces her plans to be married, questions generally start to percolate about the woman's career intentions and personal priorities. Which will be more important to her, her family or her job? Will her career come second to her husband's? Will she have children? If she does, will she continue working? If she decides to have a second or third child, will she decide to stop working then? The assumption—by managers, peers, and subordinates, whether male or female—is that the woman has to make choices, personal choices. Choices, they presume, even the most clear-headed businesswoman may not be capable of confronting until she gets there. More than once we've heard a manager say about a pregnant employee who has made a commitment to return to work, "Oh sure she says that now, but wait until she gets that baby in her arms."

For men in comparable personal situations, the expectations are usually markedly different. While the advent of marriage and the arrival of children often put a woman at risk in the eyes of business, these same life events are usually interpreted as making men better employees. The male employee is frequently viewed as settling down, being more serious about life, taking on responsibilities that will make him even more committed to being successful at work. Far from being in conflict, for a man, these life choices are considered by many companies as motivating him to be the hard-working, dedicated employee the corporate world loves.

Women face a Hobson's choice regarding commitment. A woman who demonstrates commitment to her career is often presumed to have a deficient personal life. Yet a woman with a fulfilling personal life is frequently seen as not seriously committed to her job and career. This commitment paradox is deeply disturbing, for it deals with presumptions and impressions that are more about character than performance. And concerning character, the presumptions are wrong. We believe the paradox derives from historical cultural expectations of gender roles in business, combined with traditional concepts of motherhood and fatherhood, that put work and personal lives in conflict for women, but not for men. The problem is compounded by imperfect proxies of commitment used by business, proxies that can fail to always accurately assess dedication to the job and therefore penalize women disproportionately, in comparison to men. While men, even on a male proving ground, are allowed to meld their business and personal lives in such a way that they can be committed and successful at both, women often are not allowed to do this. Women face a paradox, another either/or choice, that puts them at a disadvantage in the workplace relative to their male peers.

Chapter 7

PARADOX #4: BONDING WITH CO-WORKERS

When a woman bonds primarily with her female co-workers, she is segregated and often outside the power structure.

When a woman relates to her male co-workers as "the opposite sex," she rarely builds strong bonds.

When a woman tries to bond with her male co-workers as "one of the boys," she tends to alienate both men and women.

THE IMPORTANCE OF BONDING

It was 6:00 a.m., and the alarm was buzzing. Gerry hit the off button, stretched, and slowly started to focus on the day ahead.

"Okay, it's Tuesday, so I have the 9:00 a.m. weekly staff meeting," he thought as his mind emerged from the fog of slumber. "Then I need to finish that new proposal. That'll be tough, but at least I'll be working with Jay. He's always good for a laugh. And I'll be having lunch with Ethan and Jonathan—the dynamic duo from finance. They're good to work with. They'll be at the staff meeting, too."

As he headed toward the bathroom, he mused, "Should be a decent day."

Though Gerry didn't consciously think of it this way, the bonds he'd built at work were serving him well.

Bonding with your fellow employees nurtures the feeling that you are working in the right place. You see yourself as connected to the people you work with. You think of yourself as being part of a larger whole to which you belong and to which you are contributing. As a result, you go to work with a degree of positive anticipation, simply because it's pleasant to spend time in a place where you like the people, and the people like you. This doesn't mean that every day is wonderful, and that work is always a joy. We all have our bad days. But bonding with your co-workers diminishes the pain and expands the pleasure of the daily work experience.

In the absence of bonding, an employee can still do good independent work, but he is isolated. If the seclusion is self-imposed, the employee is often faulted for being antisocial, a loner. We heard one senior executive snidely say of such an employee, "He tends to drain personality out of a room." On the other hand, if an employee finds that despite his best efforts he has trouble bonding with his co-workers, he may experience a daily sense of inflicted loneliness. In a manner reminiscent of rejection by a high school clique, he is not included in the joke or invited to join the crowd. Rarely does this occur because an individual is misanthropic; it's usually because he does not fit in with his organization. We've each had this happen to us once or twice during our careers. Even when the pay is good, the work is interesting, and the reviews are okay, it's hard to believe that your future prospects are promising. There's a nagging sense that you can't continue to work at that company. You are too disconnected. Under these circumstances, most people will change jobs; sometimes they will even be willing to take positions with less prestige and lower pay.

Bonding with co-workers is clearly a key ingredient of daily job satisfaction, but it may also impact job performance. It begins with the simple fact that the better employees feel about the people they work with, the better they tend to do their jobs. It's a virtuous cycle that increases the likelihood of their performing well in the long run. People like you; you like them. They give you special opportunities because they like you, and you respond by doing an exceptional job because you want to please them. Your excellent work encourages them to offer you more opportunities, and the resulting expansion of your skills leads to a good reputation and more challenging assignments, and so on. Within the system of business, bonding with co-workers fosters achievement.

Over time, bonding over work builds a loyal network of business connections that can be called upon to bolster a career. A legacy of strong working relationships provides a critical support base inside a company, as well as when moving from job to job. Howard was called when he was fifty years old by someone he had worked with when he was thirty, to see if he would be interested in a high-ranking executive position. Lynn was recruited by a client to head a new department in his company. In today's mobile economy, this type of networking has been raised to the status of a major art form. Books have been written on the topic, and certain consultants specialize exclusively in teaching people how to develop, maintain, and leverage the business connections they have established over the years. Despite the current pedagogical ruminations, networking, at its core, has one and only one essential ingredient: bonding effectively with fellow employees.

From the company perspective, bonding is not just about employees feeling good about where they work; it's about positive business outcomes. For example, bonding with peers is a vital precursor to the development of effective, productive work teams. Without positive personal connections among individual employees, it is almost impossible to build a high-functioning group. This is most conspicuous in athletics. A collection of star athletes who don't get along rarely performs as well as a collection of good athletes who really gel.

A corporate culture in which employees are connected also helps companies to attract and retain good talent. When recruiting, companies are looking for capable individuals who can work well with the existing workforce and, thereby, quickly become productive. The prospective new hire looks for this, too, and typically when he finds a workplace flowing with camaraderie, it is magnetic. You can feel the energy and good spirits the moment you walk through the front doors. You see happy, smiling employees and think, "I can be happy here, too." Not only potential future hires but also current employees appreciate the ambience, which strengthens a company's retention efforts. Over the years we have seen survey after survey showing that "liking the people you work with" ranks high as a reason why people stay in their jobs. We know that employers calculate the hard-dollar cost of the high-turnover alternative—the increased expense of recruiting, the larger time investment in training, and the ratcheting up of salaries. Creating an environment that promotes positive bonding among employees can minimize these costs by keeping employees content where they are.

Investing in work environments that promote positive working relationships among employees—employee bonding—serves a valid business purpose. This is one reason why companies provide a variety of venues and sponsor multiple events where employees can connect with and enjoy each other. Holiday parties, company sports teams, company picnics, off-site meetings, golf outings—all are organized for the purpose of bringing employees together to create a cohesive, mutually supportive, engaged workforce. All promote employee bonding.

Bonding is such a natural part of the human experience that we tend to take it for granted. But in a work context it is a critical element in building a successful business and successful careers. Consequently, the basic business rule that an individual should seek to build positive bonds with co-workers makes sense. But because of the dynamics of bonding in the workplace and the overall culture of many businesses, this rule can be inherently more difficult for women to follow than for men.

A SINGLE-SEX PHENOMENON

In life, people bond over the smallest and simplest of things. Two people discover they have the same birthday; two others love reading the same mystery novels; a third pair connects over vegetable gardening. Special relationships that develop between casual acquaintances fall under this heading, as do those bonds based on broader affiliations such as ethnic background, religious beliefs, family ties, and geographic proximity, to name just a few. But characteristic of all bonding is a special chemistry between people, a sense of ease and connection between them.

Similarly, within a corporate context, bonding is associated with a degree of comfort and camaraderie between employees. Though it originates in a business association, the rapport between co-workers evolves into something more social in nature, usually made richer by things people discover they have in common, either at work or elsewhere. Two employees find they both believe a job should be done in a certain way, or they learn that they grew up in the same Brooklyn neighborhood. The bond may be built on a positive connection—shared enthusiasm for a novel idea—or even a negative connection—dislike of a particular boss. The relationship may stay within the confines of the office, but it sometimes expands beyond the boundaries of the business world to include social outings. Occasionally it may endure after both have left their common employer. We have found ourselves at former co-workers' weddings and funerals. Thinking back on these relationships, we see that they all began with something shared—interests, backgrounds, hobbies, work habits, values, or even common enemies.

With the basics of bonding in mind, companies seek venues that promote shared experiences among employees. Like matchmakers, they nudge employees into social settings where they hope people will click. Office parties, off-site meetings, community service fairs, and company-sponsored sports teams are but a few of the more traditional bonding activities of today's business world. These events are so widely accepted as contributing to the good of the business that most associated expenses are tax deductible. Company training sessions serve the same purpose by inculcating not only common understandings but also common experiences. Lynn recalls one company that had employees take the Myers-Briggs personality assessment to enhance their management skills. Myers-Briggs uses a four-letter acronym to denote opposing personality features; for example, the lead letter "I" indicates an introvert, while an "E" indicates an extrovert. The assessment's bonding potential was proven when, within ten minutes of first being introduced to each other, two women from different countries, Canada and United States, found themselves excitedly exclaiming, as if they were twins separated at birth, "You're an ENTJ! I'm an ENTJ!"

While companies support employee bonding, the goal isn't always for all types of employees to bond with each other. Rebecca discovered this when she was recruited into a major financial services company as one of its few top female senior executives.

"What a boondoggle!" erupted Rebecca to her female colleague. "And only the men are going? This is ridiculous. I need to say something."

Rebecca had just been informed that once a year, a group of senior executives from her company—all men—scheduled a "meeting" at a resort near a world-class golf course. The previous May, the men had played Pinehurst; the time before, Pebble Beach. Since these were categorized as business meetings, the company picked up the tab (other than the greens fees). The egregiousness of the gender exclusivity emboldened Rebecca to speak to her new boss.

"This isn't right," Rebecca began. "Bonding and team building are important for all executives, regardless of gender."

Her boss's response was both surprising and gratifying.

"You know, you have a point. I hadn't given it much thought. It's just the way we've always done it. Give me a day or two to figure something out."

Three days later, Rebecca received an e-mail from her boss authorizing her to schedule a planning meeting for a select group of senior female executives. He suggested she hold this near a spa, at a Caribbean resort, or at some other venue where the women could take some quality down time in order to bond. The company would cover the cost.

As in Rebecca's company, an interesting pattern becomes quite obvious when employee relationships and corporate efforts to facilitate them are examined through the filter of gender. The majority of employee bonding is single-sex. And we've found that the higher you go up the corporate ladder, the more entrenched the distinction is. This may not be as obvious as in Rebecca's organization—many company outings include both sexes. But study the interactions at any large office party, watch the exchanges at a business conference, or spy on employees at an off-site meeting, and you'll see the pattern. Men tend to congregate with men, and women tend to congregate with women. The bulk of the bonding occurs within one's own gender.

This single-sex nature of bonding within the corporate world eludes most employers and employees. They just don't see it. Or, more precisely, they don't see it as a problem. Their lack of concern is supported by what they consider to be a reasonable rationale. Bonding among employees is good for the company and good for employees. But employees' choice of whom to bond with is a personal matter and of little consequence. The goal, after all, is to make people comfortable, to help them fit into the work environment. Consequently, the company tries to sustain a corporate culture that enables employees to connect with each other and encourages them to do so. As long as the company's efforts in this regard are unbiased, the company is acting responsibly. If employees naturally bond by gender, if that's what employees are most comfortable doing, then so be it.

And the fact is that in our American culture, outside of work, men tend to have more friendships and social bonds with men, and women with women. Just ask people to list their buddies, then count heads by gender. Or watch television, or go to the movies. While men and women have lots of social contact with each other in American society, the bonding that takes place between individuals that leads to trusting, enduring, supportive friendships and camaraderie tends to be single-sex, not opposite-sex, in nature. That the current American culture outside of work should spill over into work is not surprising.

The business world has incorporated single-sex bonding into its operational protocols for some time. If anything, the corporate world has had a history of magnifying the separation of the sexes. As late as the 1970s, business categorized its job opportunities as male or female. The column headings for classified ads from that era made the distinction strikingly clear: "Help Wanted—Male" and "Help Wanted—Female." While sex-distinct jobs seem archaic today, we argue that the cultures of many businesses continue to condone and in many ways even to encourage social codes of behavior that reinforce single-sex relationships. The lament of a mid-level female oil company employee provides a typical example. Every day she worked easily with the others in her predominantly male group. Then came lunchtime, and she would sit in her office with a sandwich and a Coke, listening to the men getting together and heading down to the company cafeteria, walking right past her doorway without so much as a sideways glance. Though men and women work side by side day in and day out, casual informal interactions often continue to be surprisingly gender distinct.

Though it is commonly considered benign, we see the single-sex nature of social bonding in business as warranting more scrutiny. The simple rule that encourages employees to bond with their fellow employees does not necessarily have simple, gender-neutral ramifications. While one can understand how, absent any significant intervention, bonding in business would mirror bonding in the world at large, the single-sex pattern can have grave, if unintended, consequences. Bonding with co-workers is a cornerstone of corporate life. It helps employees feel good about their jobs, build career-supporting networks, and improve their chances of success. It helps companies build positive work environments and achieve better business results. But despite the integration of men and women in the modern work world, bonding with co-workers is still largely a single-sex phenomenon. Generally, this is not a major problem for men. But for women, it results in a disadvantageous paradox, adding to the challenges they already face in comparison to men working within the system of business.

GIRL FRIENDS

Diana was nonplussed. After returning from lunch with Nadia and "the gang," she sat in her cubicle blankly staring at her e-mail. Something was gnawing at her; something was amiss. But she couldn't quite see it. Like a camera out of focus, her thoughts were blurry and unclear.

Several months earlier, Diana had started her new job with a pharmaceutical company. Fresh out of college, she had been both anxious and excited about entering the corporate world as a marketing analyst. Surprisingly, her anxiety had dissipated faster than she had expected, as she began to acclimate to the new environment in which she worked. The people seemed nice, the work was challenging, and she was kept very busy.

Within her first two weeks of work, Nadia had reached out to Diana by inviting her to lunch. Nadia, a "veteran" of about three years with the company, planned a lunch every month with a group of four or five female colleagues. "The gang," as she called it, was great—a group of intelligent, ambitious young women giving each other support as they all aspired to achieve their career goals.

At first, Diana had been flattered to be included. But, after a few lunches, an uneasy feeling started to seep in. Why did she need to have a support group? Where were all the young guys they worked with? They had been hired at the same time. Did they have a support group, too? Why was "the gang" so competitive with the guys, always comparing and commenting on their accomplishments? While Diana was having trouble articulating the source of her uneasiness, her intuition was setting off alarms.

Though it was early in her corporate career, Diana was beginning to perceive some of the unintended consequences of gender exclusivity. The pattern of single-sex bonding, which is prevalent in American business today, can certainly be supportive at times, but it can also have limiting implications for women. First, when a woman bonds primarily with her female co-workers, she is segregated, defined by her gender. In this day and age, when most academic institutions are coed, when law school and medical school classes are fifty-fifty by sex, when even many college dormitories are coed, it feels odd that your sex can be a primary characteristic that defines you and your network. Yet with respect to the informal social protocols of business, gender exclusivity is fairly standard. Almost as if women are being told to stick to their own kind, they are regularly relegated to the female side of the house when seeking camaraderie and support. Like Diana, young women recently out of academia are often the most surprised that their gender is so distinguishing a feature in today's work world.

Besides the self-consciousness that comes with being segregated, women who bond primarily with other women will say that the exclusivity sometimes impacts their effectiveness. While women may be more comfortable with their female colleagues and feel more easily accepted as peers, they may be left at a disadvantage when dealing with the men in their workplace. This can be a particularly serious problem in predominantly male businesses. As one businesswoman from a Wall Street firm said, "I know the women so well in this organization that I can speak shorthand with them. When I talk to the men, it takes more effort to get my point across. They don't know me, and I don't know them as well."

Some women, especially those in predominantly female departments, even speak of a sense of inferiority when they are operating in the organization at large. Disconnected from the power structure, they suspect that the action is happening somewhere else and feel out of the loop of those in the know. More important, they don't seem to have input on outcomes comparable to the input of their male co-workers. They find that even though they are technically in attendance at a meeting, important decisions are finalized without them—in the case of one woman, while she was in the ladies' room.

Limits in the breadth of women's business connections present another problem with single-sex bonding. Beyond making employees feel good at work, bonding is supposed to enhance their chances of career success by building networks, which can be leveraged over time. When men and women are segregated by gender, this purpose is not served equally. The math is elementary. When women's close supportive work relationships are limited primarily to other women, unless they are in a female-dominated business, they are at a numerical disadvantage. When the formula is weighted by the number of women who are likely to rise to high places—positions of power that can influence a career—the disadvantage is increased. As a result, many working women do not have business networks that are as large or useful as those of their male counterparts.

Finally, few, if any, businesses are pure meritocracies. Who you know and how well you know them makes a difference. Those in power will tend to skew outcomes toward the employees they have a positive relationship with—the ones they have had more exposure to. Since men hold most of the power in today's system of business, the prevalence of single-sex bonding in corporate life can impede women's advancement. People in power tend to favor those they know and are comfortable with. When these are men who bond primarily with other men, women are disadvantaged. Lynn recalls talking to Howard about this when he mentioned a male employee that he met playing tennis at a company outing. Since they were partnered for several doubles sets, the two of them spent a fairly long period of time together. Earlier that morning, when Howard had left for the outing, he barely knew this man. When he came home, he said, "I like this guy. I'm going to consider him for an opening in the compensation group in my division." Exposure breeds opportunities. As a result, when it comes to bonding in business, separate but equal simply doesn't work for women.

While women may feel ambivalent about single-sex bonding, men's reaction may be even more complex. When we talk to businessmen individually, almost to a man they will say that they truly enjoy working with the women in their workplace. None have ever suggested that women's job opportunities should be in any way limited due to their gender; nor have they said that men and women should be segregated in actual work assignments. However, when men congregate as a group, especially in a more social setting, a different dynamic often takes over. When other men are around, many men seem more comfortable when the sexes are segregated. This brings us back to the notion that business continues to have some of the characteristics of a male proving ground. If men's manhood is constantly being tested, then a single-sex social dynamic prevails. When women bond primarily with other women, they are not threatening and they are actually supporting the masculinity precepts of the "flight from the feminine"[1] and "homosocial enactment."[2]

In reaction and in desperation, many ambitious women seek out all-female or predominantly female business opportunities. Seeing that women who bond primarily with women are handicapped in many large corporate environments, they attempt to solve the problem between men and women at work by moving to what amounts to the ultimate level of segregation. And, ironically, it often works. There can be no conflict between men and women in a work environment composed only of women. Women can't be second class citizens if they're the only citizens. Just as in single-sex educational institutions, the all-female business neutralizes gender. But while all-female businesses accomplish the goal of removing gender parity as a problem, they passively, if defensively, endorse a separate-but-equal principle in American capitalism.

So, what's a woman to do? If she bonds primarily with her female co-workers, she is segregated and often left outside the power structure. Since this places women at a disadvantage relative to their male peers, the doors of opportunity open a little more narrowly for them. And, just as the flap of a butterfly's wings on one side of the world can cause a chain of events leading to a hurricane on the other side, a small difference in opportunity at one point in a career can lead to a giant discrepancy later on. Understanding intuitively and analytically the limitations of single-sex bonding and not willing or able to go out on their own all-female venture, many women seek to build bonds with their male co-workers. Unfortunately, in doing so, they run right into the next aspect of the bonding paradox.

BATTLE OF THE SEXES

In business, as in life in general, the onus falls on the less powerful to ingratiate themselves with the more powerful. Thus, for the most part, it is women who must find a way to bond with men in the corporate world if they want to fully participate in that world. But how should they go about doing this? In an environment where men hold most of the power positions, how should women interact with men so that they are perceived favorably by men? Many women confronted with this challenge fall back on the behaviors that have historically made them attractive to men on a male proving ground. They appeal to men as the opposite sex.

In business, relating to men as the opposite sex is primarily accomplished by accepting and accentuating differences between men and women. Gender becomes a primary identity element at work, and relations between men and women reflect the presumption that the sexes are much more different than they are alike. Consistent with the cultural norms of the historically man's world of business, men and women are ascribed gender roles that place them in different orbits. The contrasting attributes that are taught in so many diversity training programs support these roles and supposedly form the foundation of work relationships: men are more competitive, women are more collaborative; men are more rational, women are more intuitive; men are more demanding, women are more nurturing; and so forth. While these stereotypes are in many ways absurd and offensive, they continue to be an element of many training programs and enable the notion of business as a male proving ground. For example, when women play the role of the opposite sex, men are free to bond primarily with other men because male employees are the ones with whom they have the most in common. In essence, men are given tacit permission to segregate themselves.

Infused with a little more energy, opposite-sex behaviors begin to look like courting rituals. Men and women at work may tease, preen, and banter with each other. Sometimes double entendres, sexual innuendos, and ego stroking infect interactions. And let's face it, it can be fun to flirt and play the opposite-sex game. The underlying sexual tension, feigned or real, can invigorate, adding spark to the work day and making the participants feel attractive and youthful. Spirits tend to pick up at a conference table filled with men when a woman takes a seat. Groups of women in HR departments often find that the addition to the team of a man from finance seems to perk things up.

For some women, this opposite-sex model of male-female relations in the corporate world may even provide a powerful platform. By leveraging sexual attraction—what used to be called employing feminine wiles—they can connect with some men on men's terms and gain ground in the perpetual battle of the sexes. The far-reaching nature of this power was evinced by one tall, striking, blond woman who humorously lamented about her efforts to convince a computer technician to move her job to the top of the production list. "I really tried to use logic," she said. "But when that didn't work, I just *made* him do it." In an environment where men and women relate as opposite sexes, the young, attractive female can navigate the world of men in ways that others cannot. She is often the center of attention and rarely the one left out. She may catch the eye of higher-level male executives without much effort. Frequently, she is noticed when others are ignored.

But leveraging sex appeal in business can be a dangerous game for a woman. While some do this successfully, most of those we've known have run into trouble. Jessie, a bank executive and another blond beauty, was praising a junior male colleague in a taxicab after a meeting, when the young man, thinking Jessie was coming on to him, literally pounced on her. Julie, a pretty brunette, recalled her manager dismissively saying to her, "Of course, you're charming," as the explanation for her success with clients, as if her appeal did not take effort, and her intelligence and hard work did not come into play. Gloria, an attractive, middle-aged marketing consultant, privately confessed how much time, energy, and money it took to keep up the physical façade. "The makeup, the manicures, the hair coloring, the exercise classes—it's a lot of work. I don't know how much longer I can keep it up." Unlike men, who traditionally build their power in business with time, women who follow this route may see their power wane with age.

Most significantly, though, relating to men as the opposite sex rarely builds strong, enduring bonds with male co-workers— unless the woman marries one of them. It can mask a woman's true competence by drawing attention to her form over her substance. It can repel some male peers who begrudge women their "unearned" power or who are uncomfortable with any flirtatious or suggestive behavior. It can even annoy other women who are either resentful of the advantages enjoyed by attractive women or feel that leveraging sexual attractiveness in a business setting is inherently unfair and unethical. And even relationships with the men who encourage the opposite-sex game may lead to vulnerability. Bonding—by definition—presumes an easy, enduring trust and camaraderie between two people. Relationships involving sexual attraction are based on tension, sexual tension. Leveraging sexual tension is more of a power play than a way to build strong, lasting bonds with either sex.

Even at a slightly less-charged level, the opposite-sex model is a dubious bonding technique. Women who play the traditional female gender role of being nurturing and deferential and defining themselves as definitively different from men can regularly find themselves in what Dr. Deborah Tannen refers to as a "one-down position."[3] Tannen, a noted Georgetown University scholar, discussed this predicament in-depth in her book, *Talking 9 to 5*, with regard to different gender linguistic styles in business. She explained that in American culture, women will often defer and appear self-deprecating out of politeness, expecting the person they are conversing with to do the same. However, in most business settings, men rarely return the behavior. As a result, businesswomen are regularly left in a weaker position.

Being "one-down" is a matter of relative power. Women still have influence, but a little less influence than men; women may have control, but a little less control than men; women are important, but a little less important than men. Being one-down doesn't mean you're completely out of the game; you're just always a step or two behind, waiting for your turn. Figuratively and often literally, women in this situation have to wait to be asked. But Tannen also noted that when women exercise the assertive alternative, they lose their appeal. If a woman "talks with certainty, makes bold statements of fact rather than hedged statements of opinion, interrupts others, goes on at length, and speaks in a declamatory and aggressive manner, she will be disliked."[4] The traditional gender roles of business—women as the opposite, second sex—can relegate women to an impossible and perpetual one-down position, or render them unappealing. In either case, they frequently prevent women from bonding with their male co-workers as true peers.

But most significantly, any bonding approach focusing on what distinguishes the sexes, no matter how well intentioned, violates a basic maxim of human relationships: people tend to connect over what they have in common, not over how they differ. Our basic politeness behaviors are protocols for finding mutual interests, shared backgrounds, and common under- standings. Stressing how little men and women have in common with each other and highlighting the idea that one is of the opposite sex tend to alienate rather than unite men and women. The precept that emphasizing differences can reinforce discrim- inatory values is so elemental that we recently found the fol- lowing statement in the back of the *Random House Webster's Dictionary, Classic Edition*:

Avoiding Insensitive and Offensive Language

This essay is intended as a general guide to language that can, intentionally or not, cause offense or perpetuate discrimina- tory values and practices *by emphasizing the differences between people.*[5] [emphasis added]

Taken all together, then, in today's system of business, when a woman relates to her male co-workers as the opposite sex, she rarely builds strong bonds with them. Bonding is supposed to create a sense of comfort and a relaxed connection between people. Relating to others as members of the opposite sex tends to create tension, actually thrives on tension, and focuses on dif- ferences. Those playing the opposite-sex game have to keep up their guard, always have to be "on," and have to keep up the façade. Even when sexual tension is not the focal point, the opposite-sex model of male-female relations often leaves women in a one-down position. Rather than fostering ease, trust, and equality, relating as opposites can create stress, wari- ness, and inequity. It violates a fundamental tenet of bonding— people bond over what they share in common.

ONE OF THE BOYS

For many women in today's corporate workplace, bonding pri- marily with other women frequently leaves them segregated and out of the loop. Relating to men as the opposite sex may result in relatively weak bonds with male co-workers. While bonding primarily with women and interacting with men as the opposite sex are both socially and professionally acceptable practices in business, often they do not result in integrated, easy peer relationships between women and men at work. They do not deliver for women the inclusive sense of camaraderie that employees seek when they attempt to bond with their co-workers. On innumerable other fronts—professional networks, proximity to power, broad-based support—these traditional approaches have also left women disadvantaged as they work within the system of business.

In trying to break through, many women try a different tactic. They reject the traditional gender roles of the business world and attempt to bond with men as "one of the boys." These women seek to put their sex aside and focus on what they have in common with men. In essence, they try to bond with men as men bond with each other.

Trying to be like men is far from a new strategy for women in the world of business. Remember the 1980s female uniform of pinstriped man-tailored suits and crisp, white shirts with red bow ties? Recall the decades of self-help books admonishing women to behave more like men if they wanted to succeed in a man's world—be more assertive, more competitive, more hard driving, more take-charge, less "nice"? Recollect the regular counsel that businesswomen should learn to play golf? All of these strategies operate on the premise that if women are to excel in a man's world, they need to learn the rules of the game and adopt the behaviors that have worked for men. They need to go about business as men do. Many women have really tried to heed this advice. From their style of dress to the sports they play, women have mirrored the practices and behaviors of corporate men in the hope of nullifying their gender and blending into the corporate world. Some have even rejected procreation so that, like men, their careers won't be interrupted by pregnancies and maternity leaves. The problem is that when these women try to bond with men by minimizing their differences from men and highlighting what they have in common with them, they rarely achieve their desired result. To their chagrin, their strategies frequently have exactly the opposite effect. More often than not, when women try to bond with men as one of them, "one of the boys," they alienate the men they are seeking to connect with.

Men's reactions will often catch women by surprise, as in the case of Laura and Adam. Assigned to work with Adam, the head of sales, on a huge Fortune 100 request for a proposal, Laura really wanted things to go well. This was the first time she had teamed up with Adam, and she was keenly aware of his popularity in the office. Easygoing and affable, he was the Bing Crosby or, in more contemporary terms, the Justin Timberlake type. And, as everyone in the office knew, he was a superlative golfer. Laura wanted Adam to like her.

So how to connect? Laura didn't play golf. And though Adam was nice enough to her, there was something slightly aloof in his manner whenever they met. Laura needed to find something she and Adam had in common. Some trait, interest, or activity that they could bond over.

One night the two of them were working late into the evening together when Adam said to Laura, "I really want this piece of business. I'm really competitive."

Adam had just said something that rang true to Laura. All her life she had been extremely competitive, much to her mother's consternation at times. She loved competitive sports, or, for that matter, any game that gave her a chance to win. She hated to lose. "You're too competitive, let it go" were regular refrains she heard as she was growing up. But now that she had found her calling in business, she felt her intense drive would serve her well. This was what she and Adam had in common, she thought. This was what they could bond over.

"Me too," she enthusiastically responded. "I've always been competitive."

Abruptly, Adam stopped what he was doing, deliberately

put down his pen, and looked directly at Laura. Clearly, she had done something wrong. Then he stated, as if spitting out a pit, "But I'm *really* competitive."

Laura and many women like her focus on what they have in common with their male co-workers in an attempt to bond and be accepted. Logic guides these women to believe that if they connect as men do, then they will achieve a similar result. But it rarely works. Guileless, they are caught speechless when what brings men together clearly doesn't work for them. In Laura's case, she had seen men high-five each other over much smaller, less pertinent personality traits that they had in common. Not only were there no high fives for her, but the insinuation that she and her male co-worker weren't all that different seemed to be taken as insulting and downright distasteful. Not only did this leave Laura perplexed, but it can make her and women like her feel that there must be something wrong with them—something in their personality or behavior that makes it difficult for them to get along with people in the business world.

We have examined this issue long and hard. Our first and perhaps most important conclusion is that it is not personal. Though many women may think that they're at fault, that they are fundamentally unlikable, the pattern is too common and too skewed toward women to be a personal issue. In addition, these women with supposed problem personalities rarely have similar issues with either men or women outside the corporate setting. Rather, we believe that women who try to relate as "one of the boys" are running head-on into not one but two of the three primary behaviors that are vestiges of business as a male proving ground.

The first collision is with the principle that, no matter how hard women try to blend into a man's world, they cannot be men. Obviously, we are not talking about the physical aspects of being male or female. Rather, we are referring to women seen as the opposite sex. When women try to bond with men in the business world by adopting the behaviors and approaches that have served men so well, they are up against the wall of the way

manhood is defined on a male proving ground. Under the traditional rules of masculinity, you cannot be a bona fide man if you
have a lot in common with a woman. The closer women get to
infiltrating the practices and protocols of manhood on the
proving ground of business, the more some men seem to push
back and separate themselves in order to preserve their identity
as men. Their visceral negative response to women who innocently imply that "we have a lot in common" is a major "tell."
Generally, the more deeply a man feels the need to prove his
manhood, the stronger will be his reaction. This was the barrier
that suddenly appeared and perplexed Laura when her attempt
at bonding led to her co-worker's negative reaction.

The second precept of a male proving ground that women
are confronting when they try to bond with guys as guys is
exclusivity. "Real men" want to band with other "real men"
and exclude all those they see as on the fringes—minorities,
homosexuals, and definitely women. When practiced aggressively, white male exclusivity has clearly been racist, homo-
phobic, and sexist. But over the years, as the edges on the exclusion of minorities and homosexuals have softened, the nonin-
clusion of women has often been positioned in terms of a more
positive, socially acceptable spin—called male bonding.

Exclusivity builds a barrier that protects the concept of masculinity inherent in a proving ground and is generally guarded
most vigorously when men congregate as a group. We've seen
instances in which, even if a male and a female co-worker have
been working closely and effectively together, once other men
are around, the man distances himself from the woman. "It's
like I've been dropped," is how one woman described it. "Bob
and I had been working on this project together for a month,
talking on the phone almost every day, joking and laughing.
Then I see him at a business meeting standing with a group of
men, and I go up to him and he acts like he barely knows me. I
felt like such a fool." In the presence of other men, far from
readily bonding with their female co-workers, it's as if some
men do not want to be seen "playing with girls."

Many women, and even some men, would say that men should be held accountable for such behavior. While we agree, we believe that at the same time these men feel pressured in the workplace to live up to the cultural standards of their corporate environments. In some business settings, too much association with women can lessen their manliness in the eyes of those who are testing their manhood. One young man learned this hard lesson early in his career. In high school and college, Joseph had never had strong, platonic female friendships. Then, in his first job out of college, he befriended a young female co-worker who started about the same time he did. They enjoyed each other's company. They shared their newbie mistakes and laughed about them. They went out to lunch regularly. They bonded.

But after a year, Joseph started to suspect that this friendship was negatively impacting his prospects at the company. Not that anyone said anything explicitly, but he'd have trouble clicking with the other guys in the office, a problem he'd never had with his fraternity brothers in college. Though there was no romantic involvement between Joseph and his female friend— both were already in serious relationships—others in the office acted as if there was and chided him about it mercilessly. Even his performance reviews seemed to underrate his contributions. He ended up leaving the organization after three years. Though he couldn't isolate any one specific factor, he felt certain that his work relationship with his female colleague contributed to his lack of success on the job, since it inhibited him from effectively bonding with his male peers.

While women who try to be "one of the boys" at work can alienate many men, they can alienate some of their female co-workers as well. Too often, the woman who tries to cross the invisible gender divide is resented by her women co-workers who stay on their own side. You can almost hear these women saying, "Just who does she think she is?" As in ethnic, racial, and religious groups, those who stray outside of their group, those who try to assimilate into the opposing culture, can be considered uppity and elitist. Or sometimes there is just a sense of betrayal. Almost as an intervention, women will plead with other women over lunch, arguing that "we have to stick together. And besides, we are smarter than the men." Some female co-workers may feel abandoned and repudiated by women who try to play down the feminine in their attempts to bond with the masculine.

Women who try to bond with men as "one of the boys," then, can often end up alienating everybody. They may alienate men by violating fundamental precepts of a male proving ground. They may alienate some women at work by defecting to the other side. This can leave the woman who tries to bond with men in this manner in a confusing "no-man's" land— neither one of the boys nor one of the girls.

Women face a discouraging paradox when they try to follow the rule of bonding with their co-workers. When a woman bonds primarily with her female co-workers, she finds herself segregated and often outside the power structure. When a woman tries to relate to her male co-workers as "the opposite sex," she rarely builds strong bonds. When a woman tries to bond with her male co-workers as "one of the boys," she tends to alienate both men and women. This paradox leaves many women disconnected and disheartened. They feel like perpetual misfits, never able to achieve a sense of belonging in the business world. As one woman put it, "The environment is uncomfortable. It's as if the furniture never seems to fit me." Though many women fear they may be personally at fault for not being able to bond with their male co-workers, we believe this, like the other parity paradoxes of business, is a matter of corporate culture that is beyond their control.

Chapter 8

PARADOX #5: CHALLENGING THE POWER STRUCTURE

**Employees who imprudently challenge the power structure are stigmatized and their careers suffer.
If women accept the power structure, nothing changes.**

THE NEED FOR ORDER

Lenny was frustrated. He was sitting in a conference room with Jason, Nancy, and Bruce. Two weeks earlier, they had all been peers. But Bruce had just recently been promoted to senior manager, so today he was their superior in the corporate hierarchy. Bruce had called the meeting because Lenny, Jason, and Nancy had been working on a proposal for a mega-multinational financial institution for three days and could not agree on the right way to price it. Bruce wanted to hear what each of them had to say.

"My thinking is this," began Lenny. "This is the first time we've bid on work for this company. If we win the contract, it will give us a foothold in their organization. We should be able to sell the add-on work without going through an expensive and time-consuming competitive bid. Also, having their name on our client list will position us well for opportunities with other companies this large. All in all, I think it makes sense to price this a little low and take some upfront loss to get more profitable work later on down the pike."

"I disagree," Jason interrupted. "I don't think it's worth taking a loss on this one. Word on the street is that these guys are notoriously cheap and inefficient. If we price this low, I think we are going to lose our shirts. And even if they give us the communications and systems work, I don't think we will make much on it. Actually, I think we should price this high in anticipation of the extra time it's going to take. I think our competitors have more history with this company and will be doing the same thing."

Nancy saw things differently. "It's not that they're cheap, they're just value buyers—they'll pay a lot if they think the value is there. And I don't think we know enough about them to say they are going to be hard to work with. We have the most experienced team and the deepest resources for this type of project. We should price our proposal according to what it would normally cost to do the work. No more, no less."

Round and round they went for about fifteen minutes, with each of the three becoming increasingly vociferous in advocating their point of view. Finally, Bruce cut in and ended it: "Okay. Let's go with Jason's approach and price it ten percent high."

The room went quiet. In his gut, Lenny knew that Bruce had made a poor decision. They would not win this important piece of work. Lenny had been in sales just as long as Bruce, maybe a couple of years longer, and truly believed that Bruce was no better qualified than he was to make this call. Yet he also knew that it was Bruce's call to make. He was the senior manager now. Lenny swallowed hard and said to himself, "Let it go."

Like every other corporate citizen, Lenny knew he must bow to his boss's authority. He and the others in the conference room understood that, as Bruce's subordinates, they were expected not only to accept but to support Bruce's final judgment. Regardless of how strong their feelings were, or how cogent their arguments were, they needed to stop challenging. Certainly, there was room for disagreement and debate. But the last word always goes to the one in the room who ranks highest.

Business and its power structure are indivisible. Every company is a hierarchical entity where power consolidates at the top. Respecting the power structure and following the chain of command are requirements of the system. In most companies, the pecking order is set out in meticulously designed organizational charts. Domains of responsibility and lines of reporting are plainly and publicly delineated. Job titles are carefully chosen and conspicuously printed on every piece of stationery to ensure that the power of a position relative to others is commonly understood. Even corporate office space is usually designed to visually reinforce relative power and status—big office, big position; corner office, big shot.

The power-laden, top-down organizational structure of the corporate world keeps the well-oiled machines of commerce running smoothly. Decision-making authority is commonly understood to be concomitant with an employee's position on the ladder. In this way, dissent, debate, and disagreement are kept in check. The behavior required of employees is analogous to the discipline demanded of military personnel. Be a good soldier, march in step, salute the stripes, follow the chain of command—all are pithy principles applicable to corporate life. The structure and strictures of the corporate power system keep order. Without them, the wheels of business would be slowed, inefficiency would mushroom, and business results would deteriorate. The need for employees to respect the authority of their managers is so important that insubordination—the ultimate violation of the rule—is seen as a surefire path to involuntary termination.

Respecting the power inherent in the hierarchy involves accepting your role as a cog within the complexity of a large organization. On a day-to-day basis, this means understanding when to speak up and when to hold your tongue, when to push back and when to give in, when to join a group and when to step aside, whom you can approach directly and whom you can't, which topics are fair game and which are sacred cows. To some, the requisite subservience may sound like sycophantic obsequiousness. But for most employees, respecting the power structure is about being attuned to your environment. You are part of a larger whole in which you only succeed if the business succeeds.

Companies go to great lengths to define and document their organizational structure, the work flow it dictates, and an employee's place in it. At most companies, the written job description is the foundation; it details the requirements of a role, including responsibilities, accountabilities, necessary knowledge and skills, reporting relationships, and level within the corporate hierarchy. Lynn once had the mind-numbing consulting assignment of writing the job descriptions for the human resources department of a major insurance company. For three solid weeks she did nothing but parse words to ensure that each position had its distinguishing description. Her sympathetic manager's comment at the time captured the experience: "I know, it's a real how-many-angels-can-dance-on-the-head-of-a-pin sort of thing." Nevertheless, employees rely on these descriptions as guideposts and learn fast that their job is as big—and as small—as what is written on that piece of paper. Staying within their defined scope of authority may be even more important than fulfilling their job's stated requirements, regardless of the additional talents and abilities that employees may bring to the table. This is why corporations are often reluctant to hire the overqualified—the temptation for such an employee to step outside the bounds of his jurisdiction is too strong. Even if the employee is highly experienced and well intentioned, such overstepping can wreak organizational havoc. For an employee, recognizing where his or her authority ends and someone else's begins is an essential corollary of respecting the power structure and a necessity in keeping the system of business at a high-performing level.

While the corporate ladder provides the framework, organizational culture is one of the mightiest enforcers of the power structure. Though they are rarely found in writing, the dictates of a corporate culture define the appropriate and inappropriate manifestations of respect. From an employee's knowing who can be addressed by their first names to his knowing what tables he can join in the company's cafeteria, corporate cultures are replete with dos and don'ts that buttress the business rankings. As consultants visiting multiple major companies, we found it startling to see that what was considered an over-the-top display of respect at one company would be deemed minimal to inadequate at another. We've seen a CEO who went out of his way to chat up employees as they rode up the elevators together in the morning, insisting that everyone call him "Bob," irrespective of their station. And we recall one unbelievable story that swept though a major company like a cautionary tale. A friendly flight attendant supposedly greeted the chairman directly as he stepped onto the private company jet, saying, "Good morning. Looks like it's going to be a nice day, don't you think?" She was terminated at the next stop for being inappropriately familiar.

Respect for the power structure means that the boss's priorities become the employee's priorities, at least from nine to five. Most managers allow something in the range of a two- to three-month grace period in which minor missteps are forgiven. But after that, if an employee wants to get ahead, he must learn to recognize the requirements and conform to what is expected of him. One employee told of a time when he worked for a manager who was downright anal in insisting that all those who reported to him "clear their graphs" when making a presentation, by taking a moment to define the X and Y axes before going into the content details. At the time, this employee was a forty-something new hire with years of stellar experience making effective presentations. For his first meeting with his new boss and some of his peers, he had put together a colorful, insightful, and comprehensive presentation, overflowing with clarifying charts and graphs. Still, he swore that his manager audibly gasped when he did not follow the clear-your-graph protocol and was displeased to the point of distraction. "How silly," was this employee's initial reaction. But then, he never failed to clear his graphs again.

While respect for the power structure may require some small personal concessions, it's of major importance to a company's success. Some degree of order and structure must be enforced, otherwise confusion and chaos would ensue. But creating that well-oiled machine where everyone works in concert to achieve peak performance is far from an easy task. Companies constantly need to deal with conflicting priorities and competing needs. While a hierarchical power structure and standard operational protocols promote efficiency, too much rigidity can stifle creativity and innovation. The sheer magnitude of large organizations and their networks of authority can lead to a heavy bureaucracy, which ironically defeats a prime purpose of the power structure by preventing nimble reactions to market forces and efficient operation. Many corporate employees have had the exasperating experience of needing to complete multicopy forms and obtain a department head's signature when all they wanted to do was buy a box of pencils.

The challenge of reaching the right balance is so imposing that academics at business schools and consultants in the marketplace have made careers out of analyzing it. Whole areas of business science, such as organizational development, organizational effectiveness, and organizational psychology, have emerged to focus on how to aggregate a group of individuals into a productive force that results in a competitive, profitable, and sustainable company. Though requiring respect for the power structure may seem rudimentary in comparison to today's sophisticated organizational theories and management strategies, it is the basic principle of business that enables the theories and strategies to work.

PICK YOUR BATTLES

While respecting the corporate power structure is essential to understanding your place in the business world, this is not to say that you can never challenge the system. Knowing who has power and who doesn't, relative to you, may be necessary for survival, but lemmings rarely get ahead. Rather, respecting the power structure means knowing how to challenge prudently.

In the fast-paced global marketplace, speed usually trumps precision. As one business executive preached, "It's better to make a mediocre decision fast and clean up afterward, than to make a good decision too late." Companies need to keep moving, keep pursuing their business goals. They can't afford obstacles that distract them or unnecessarily slow them down. Relentlessly questioning and rethinking decisions spins wheels. Arguing over minutiae creates drag. At the same time, business expects employees to be more than automatons who mindlessly follow orders. The ideal employee has perfect pitch when it comes to identifying problems as they arise, thinking independently, fashioning creative solutions, and pushing back when necessary to achieve better results or avoid negative consequences. The delicate balance between choosing when to challenge and choosing when to acquiesce requires employees to be keenly aware of the limits of their position and their current environment. Whereas management values the employee who is prudent and politically adept at questioning, it derides his close cousin who doesn't know when to quit.

As a result, employees need to pick their battles. They need to be judicious in what they question, selective in deciding when to push back, and cautious in how they confront. Those who challenge imprudently and indiscriminately may offend authority, step on people's toes, and cause disruption and distraction. They are often viewed as instigators of dissatisfaction and as potentially destructive to the system. Consequently, they run the risk of poor performance reviews, small or nonexistent pay increases, demotion, and, if deemed insubordinate, termination of employment. They are frequently stigmatized and often socially ostracized.

The battles that an employee chooses to fight and the way he or she goes about fighting them are viewed as prime indications of judgment and maturity. The subtle sensitivity needed to balance the power of one's argument against one's current place in the hierarchy needs to be mastered. Young employees straight out of academia usually need the most help. Howard recalls his first, lowly corporate job out of college working in the back office of an insurance company. Sitting at his gray, metal desk, he questioned why he had to wear an uncomfortable, constraining, and costly suit and tie to work every day. After all, he never saw anyone aside from the fifteen people in his department, let alone anyone outside the company, so why be so formal? While this seemed to him to be a very reasonable query, young Howard crossed the line by raising it often with others and by being particularly persistent with his manager. Fortunately for him, the vice president of human resources took an avuncular interest in his development. He called Howard down to his office one day and kindly, gently, but firmly told him to drop it. "You have a promising future at this company," he counseled, "but not if you don't let this go." Given today's ubiquitous casual dress code, twenty-three-year-old Howard could be considered prescient. But at his level, at that time, challenging company-wide dress code policy was well beyond his purview—a bad battle to pick.

Effective challenging requires a sensitive touch. While the degree of debate and questioning that is acceptable will vary by company, within every company there is a fairly consistent, typically tacit internal code for what is encouraged and tolerated and what is deemed unacceptable. Employees need to learn the boundaries defined and enforced by their corporate culture. Knowing which topics are considered toxic or trivial, which approaches are considered too aggressive, what's politically incorrect, when you are crossing over into complaining, when your raising a problem makes you a problem—is not easy. The standards not only change from company to company but according to your position and status within a company. How much you can challenge and what issues you can question are very different for a senior executive than for a junior assistant, regardless of whether both are making exactly the same points. Even when employees are at comparable levels, those held in high regard in an organization have more latitude than those who are not.

Neil remembered a time when his manager made a teachable moment out of his judgment of when to challenge. Neil had just been promoted to a position in which he was entitled to a valuable new benefit: a company car. In truth, Neil had very little business use for the car. He worked in an urban office with good public transportation, so he rarely needed to drive to see his customers. But he really wanted the car—it was a great perquisite. The company not only gave a generous amount to cover the cost of the car of one's choice, but it also paid for the upkeep of the car. Neil had his eye on a tan BMW convertible with a black top. Delighted, he found that the price was within the allotted allowance, so he put in his request to headquarters. Then the people in finance got back to him.

"We do not want a convertible in the fleet," was their dismissive reply. Neil was furious and went storming into his manager's office waving a printed copy of the e-mail from finance.

"Can you believe this? They don't want a convertible in the fleet! Those bean counters are such idiots. There is nothing in the car policy prohibiting convertibles. I just read it," he fumed. Taking a deep, calming breath, he turned to his manager and mentor: "It's not right, Kevin. I really wanted that car. I earned it. Can you help me out here? Can you call the CFO?"

Kevin was the prime supporter of Neil's recent promotion and felt it was well earned. But he also saw clearly that Neil still had a few more things to learn about corporate life.

"I can call the CFO, if you want me to, Neil. But are you sure that's what you want me to do? You haven't had that much exposure to him, or anyone else at his level. He's a good guy, but is challenging the company car policy really the issue you want him to identify you with?"

No call was made. Neil may have been brash, but he wasn't stupid.

Because being smart about challenging is such a tricky business, there's plenty of advice to go around. Don't be petty. Avoid personal issues. Wait until your boss has had his morning coffee. Spin it so that it's about improving the business. Steer clear of politically sensitive issues. Come to the point quickly. Don't generalize from the personal. Bring solutions, not just problems. Avoid self-righteousness. Don't embarrass your boss. Don't embarrass your subordinates. Make it look like it's your boss's idea. From the small to the strategic, employees learn ways to selectively, effectively, and prudently make their points. But the most important point is to "let it go" if your boss indicates that this is a bad battle.

THE RIGHT TO CHALLENGE

Since challenging the power structure is a delicate business, learning a company's unwritten guidelines can take time. But what if your actions and behaviors are perceived as challenging when your aim is not? What if an attitude is ascribed to you that is contrary to your intent? Toni was grappling with these questions at her job.

"I think that number representing the size of this market is wrong," interjected Ray. "I recall seeing something different recently in the *Wall Street Journal*."

A dozen managers were listening to a presentation being given by the marketing department on the launch of a new product. The meeting attendees included product managers, production managers, salespeople, and marketing staff. Ray and Toni were keenly interested in this presentation, as they were the sales managers who would be responsible for the new product.

The presentation progressed smoothly, with periodic interruptions for questions and comments. At one point, Toni spoke up.

"I'm not sure the Pew research is the best source for this product. The other night, I was looking at a study done by Gallup and I think it's really good."

When the meeting was over, Toni stopped at the coffee station and overheard a conversation around the corner.

"I'm glad Ray's one of the lead sales guys on this. But Toni I'm not so sure about. Did you see how she went after Martin regarding the research?"

"Yeah, she was pretty aggressive."

Toni froze. "Aggressive? Went after Martin? Really?" Thinking hard, she replayed the entire meeting in her mind, focusing on what she had said and how she had said it. "All I did was raise a point about the market research. I didn't talk any more than anyone else; actually I spoke less. I wasn't particularly caustic or forceful in my comments. I think Ray was stronger and more critical than I was when he said Martin made a mistake in the size of the market according to the *Journal*. These guys are making me sound like I'm some challenging pain in the ass. What's going on here?"

Toni's sense of being misunderstood is a frequent experience among women who, in the normal discourse of business, present themselves as strong, definitive, and confident. They are often perceived as aggressive. Their demonstration of competence somehow causes offense. We've seen a man and a woman use the same words, speak with the same intonation, deliver their words with equal degrees of power, yet elicit markedly different reactions from co-workers—of either sex, whether they be superiors, peers, or subordinates. One female manager recounted her experience in this way: "Men would always talk over me at meetings, so I learned to talk back over them. Then my anonymous feedback came in, and people said I was rude. The guys trounce each other in meetings all the time and no one says they're rude!" Another female executive described it simply: "When my male colleague is hard on people, they consider him demanding, with high standards. When I'm hard on people, I'm a bitch."

For women, the acceptable degree of power they can use in their personal expression in corporations tends to be lower than for men. A male executive can raise his voice and pound on a table with impunity, while a female executive who does so is often considered "shrill," "harsh," or "a ball-buster"—adjectives reserved almost exclusively for women. This disparity exists both inside and outside the corporate environment. John McEnroe can verbally assault line judges throughout his tennis career and be a role model of intensity, but when Serena Williams does so once, the USTA and the world are horrified. The standards of acceptable behavior for wielding power, even in the outside world, are simply different for men and women. The reaction to women exercising power tends to be more extreme and more pejorative than it is to men using basically identical words and behaviors.

The disparity has disconcerted many women in the corporate world. Frequently feeling misunderstood, they fail to recognize the way they come across in a business world that has been, and often continues to be, more comfortable with men incorporating power into their speech and demeanor than with women doing so. Lynn recalls receiving written feedback from a subordinate saying that Lynn "really challenges me and, though she can be tough, she makes me produce my best work." Lynn's manager characterized the comment as "negative." Clearly, to him, Lynn was supposed to be nurturing, not demanding. However, when Howard received similar feedback at the same company, it was deemed an indication of his leadership capacity and his ability to motivate people.

Acceptable modes of behavior for women on a male proving ground tend to be those that are more acquiescent and less challenging. We see this as deriving from traditional gender roles that required women to be supportive and deferential. The different standards of acceptability put women in a difficult predicament. In order to avoid the negative perceptions of their colleagues, they must tone themselves down in comparison to men. Yet if they decrease their degree of forcefulness, they often don't get heard, or they are ignored all together.

In a business world with vestiges of a male proving ground, women who come on strongly, definitively, or confidently are challenging embedded gender roles, even if they are doing no more than trying to be equal to men in the normal interchanges of work. Unfortunately, women such as Toni are frequently perceived as challenging when they are merely being themselves and acting as men do. In these environments, the only way to avoid being pejoratively defined as a "challenging woman" is for women to diminish themselves by playing themselves down, being a bit deferential, a bit quieter, and a bit weaker, and using less power in personal communications.

Often, as women progress through their careers, the double standard regarding acceptable behavior becomes more of an issue in corporate environments. That's because expectations surrounding the ability to challenge the power structure and the necessity to do so change with seniority and advancement. Employees entering the workforce at lower-level positions have little leeway in challenging others. Their new entrant status requires similarly obsequious behaviors from both young men and young women, since all are at the bottom of the hierarchy. "Bag carriers" is what we used to call ourselves, since our primary responsibility, regardless of gender, was to transport materials to meetings for our managers. Further illustrating our lowly rank, we both recall being invited to meetings on a K-Y-M-S basis—keep your mouth shut. But generally, as you get older, as you gain experience and knowledge, the boundaries are broadened. Assertive behavior that may be considered inappropriate for a young employee becomes permissible and even expected of a more mature, higher-ranking individual. Challenging the system, questioning how work gets done, and pushing back on the status quo become more feasible and more the norm as you rise through the hierarchy of business. This should be true regardless of gender. Rather than deferring to others, you expect others to defer to you.

Ellen found herself at a point in her career where she felt others should be deferring to her. She and Jackson were the two highest-ranking managers in the corporate communications department, reporting to Ira, the senior manager responsible for the whole area. For the previous six months, Ellen and Jackson had been sharing with each other their confidential concerns about dysfunction in the department and Ira's ability to continue managing it. Given her position, Ellen was starting to think that maybe something needed to be done—perhaps to challenge the power structure.

"Our department is struggling, but Ira doesn't seem to notice. He seems to have lost interest in running the group," was Jackson's concern. "He spends all his time outside the office on the launch of the new product line and ignores all the people issues here that need to be dealt with."

"Yeah, I know," Ellen said in agreement. "I really like Ira, and I think he's really good, but I think he's no longer interested in managing. Maybe it's time for him to step aside and let someone else take over."

"It may be, but I doubt that Ira would do so unilaterally," replied Jackson. "We could go around him and talk to Chuck, but that's a risky move. If we do that at all, we'd have to do it together to lessen the risk."

"I don't know. That's a high-risk move," Ellen noted warily. "Let me give it some thought."

A few days later, Jackson and Ellen jointly approached Chuck, Ira's boss. To their delight, it worked out better than they had ever imagined. Ira was transferred to another job without much protest, and Jackson became the head of corporate communications. Ellen felt she had been forthright and adroit in handling a delicate situation, resulting in a higher-functioning department, which had benefited the entire company. Even though it was probably a coin toss as to whether she or Jackson would replace Ira, she was okay with the outcome, almost feeling safer as Jackson's subordinate.

A good example of a high-ranking individual's need to challenge the power structure and doing so prudently, right? Not quite. Revisiting the scene several years later, we find that Jackson was highly praised as a dedicated manager and a strong leader who was willing and able to face difficult situations. He'd actually been promoted to a higher-level executive job. Ellen, on the other hand, had left the company, opting for a very early, unexpected retirement. Following the incident with Ira, a feeling spread through the corporate communications department and more broadly through the company that Ellen had acted inappropriately, that she had figuratively stabbed Ira in the back, that she had abused her power and could not be trusted. The feeling was so strong that when Jackson was promoted to a higher-level job, the company passed over Ellen and named someone else to run the department. Frustrated and angry, Ellen chose to leave. It appears that actions that were prudent for Jackson were not so prudent for Ellen.

Throughout the business world, we've witnessed women laboring under a double standard with respect to challenging behavior. On one level, behavior that is considered strong, forthright, and confident in a man is often considered inappropriately challenging and aggressive in a woman. For the man, the perception is positive; for the woman, it's negative. Moreover, women who challenge the power structure are often judged more severely than men. While challenging the power structure is risky, it appears that men have more room to maneuver than women. What's prudent for men is not necessarily prudent for women. To make themselves acceptable, women must often dilute their strength and come across as more accepting and less demanding. Yet this leaves women in a less-than-equal position relative to men. In this way, the boundaries of appropriate behavior in business tend to be narrower for women than for men. Women who cross these boundaries, who attempt to be as forceful as their male peers, are likely to be labeled as offensive challengers and suffer the consequences.

A TOXIC TOPIC

Adding insult to injury, not only is a woman who challenges often walking a fine line regardless of the issue, but a woman who specifically raises questions of gender inequity can be at even greater risk. She has moved from representing implicitly to stating explicitly that women are constrained by their gender in their corporate environment. Putting forward concerns about gender problems gives public voice to a topic the hierarchy would generally prefer not to hear about.

Employees are supposed to acquire over time the finesse needed to be effective challengers. They learn primarily by watching the way others go about it, then trying it themselves. When do you bring up an issue? To whom should you be talking? How should you broach the topic? Is the topic worth bringing up at all? But pushing back on some issues is tough, no matter how experienced or adept you may be and regardless of the tactics you use. In our experience, gender equity is one of the toughest issues. It's a toxic topic.

To understand why issues related to gender are such a problem, you have to start with the situation in which an employee would bring up gender inequity in the first place. What occasion would lead a woman to talk to her boss, her co-workers, the human resources department, an executive, or anyone else in the organization about her concerns that the company may not be treating her fairly because she is female? In our experience, women who raise this issue are usually motivated by something concrete that has happened to them. It can be a dispiriting personal experience or the last straw in an accumulation of events, but generally the woman feels unfairly disadvantaged because of her sex. In reality, it's typically a firsthand experience of victimization due to gender bias that will most often get a woman thinking about fighting the gender battle.

Ginger was just such an employee. An experienced CPA in the finance department of a large industrial corporation, she was stunned when Marty was picked to head her group and not herself. She kept going over the facts, and they didn't add up to her.

"I've been in this industry longer than Marty. I have an extra two years of service with the company. I received great feedback on the job I did managing the new process for receivables, and good reviews on my leadership and management skills," she thought as she walked toward the coffee machine. "Granted, Marty's had more exposure to the CFO than I have, but that's because he was picked by his buddy in the marketing department to work on that special sales compensation project."

Ginger's anger and frustration continued to mount as she reexamined her situation. Sitting in her cubicle, too riled to focus on her work right then, she hit on something. "Now that I think about it, the same thing happened to Belinda in systems. She was passed over for a promotion even though she was clearly the most qualified person in that department. At the time, I suspected that they didn't give her the job because they couldn't handle having a strong woman as a boss. But I thought that was just the systems group; they're pretty macho over there. I didn't think this could happen to me, not here."

As the sense of being a victim of bias sank in, Ginger's mood darkened. She realized she was in a weakened position, having just been passed over for promotion. Yet she felt the need to say something. She'd worked so hard for so long that it just didn't seem right. "Maybe I should talk with the CFO directly. Ask him what happened? Tell him that I think I was passed over due to my sex."

Ginger visualized herself sitting in the CFO's majestic office, listening to him across his massive mahogany desk. "Yes, Ginger, you're absolutely right. Marty got the job because he's male, and you didn't because you are female. We prefer to have men in leadership positions in finance. Our group is biased. Consequently, it's more difficult for women to get ahead here than for men. We should fix that, and the first thing I'm going to do is take that promotion away from Marty and give it to you." Ginger smiled to herself at the absurdity of contemplating such a response.

Moving on to a more realistic assessment of what was likely to happen, Ginger reevaluated her options. "Of course, any accusation of gender bias will be met with a denial. The reasons for my not getting the promotion will be justified by a litany of why Marty was a better choice. I'm not as qualified as Marty. I don't have the management talent that he does. Senior management is more comfortable at this point with Marty. Yes, I did a good job on the receivables, but Marty did a fantastic job on the more important sales comp project. I just need to hang in there and be patient. My turn will come. Blah, blah, blah. Whatever the particulars, the rationale for the decision will be based on a painful personal assessment, and I will come up short."

After thinking it over, Ginger reached the depressing realization that nothing good would come out of raising this topic with the CFO.

Ginger's assessment of management's reaction was spot on, based on what we've seen of the corporate world. No man wants to hear from a woman that she thinks he is gender biased. Accusing anyone of being sexist is insulting and offensive. And most managers don't think they are sexist. Suggest to almost any man that he is prejudiced against females and he will instantaneously list for you all the women in his life—his wife, mother, sister, assistant—with whom he gets along just fine. Tell a female manager that she is biased against women, and she will likely laugh you right out of her office.

Most senior executives who are running companies today honestly feel that their businesses treat men and women with equity. If there are any prejudicial outcomes in the system—more male executives, higher average pay for men—they see these outcomes as a consequence of an inherently fair system. Therefore, confronting a company on gender issues will almost always put management on the defensive. Executives will point to myriad actions or facts that they feel prove their egalitarian nature. "Didn't we just name Jane Smith to the executive team?" or "Don't we provide mandatory diversity training as part of our management development approach?" or "Aren't more than half the employees hired through our college recruitment program female?" And they are right. Based on today's accepted diversity practices, most companies have done a lot.

As a result, any woman who brings up gender inequity as a problem may find that, rather quickly, the topic turns. Since typically the woman who claims gender bias has just suffered a career setback, the accusation can be dismissed as an excuse, a lame excuse. The woman's allegations are often viewed as an attempt to divert attention from her personal inadequacies or lack of qualifications. The real problem is her own shortcomings, and she's just not facing facts. Consequently, unless the discrimination is crystal clear and blatantly illegal, such as physical or psychological sexual harassment, the woman raising the problem will often be seen as the problem.

The lack of tolerance for those who raise gender inequity issues at work also derives from a weariness that has set in after years of arguing, fighting, and remedial effort. Many people in management are tired of constantly drawing battle lines and being adversarial. They often feel that they've made all kinds of concessions already. For these people, it is time to accept where we are. They just don't want to hear women complaining about being treated unfairly anymore. Not to mention that fights about gender can get messy fast. Publicly, lawsuits, bad press, and internal investigations can rapidly run out of control. Privately, presumptions about appropriate gender roles and male-female relationships can be sensitive. The accusations on both sides create feelings of guilt and defensiveness. Not surprisingly, the win/win solutions that business loves to champion are elusive when it comes to addressing gender issues at work.

Gender equity is a toxic topic. The casualties are almost always high, and the bruising battles rarely result in any real victors. Women who take on this fight, who challenge the power structure by saying they are treated inequitably due to their gender, often become pariahs, and their careers suffer. The issues quickly become personal, and a woman can become a double victim. First, she's a victim of the gender bias she is identifying, and second, she is targeted as a problem when she broaches the sex-discrimination topic. The risks and consequences can be severe. Ask any woman who has hired an attorney or ended up in court in pursuit of fairness. The cost is high in both dollars and personal exposure and thus she suffers whether she wins or loses. She becomes permanently marked within her organization, and often within her profession or industry. Things can never return to business as usual. Still, on occasion, a lawsuit does result in a monetary judgment in her favor. But it's a grueling and disheartening process.

For most women, though, the battle is not fought in court; it's fought within the corporate walls. And business is a formidable foe, which expects employees, especially women, to respect the power structure and operate within the confines of appropriateness, as business defines them. Even though most companies today have formal processes for handling claims of discrimination, such claims are far from welcome. Rarely will anyone thank a woman for initiating a charge of gender bias, even her female colleagues. The issue is too divisive; it forces people to take sides. Accusations of gender inequity create a time-consuming conflict that distracts from an organization's primary business purpose. Thus, the woman who challenges usually ends up isolated, frustrated, and resentful. More often than not, she eventually leaves the organization with the aim of making a fresh start elsewhere.

Legislatively, we've made progress in the United States in providing some protection for those women who publicly claim harassment or discrimination at work. But the fact that we need such laws is in and of itself indicative of the risks women take in challenging today's power structure. As the gender problem in corporate America has moved from the issue of women getting into the system to the issue of women working within the system with parity, the forms of bias and discrimination have become more subtle, more passive. In many ways, this makes it even harder to challenge gender equity, because the inequities are less obvious. And it makes the expected response from corporate America more defensive, more personal in its counter-attack. So, despite the progress we've made, the woman who challenges on the toxic topic of gender bias will lose the battle far more often than not.

STATUS QUO

Today, women hold less power, make less money, and suffer more setbacks than their male counterparts in the corporate world. If they work within the system to effect change, they run a serious risk of being stigmatized as imprudent challengers of authority, of not respecting the power structure. Their career prospects can be limited, and they can even be pushed out the door. Women's generally lesser status in the system of business (even though they may have the same title and be at the same level in the hierarchy as their male counterparts), combined with the toxicity of gender inequity as an issue, produces a subliminal yet powerful message to women: picking gender equity as your battle puts *you* at risk.

A senior female executive told us that she feels the key to her relatively stable career is that she never, ever makes her gender an issue. "I assiduously avoid the topic and refuse to be drawn into discussions or debates about the equality of men and women at work." Rather, she focuses myopically on work, continuously hones her skills, and stoically performs her assigned duties. Privately, she acknowledges that she sometimes feels she has been disadvantaged due to her gender, but she's vowed never to let that sentiment pass her lips within earshot of anyone she works with. Her point is brutally direct: whether or not the playing field is level is immaterial. It is what it is. If the field is tilted against women, so be it. That doesn't mean women can't still play the game. They just need to discover how to do it to their advantage, given the lay of the land. As in the operating philosophy of some men in business, it's every woman for herself.

This works for some women. And, without question, certain women have "won the game" by rising to the top of the corporate hierarchy despite the difficulties that are more prevalent for women than for men. Similarly, many women do not choose to raise gender equity as an issue and risk the consequences. Rather, they comply with the system and try to stay inside the boundaries of what is deemed appropriate behavior, as defined for them by business. They may vent their frustrations with their friends, or grumble to their spouses, but just like the successful female executive quoted above, they continue to focus on their work and do the best they can within the confines of the system.

But the accumulated inequities can take their toll. Most women, in fact, do not do well in the game, and few rise to the top. Instead of being inspired and motivated by the demands of playing on an unlevel playing field, they can find the daily inequities wearing and discouraging, especially in the later years of a career of devoted work effort. But they are also concerned that by not challenging they are tacitly accepting the status quo. Conflicted and relegated to secondary positions, some women opt out of the mainstream corporate world altogether, even though this can mean reduced income, higher risk, and lower prestige in the business world. They seek positions in predominantly female companies, start their own businesses, work in different economic sectors (for example, nonprofit, education, government), or simply don't work for pay at all. They reach a point when work doesn't work for them anymore, when the rewards of employment in the corporate world no longer outweigh the indignity of being overlooked and underpaid in comparison to their comparable male colleagues.

Those who stay within the system, who continue to work at their corporate jobs, despite the inequities they experience, often believe or hope that business will continue to evolve and women's place in it will improve. They point to the tremendous progress that has been made over the past forty-plus years, since the beginning of the modern-day women's movement. They note that business is a dynamic force that both shapes and reflects the broader social, political, and economic trends, so that change will continue in the future. They acknowledge that life in business has been easier for them than for their mothers, and they expect that their daughters will have an easier time than they've had. If change takes literally a lifetime, at least it's progress.

We don't think patience or faith in the future is the solution. It can't be denied that inequity at work between men and women persists. Furthermore, the employment data clearly show that we're stuck at a point where the rate of progress has slowed almost to the point of regression. A focus on access—on getting into the system—is responsible for the progress that has been made to date. Today's problem, though, is about men and women working *within the system with parity*. This issue is at the heart and soul of the challenging-the-power-structure paradox. If women don't raise questions of gender inequity in business, little will change. Working within the system will continue to be more difficult for women than for men for a long time, if indeed the situation ever improves at all. The underlying causes of the disparity will remain unaddressed, and the likelihood of a positive and permanent resolution will be depressingly low.

For an individual woman, raising questions of gender inequity can be career limiting at best, career ending at worst. Overall, this risk to women reinforces the we/they attitude that exacerbates the problem of gender inequity and worse, reaps no results. Rather than continuing what many see as the battle of the sexes, we suggest a collective effort by men and women to understand the subtleties of the situation, for understanding is the first step to resolution. The parity paradoxes are bona fide problems that women face on a daily basis. The rules that underlie the paradoxes—be a team player, find mentors and win advocates, demonstrate commitment, bond with co-workers, be prudent in challenging the power structure—just don't work as well for women as for men. When women try to follow the rules, they find themselves in untenable, no-win situations. If a woman is a good team player, she rarely receives the recognition she's due. Yet, if she raises the issue of the disparity, she's frequently seen as not being a team player. Moreover, women who work just as hard as their male colleagues, and are equally talented, often don't win the mentors and advocates that men do. Women who demonstrate commitment, or try to bond with their co-workers, face additional, even more personally painful paradoxes. No matter what a woman does in trying to follow these basic rules of business, she frequently finds herself in a position of disadvantage relative to men, with no way of achieving true equality.

The parity paradoxes confound both men and women. For the most part, each sex believes in equal employment opportunity, regardless of gender. Both women and men want the problem to disappear. As corporate citizens, both men and women want to succeed as individuals and want their businesses to succeed. We believe a recognition that businessmen and businesswomen have these and other objectives in common can provide a strong foundation for a solution.

Chapter 9

THE COED COMPANY

In a coed company
- gender is immaterial,
- integration of the genders is essential, and
- parity between the genders is paramount.

THE STEALTH FACTOR

Sexism is an ugly word. Having misogynistic overtones, it connotes the conscious and deliberate discrimination and exclusion of women. But this is not what we generally find in today's business world. Most of the overt sexism in the workplace has been extinguished. Yet women continue to lag behind men in critical ways. The data clearly show that men make more money than women, even when women are in comparable positions with equal qualifications and experience. Men rise to a disproportionate number of the power positions in the corporate world, even though men and women have had similar career patterns up to the point when the men are elevated. While the problem of women getting into the system of business has largely been addressed, the problem of women working within the system in parity with men is far from resolved. In today's world, working in the system of business is just more difficult for women than it is for comparably positioned men.

Our identification and examination of the parity paradoxes are intended to shed new light on women's predicament in the business world. But we don't want to stop there. Collectively, the parity paradoxes pose both a conundrum and an opportunity. The conundrum is how can a woman deal with a business system whose intrinsic way of operating subtly but definitively keeps her in lower regard than her male counterparts? How can she excel if the system is working against her? The opportunity is that by articulating the parity paradoxes we can begin to understand today's problem of gender inequity and develop true, enduring solutions. So let us focus on the opportunity that now exists. Despite the negative picture of gender conflict in the workplace that the paradoxes reveal, we believe they can also open the door to a better future.

We begin with the observation that each paradox is predicated on a basic rule of business. In general, when women try to follow the dictates of the rule, the benefits they reap are significantly smaller than those accorded to comparably situated men. Yet if women ignore or go against the rule, the consequences for women are substantially more punitive than they are for men. This is the essence of each paradox. In examining this problem, our first instinct was to say that there must be a problem with the rules themselves. There must be something inherent in these basic laws of business that benefits men more than women or demands more of women than of men. But upon further reflection, we don't think this is so. In fact, we have concluded that the rules are powerful and fundamentally sound. Each rule is intuitively reasonable and pragmatically good counsel. Consider finding a mentor and winning advocates. This is certainly wise advice for any employee, male or female. The fact that men find more mentors and win more advocates is not a direct consequence of the rule as written. Similarly, being a team player, demonstrating commitment, bonding with co-workers, being prudent in challenging the power structure—all of the rules meet this test. All are gender neutral in content and intent. Together, and in concert with other standard operating procedures of business, they form the foundation of the American system of capitalism—the most powerful and successful economic force in the world.

Yet these standard rules of business lead women into paradoxes that men don't typically encounter. So perhaps the issue is in the execution of the rules. Are men simply better at executing the rules than women? Do men have more experience with them earlier in their lives and therefore follow them more effectively in business? This may have been true in the past, but we don't think it's the case today. Certainly in years gone by, men were prepared for a career in business in ways that women were not. Single-sex education, participation in athletics, and military experience equipped men to fall in line and succeed in business to a much higher degree than women. But over the past fifty or more years, these differences have largely disappeared. Today, women have access to the same types of formative experiences and education as men. The lessons taught formally in the classroom, informally in the sports arena, and through military service are available to women and men alike. Now that we have reached the point in history where women share in the advantages gained in these preparatory forums, it is hard to argue that men are more experienced and therefore better at following the basic rules of business than women. Inside and outside the business world, we see women who are just as capable as men of comprehending and following the rules.

So, if the rules are gender neutral and women are just as capable as men of following them, then perhaps it is men who are creating the paradoxes that entrap women. After all, men retain the vast majority of the power and influence in the business world. If business is biased against women, if the playing field is tilted in favor of men, it might be logical to conclude that men are protecting their position and preserving their power by making the business world more difficult for women than for men. But exploring this premise exposes a puzzling dichotomy. On an individual level, we have found almost universally that men say they firmly believe in and support gender equity at work. Women we have spoken with validate this view when they list numerous men in business with whom they interact one-on-one on a nonbiased basis. Yet the disparities that exist and the challenges that women uniquely face are hard to deny. Like women, men seem to be stuck in a game that is producing unwanted results. Individually they say they support gender equity, but in the aggregate they pose obstacles for women. Men seem blinded by the broader forces at play and, therefore, can't rectify the situation, even when they have good intentions.

We believe group dynamics are the problem. We have found that the vast majority of men and women in business are not consciously sexist—they believe in the equality of men and women in the workplace. We have also seen that the basic rules of business are gender neutral. But, when gender-neutral business rules are mixed together with men and women who personally believe in gender equality, the perplexing result is parity paradoxes that plague women and not men. The only power we know that is strong enough to create this conundrum is the pressure to fit within social norms. Just as we see that adolescents can be such good kids when you deal with them one-on-one but complete monsters when they are with their clique, we see that the power of the group dynamic in the work environment can override the good nature of individual employees.

Corporate culture is the stealth factor that perpetuates the behaviors creating conflict and inequity between men and women at work. As we've defined it, corporate culture is that amorphous totality of acceptable social behaviors and shared attitudes that pervades an organization's way of operating. It's a powerful, invisible force that establishes, enforces, and sustains a company's values and sets the parameters for the way employees treat each other. As consultants working with a variety of companies, we are regularly struck by the potency as well as the wide range of corporate cultures, not only across industries but within them. One cosmetics company is stylish, another stodgy; one entertainment company is high-energy, the other flat. Nevertheless, within a company, employees will go to great lengths to conform to their company's cultural standards. Gap khakis are the unspoken uniform at one organization, whereas nothing but Brooks Brothers pleats will do at another. Employees at one beverage company never use contractions in their internal communications, while employees at another seem never to use complete sentences. Be it in style of dress or style of writing, the consistency of employee demeanor and work habits within companies is strong and widespread. We see employees from the CEO to the front-desk receptionist displaying stunning similarities, down to what might be considered personality traits: patterns of speech, levels of energy, tastes in food.

Because a corporate culture is ubiquitous and loosely defined, its impact is often missed. As with the air they breathe, employees have difficulty seeing how their culture drives their actions regardless of their best intentions or deeply held beliefs. The work community both formally and informally reinforces certain behaviors and shuns others. The result is a consistency in the corporate population in general, and ever more pronounced similarities as you move up the management ranks. When we work with a client company's senior management team, we are regularly amused by the number of these executives who literally look like each other. And as with familial resemblances between siblings, they rarely see it in themselves.

When a corporate culture's conventions are haunted by biases from the past, the pressure to conform to that culture's norms can often be noxious to gender parity. This is because deeply embedded in its standard ways of operating are dated expectations of how men and women should interact at work. Originally established when the roles of men and women with respect to work, especially corporate work, were markedly separate and distinct—men were managers, women were secretaries or wives—many business protocols continue to enable behaviors that reflect that bias today. Many corporate codes of conduct impose on men and women gender stereotypes and social strictures that prevent the sexes from working closely together with parity. The clash between the old gender roles of business and the new American woman results in paradoxical predicaments.

Corporate culture is the prime culprit today. It is the root cause of the gender disparity in many work environments—not the basic business rules or personal biases (though the latter can exacerbate the problem). That's not to say that corporate culture is always a malevolent force. Quite the contrary. The power of corporate culture can be managed to accomplish great things. Most management consultants will tell you that the most highly successful companies are the ones that have cultivated strong and durable corporate cultures. In *Built to Last: Successful Habits of Visionary Companies*, James C. Collins and Jerry I. Porras devoted an entire chapter to the topic. Their analysis of prosperous, enduring companies, such as General Electric, IBM, American Express, and Sony, identified "Cult-like Cultures" as a common distinguishing trait contributing to their success. "Joining these companies reminds me of joining an extremely tight-knit group or society. And if you don't fit, you'd better not join. If you're willing to really buy in and dedicate yourself to what the company stands for, then you'll be very satisfied and productive—probably couldn't be happier. If not, however, you'll probably flounder, feel miserable and out-of-place, and eventually leave—ejected like a virus. It's binary: You're either in or you're out, and there seems to be no middle ground. It's almost cult-like."[1] In Thomas J. Peters and Robert H. Waterman's classic *In Search of Excellence: Lessons from America's Best-Run Companies*, the authors strongly attested to the value of corporate culture, as well. Their research led them to conclude that, "Without exception, the dominance and coherence of culture proved to be an essential quality of the excellent companies."[2]

Beyond what to wear or what to say, corporate culture signals to employees through its value system what's important and why they are there. The potency of its directives can be astonishing. Whether explicitly written in a mission statement, orally handed down from an older generation of managers, or just palpably evident, a company's values are the philosophical foundation on which a culture is built. Their importance was captured in a *New York Times* article entitled "Many Find an Office's Culture Is More Than Dress-Shirt Deep." In the story told in this article, a young woman had moved from journalism to banking and was commenting on the adjustment: "It was . . . a shock to have to show up for work at 9 a.m. sharp every day, wearing subdued colors and Calvin Klein skirts. The calm, polite tenor of the frequent meetings she was required to attend also took some getting used to. . . . So did Ms. Hansen begin to yearn for the old days as a reporter? Not a bit. Instead, she learned an important lesson about the workplace: surface manifestations of a company's culture don't matter; what counts are its core values."[3]

The way male and female employees are expected to relate to each other at work is one of those core values. While every company will say it is an equal opportunity employer—it has to by law—the reality is found in the acceptable work and social behaviors of a company's culture. We've found that the prevailing underlying value in most organizations today is the belief that men and women are fundamentally different. Any similarities between the sexes are far outweighed by innate dissimilarities. This is not to say that men and women are not equal. Rather, they are distinct. Therefore, it is appropriate for gender to be a consideration at work and for men and women to be socially segregated. Unfortunately, the parity paradoxes are the inevitable outcome of such a value proposition. This is why many women have difficulties being team players, finding mentors and winning advocates, demonstrating commitment, bonding with fellow employees, and challenging the power structure prudently. This is why gender disparity persists. The parity paradoxes are manifestations of the problem. The root cause is a culture of business haunted by a belief system that accepts gender differentiation—a culture that continues to drive a wedge between men and women at work.

A DIFFERENT WAY

Kate, a businesswoman in her mid-thirties, was sitting in her ten-by-ten office, having trouble concentrating. She was an account manager with a global consulting firm, and she wanted to make partner this year. She really, really wanted to. In the conference room next to her office, three men of corporate importance—the head of her local office, the regional manager, and the head of new business development—held her fate in their hands. But they were not determining who would be nominated for partner; rather, they were deciding who would be the account manager for a prestigious new client. If given the opportunity, Kate knew she could do this job well and that her success with this particular client would elevate her to the stature of partner. And, as she'd been repeatedly told, "You have to be doing partner-level work before they'll make you a partner."

Kate also knew that the men in that room would not, when her name came up as a possibility, mention or even allude to her sex. They wouldn't talk about the fact that she was the mother of two or whether that would impede her ability to handle this demanding, important client. In this context, it was a nonissue to them. She had worked closely and successfully with all three of them over the previous five years on a variety of projects. They were office buddies, both on and off the job. She actually considered Bob, the regional manager, to be a mentor of hers and couldn't imagine Bill, the local office head, being anything but a strong advocate on her behalf. Given her prior experiences at this company and with these three men in particular, Kate had complete confidence that she would have a totally fair shot at this career-making opportunity. If she got it, great. If she didn't, she knew that it would be for a substantive reason—certainly not her sex. She'd seen how men and women worked together at her company. She'd noted how they advanced with parity. She knew she would be treated fairly. And she was.

On the desert landscape of corporate America, where gender conflict is more often the norm, Kate's experience stands out like a freshwater oasis. In her company, men and women work together in easy harmony and with unforced parity. The lack of self-consciousness about an employee's sex impacts both work-flow and mind-set. In our thirty years of working in and consulting to corporate America, we've seen similar situations sparsely scattered through the corporate world. We've also personally experienced isolated instances in which genuine gender parity has been a reality. Sometimes it's an office, or a department, or even a unit within a large company. Once or twice, we've even seen it throughout a business, primarily in small businesses. We've rarely found this state of parity throughout a major American company, though. Nevertheless, the fact that it exists within any business gives us hope and motivation.

In such work environments, the basic business rules remain intact, but the parity paradoxes that are so prevalent throughout the business world seem to simply disappear. Employees still need to be team players, find mentors, win advocates, demonstrate commitment, bond with peers, and challenge prudently, yet following these requirements doesn't seem to put women in secondary positions. As one woman at a major cosmetics company put it, "My gender doesn't matter here. Nobody's gender matters here." This type of environment can be incredibly liberating. A certain lightness pervades the workplace for both men and women because neither sex has to carry the burden of gender roles or gender conflict. As a woman in a staff function at an insurance company said, "Nothing is limiting me, except myself."

One of the more intriguing gender parity environments we have ever been exposed to involved teenagers. Our son, a master scuba diver, would go on summer trips with an organization called Broadreach. He went on three or four of these expeditions, and his e-mails and photos resulting from the experience were surprisingly gender neutral. One particular excursion placed sixteen adolescents on a catamaran for six weeks, sailing around the Caribbean. Independent of gender, the boys and girls were assigned not only daily crewing responsibilities but also, since they were diving, jobs requiring them to fill and carry heavy air tanks and other cumbersome scuba equipment. For the most part, friendships between the boys and girls on these trips developed without regard to gender. To us this was all the more astounding since these kids were at an age where hormones are raging and excessive machismo is often a consequence. We spoke with Broadreach's founder, Carlton Goldthwaite, and asked how he created such an egalitarian environment. "We set up our programs to avoid gender stereotypes," he explained. "We operate on a principle of each to his own ability. We don't make assumptions about physical strength or other abilities based on gender. Everybody does what they can do. If you have trouble, whether you are a boy or a girl, you are told to ask for help."[4] The principle seems to set the tone. Goldthwaite went on to say that the adult supervisors that are employed by Broadreach try to model the same behavior.

Our own firsthand experience of a gender-neutral environment occurred during our thirties, when we were working in a small office of a professional services firm. The office was headed by a gray-haired sage of a manager and his sprightly, talented, female number two. They had a certain CEO-COO dynamic going between them: he set the strategy and she executed it. Though this office employed only about twenty professionals, it was one the most successful within this global service firm and had a reputation for creative solutions. The office ambience was urbane, energetic, and entrepreneurial. But what made it truly different was the way in which the men and women related to each other. There were no exclusions, no gender cliques. Men and women were friends, or at least friendly to each other. The office's strong camaraderie was genderless. Social interactions were all mixed-gender, including lunchroom seating, dinner outings, baby showers, and so forth. The work processes seemed to ignore gender. Decisions on client assignments, team composition, and professional development were based on individual merit and ability. No one felt advantaged or disadvantaged by her or his sex. It was a great place to work.

But not for everyone. We noticed that some employees who transferred into the office were not particularly comfortable with the culture. They brought with them customs and practices that didn't fit into the norms of the office. One male employee was always trying to organize "boy" outings—golf, baseball games, drinking nights—that others really didn't want to attend. Similarly, a female employee who liked to go shoe shopping with the girls during lunch was frustrated by the lack of enthusiasm for this gender-exclusive activity. These employees did not last long. They tended to transfer to other parts of the company, and some ended up doing very well in their new locations.

Unfortunately, our experience was fleeting. As leadership was transitioned to others, as personnel changes took place, and as the business evolved and grew, the gender parity that we experienced in our small, sheltered office evaporated. Somehow that sense of oneness that comes when gender differences are minimized disappeared. We've witnessed this phenomenon at other companies as well. There seems to be an ephemeral quality to many of those corporate situations where gender equity has become an operational norm. It lasts for a brief period of time, then it disappears, and the situation reverts to that of the more typical corporate environment, in which gender conflict is rife and women are disadvantaged on a regular basis relative to men. Though some employees lament the loss of gender equity, often they cannot identify just what happened to change their situation.

In thinking about these passing experiences, we've noticed that the cultures of gender parity that we've seen share several distinctive traits. First, the tone comes predominantly from the top and filters down. Whether it's in an office or a department, the top manager or management team in the business unit will set the standards and personally model the way men and women relate with respect to gender. Second, discussions and issues about gender seem to disappear. The culture is marked more by the absence of gender references rather than by overt discussions about supporting female employees. Third, the norms with respect to gender are rarely spoken of. Rather, the culture seems to materialize from the tone set by management and the tacit buy-in by the employees. Fourth, the culture tends to be temporary (though this is not always the case) and is subject to random change due to a variety of factors that are difficult to pinpoint. While the arrival of new employees or managers, whether male or female, who are of a different mind-set can change the dynamics, this is not always clearly the cause of the shift. Fifth, and finally, the isolated business units practicing gender equity are relatively high performing. In terms of internal benchmarks and in comparison to external competitors, these business units do quite well.

This last observation was initially surprising to us, but on further consideration it seems to make sense. Positive business performance and general employee satisfaction have been clearly correlated. It is not a big leap, then, to assume that relieving employees of the pressure of gender conflict and the distraction of gender disparity will lead to higher employee satisfaction and consequently better business results. A recent study by Catalyst, the leading nonprofit organization focusing on women's issues in business, seems to support this conclusion. Catalyst found that "Companies with the highest representation of women on their top management teams experienced better financial performance than companies with the lowest women's representation. This finding holds true for both financial measures analyzed: Return on Equity (ROE), which is 35 percent higher, and Total Return to Shareholders (TRS), which is 34 percent higher."[5] While headcounts may not be a definitive indication of a culture of gender parity—the fact that a company has a larger number of women in top management roles doesn't necessarily mean that the company is a better place for women to work in—the results of the Catalyst study are consistent with our personal observations.

Cultures of gender parity are achievable and financially beneficial but often transitory. The question then becomes how to take those isolated, short-lived instances that we've observed and make them practicable and permanent for a broad cross-section of the business world. How do you build and sustain a business culture of gender harmony and equality? We begin by noting that there is no common word for the type of environment we seek. And without the proper language, it's difficult to recapture the experience. To start, what's needed is a vocabulary that encapsulates the values and behaviors that are required to promote parity between men and women at work—in what we call a *coed company*.

A COED COMPANY

A corporate culture in which men and women work with parity within the system of business is our definition of a coed company. The core of a coed company—of any corporate culture, for that matter—is the system of values on which it is built. Like the rudder of a ship, cultural values allow a company to set a direction and keep on course. They guide the behavior of employees by setting standards for how they should act. They help translate corporate requirements into personal requirements, providing the ultimate answer to the question, "Why are you doing it this way?" At Avis, "we try harder." New York Life is "the company you keep." American Express is "the card you don't leave home without." While all are recognizable advertising slogans, each communicates a prized value that is paramount within the culture of the organization. Hence, above-and-beyond effort is prized at Avis; enduring financial trustworthiness is prized at New York Life; and worldwide, reliable customer support is prized at American Express. Employees at these companies know the values upon which their companies were built.

A company's values are most effective when they are succinct and widely communicated. One major alcohol company prominently displayed in each of its many conference rooms an elegantly printed, sapphire blue poster with silver lettering that stated the company's mission and values. It was not uncommon for these values to be specifically drawn upon during meetings. When discussing an extremely youth-oriented marketing campaign for a new wine cooler, a participant interrupted a spirited debate by pointing to the wall and saying, "One of our values is to promote the responsible use of alcohol. Does this approach really do that?" At times of crisis, when caught in a bind, going back to basic common values can be stabilizing and clarifying in a work environment.

Familiar with the power of articulated corporate values, we set out to define a coed company's values. To do this, we needed to extract, from those cultures in which we have witnessed gender parity, and synthesize the underlying, if tacit, principles that guide gender relationships. These principles were more difficult to discern than we expected, as we found a number of characteristics that were counterintuitive. For insistence, coed companies seem less focused on gender diversity than one might expect. We did not find extensive support networks in place. Nor were these cultures particularly proactively pro-female. Women in general were not especially championed, and high-ranking women were rarely held up as icons. Rather, in cultures of parity, we found both men and women very focused on their common work. Their actions and behaviors, as well as management's attention, seemed to indicate little regard for gender at all. This led us to the first of three core values.

In a coed company, *gender is immaterial*. We find this simple value quite profound. It asserts that the gender of an employee is of no consequence, no importance, and no relevance in a work environment. Gender says nothing about an individual's ability, intelligence, motivation, work ethic, or domestic responsibilities. When making work-based decisions such as those regarding job assignments, team composition, reporting relationships, compensation adjustments, bonus awards, and so on, gender is about as relevant as eye color. It's not that different physical features don't exist; it's just that at work they're not germane. Whether the employee is male or female just doesn't come into play.

Gender immateriality also has a more subtle implication for the way men and women behave at work. In a coed company, assumptions based on gender stereotypes are discounted. Statements that begin with "Women are always . . ." or "Isn't it just like a man to . . ." conflict with the core value. Such focusing on differences tends to drive men and women apart. This perspective is founded on the belief that men and women are more dissimilar than similar. The value that gender is immaterial moves the focus to what men and women have in common.

The depth and breadth of the precept is best illustrated by a story that has made the rounds of mergers-and-acquisitions specialists. Meant to be illustrative of the perils of merging incompatible business cultures, it captures perfectly the impact of the value that gender is immaterial. Supposedly, two companies were about to enter a joint business venture. Company A wanted to market children's toys based on characters from its television programs and it approached toy Company B in the hope of partnering with that company. Company A was a relatively young organization that had grown rapidly as a producer of children's television programs, and one of its sacrosanct operating principles was gender neutrality in its programming. All its TV shows were designed to appeal to children irrespective of gender. Company B had a long, successful, but different history in working with children. It considered designing gender-distinct toys a cornerstone of its success.

The business world anticipated great things from the partnership: Company A was the voice of the future and Company B had a successful operational past. At the first meeting of representatives from both organizations, Company B took the lead. Using its proven process for developing any new toy, the Company B representatives began by asking their standard first question, "Is it a girl toy or a boy toy?"

"It's a kids' toy," responded the Company A people.

"Yes, but for a girl child or a boy child?"

They never got past that first meeting. Company A genuinely didn't see its characters as exclusively for one gender or the other. They honestly couldn't answer the question. Company B, on the other hand, was organized according to girl toys and boy toys. Its business divisions were set up this way. Each company was so staunch in its perspective that the companies could not find a way to work together.

Making gender immaterial at work demands more discipline and vigilance than may be immediately obvious. The simplicity of the value belies the degree of change required in the mind-set of employees. To obtain relief from the expectations and limitations derived from gender roles in business, both men and women need to relinquish the benefits they've experienced due to their gender. Men, because of the strong link between work, identity, and masculinity, have to let go of the workplace as a proving ground for manhood. Men have to loosen the tie between their gender identity and their work identity, and give up any sense of entitlement derived solely from being a man. Women, on the other hand, need to give up their sense of being victimized (unless they are). They need to accept responsibility for their work successes and failures, and compete as equals with other women and men. Frankly, making gender immaterial at work is probably more difficult for men than for women, given the historical connections between masculinity and work. But the rewards are significant for men as well as women, in that both genders are freed from the rigid strictures imposed by gender roles at work. Once gender becomes immaterial in business, men and women can work side by side as individuals, absent any advantages or disadvantages due uniquely to their sex.

The second core value of a coed company is that *integration of the genders is essential.* Gender should have no influence over the groupings of employees. Inclusiveness becomes the overriding principle for office events, intraoffice gatherings, and daily interactions. Single-sex groupings, either formal or informal, are at odds with this core coed value. As opposed to the passivity of the past, the value demands a proactive stance. It makes it incumbent on both men and women to recognize behaviors at work that tend to devolve into unisex groupings and to consciously take steps to integrate a situation instead.

In practice, the effect of this particular value can be startling. Janice, a mid-level employee of a financial services company, noted its influence on the lunchtime routine at two locations. Same company, same activity, same professionals, entirely different social protocol. In the Connecticut office, the men ate lunch with other men. Noontime came around and they gathered each other up and found a table together. A woman could be working side by side with her male peers all morning, but they would never ask her to join them. It would have violated some unspoken rule among the men if a guy were to ask a woman to come along. The New York office seemed like a different world. Men and women mingled in the lunchroom. The topics of conversation naturally allowed both men and women to participate. It was considered rude to exclude people by gender. This didn't mean what they discussed was bland and sexless. Janice recalled Matt waltzing in, plopping himself down, and announcing to no one in particular, "I just read that twenty-two percent of employees have affairs during their lunch hour. I don't understand how that could be. Is anyone here having an affair?"

When the integration of the genders is deemed essential, employees are required to give up some of the traditional comfort zones that many of them have sought at work. The cliquish behaviors of women and the homosocial thinking of men are replaced by conscious efforts to interact in ways such that both sexes are unselfconsciously included. To some it comes naturally from the beginning, like relating to a brother or a sister; for others it takes a little practice. When fully evolved, the concept of "work friends" emerges, in which friendships between men and women at work are comparable to, and just as common as, friendships between employees of the same sex. When this is the norm, men and women who are work friends don't raise alarmist suspicions of sexual intimacy or inappropriate favoritism that may compromise their judgment. Rather, mixed-gender work friendships become a natural part of the work environment.

As an aside, we should say we are not so naïve or utopian as to deny that office romances won't develop. In almost any collection of people, sexual attraction between individuals will be present and will influence the way they relate to each other. Some attractions will lead to romantic entanglements and illicit affairs, though many will not. This is true in a coed company as well as in more traditional corporate cultures. In the case of those relationships that do cross the line, a strong corporate policy of early disclosure can be used to address some of the conflicts of interest that may emerge. The coed company tries to counter possible problems by encouraging an environment in which men and women are free to have nonsexual, mixed-gender friendships without having to be concerned that they may be looked at askance.

The third value of a coed company is that *parity between the genders is paramount*. Men and women should share equally in the opportunities, rewards, responsibilities, and power of an organization. No individual man or woman should be advantaged or disadvantaged due to gender, nor should either men or women as a group benefit disproportionately in comparison to the other. This value goes beyond providing equal opportunity for all. It implies that a business should not operate in such a way as to regularly favor one gender over the other. So, if a certain position is available to an equal number of qualified male and female employees, but in reality many more men are promoted to that position, then the company is not abiding by this value. Parity between genders means that the result, as well as the opportunity, must be balanced between men and women. Making parity paramount means committing to the value in intent and in practice.

The value of parity between the genders requires employees to change some of their patterns and practices of the past. When making business decisions, employees and managers will need to regularly add an additional question to their evaluation: "Will this decision result in a disparity between men and women?" The consequences of actions such as the awarding of pay raises and bonuses will have to be measured to assure equitable outcomes. The assignment of responsibilities and promotions to power positions will need to be subjected to a final review to ensure a lack of gender bias. Employees, male and female alike, will have to look at their daily interactions and behaviors and ask themselves if they are acting in ways that promote parity or disparity. These steps may represent a tedious challenge to some traditional business protocols and customary employee behaviors, but they are key to creating a culture in which gender parity is the norm.

The three values underlying a coed company—gender is immaterial, integration of the genders is essential, parity between the genders is paramount—are interconnected and complementary. Ideally, the immateriality of gender would be sufficient in and of itself to assure productive integration and gender parity. In some ways, focusing on gender for the purposes of integration and parity even seems to contradict gender immateriality. But companies exist within the larger society, and our society tolerates and sometimes actually promotes segregation and disparity between the genders. Single-sex education, single-sex socializing, gender roles in religion, sex distinctions in sports—all convey an acceptance of gender separation and gender differences. In a coed company, employees need to know that the values and associated behaviors at work are different. Making integration of the genders essential and parity paramount will kick-start, rather than contradict, the goal of making gender immaterial. This will raise gender relations in employees' minds from subconsciously reflexive to consciously purposeful.

The coed company represents a new cultural mind-set. Its values provide a framework within which men and women can work together as true peers in the system of business. Employees may feel clumsy and uncomfortable at first, but personal discomfort does not mean the approach is inappropriate. A good analogy is the judicial concept of presumption of innocence. If you have ever served on a jury, you have been instructed to adhere to the principle of presumed innocence. It is a weighty and at times counterintuitive concept that requires all citizens to consciously discard their preconceptions while they are in the jury box, in order to make the judicial system work. Similarly, in a coed company, certain gender preconceptions are discarded in the workplace, and every element of the corporate culture needs to support this.

We've seen it work in reality. In a coed company, people simply don't refer to gender as a pertinent distinguishing characteristic. In both work and associated social settings, the sexes are fully integrated. In making business decisions and in casual conversations, employees don't make generalizations about the abilities of men and women. Paula Madison, president and general manager of NBC4, Los Angeles, captured the essence of this sentiment when, upon receiving an award from the New York Women's Agenda, she said, "If someone asks you who is the better boss, a man or a woman, don't answer that question."[6] In a coed corporate culture, the powerful force of group dynamics guided by common values works to ensure the avoidance of biased behavior.

RESOLVING THE PARADOXES

The parity paradoxes are obstacles that prevent true equality between men and women at work. They confront women and not men, and they keep women in a disadvantaged position in the business world relative to men. Understanding that the parity paradoxes are manifestations of a business culture plagued by biases and gender roles from the past leads us to a way out. The root cause is cultural norms, and so the only lasting solution has to involve cultural change. From our perspective, the coed company—a business culture of parity between men and women as they work within the corporate system—is the cultural antidote to the parity paradoxes. The key to resolving the paradoxes is, ironically, not focusing on the paradoxes themselves but living the values of a coed company. By adopting the three values that form the foundation of a coed company, then making them real in daily operations and interactions, an organization can eradicate the parity paradoxes that beset women and perplex many employees of both sexes.

To understand how this works, we need to look at each paradox separately. We begin with the teamwork paradox: if a woman is a team player, she rarely receives recognition commensurate with her contribution. If a woman seeks recognition for her contribution, she is seen as not being a team player. The central issue of this paradox is the inequity in rewards and recognition between the sexes despite equivalent performance. A woman can be just as good a team player as a man, following the rules of team play and playing the game quite comparably and capably, yet not receive the same degree of credit—monetarily or psychologically—as her male peers. The disparity is evidenced statistically in the hard pay data for men and women, and anecdotally by women's expression of frustration with a system that seems to keep them perpetually a step behind men.

A coed company addresses the team-player paradox through its value of making parity between the genders paramount. The sine qua non of this value is the delivery of equitable rewards for men and women. Now, one might say that most companies today already have policies regarding equal pay. Corporate statements such as "We believe in pay for performance" or "Our policy is equal pay for equal work" are ubiquitous. In addition, for over forty years, the Equal Pay Act of 1963 has required that "no employer having employees subject to any provisions of this section shall discriminate . . . between employees on the basis of sex by paying wages to employees in such establishment at a rate less than the rate at which he pays wages to employees of the opposite sex in such establishment for equal work."[7] To underscore the efforts even further, in

2009, the first bill President Obama signed into law was the Lilly Ledbetter Fair Pay Act. Still, none of these acts or policies have erased the pay differential between men and women, so why would the parity value of a coed company be any different?

The difference is this: a coed company separates itself from past practices by demanding parity as a result, not just establishing it as a goal. It adds a final step to business and human resource reward allocations, a step in which employees and managers ask themselves and their subordinates if the process has resulted in parity or disparity based on gender. The vast majority of rewards in the corporate world are measurable, either through the analysis of data or through the statistical evaluation of information-gathering exercises (for example, employee focus groups and surveys). This ability to quantify the distribution and perception of rewards allows organizations to directly assess and compare outcomes by gender. A coed company uses this capacity to discover disparities and then address and correct them.

A company that is proactively making gender parity paramount will be rewarding men and women equally for their self-sacrificing team-play behaviors. Then, once parity in recognition of good team play is achieved, the second part of the paradox is neutralized. There is no need for women to seek recognition for their contributions because equitable treatment has become the norm. Even when questions of inequities arise, as they surely will since no organization is perfect, the coed company does not punish the woman who brings the issue to the fore because the concerns of the woman and the values of the company are aligned. If a business regularly double-checks its reward allocations and actions for gender disparity, then it will take seriously and respectfully the questions of inequity of recognition that are raised by employees.

A coed company deals with the mentor/advocate paradox in a similar fashion, although different values are involved. This paradox states that hard work and talent attract mentors and advocates, but that talented women who work hard rarely attract highly regarded mentors or win influential, loyal advocates. The issues here are primarily selection and strength of support. Senior employees choose to mentor men more often than women and advocate more forcefully for men. The reasons for this are subtle and complex, relating to the risk a senior employee assumes in selecting someone to mentor or advocate for, the degree to which the senior employee identifies with the junior employee, and the cultural norms of segregating men and women. The impact of the mentor/advocate paradox on women is hard to measure explicitly. The informal nature of the processes makes the gender inequities difficult to quantify, yet anyone who has spent time in the corporate world is aware of the single-sex nature of most strong mentoring and loyal advocating.

Crucial to addressing the mentor/advocate paradox is a change of mind-set regarding male/female relationships at work. Older employees need to be able to mentor and advocate for younger employees without arousing suspicions of sexual relationships or triggering sexual innuendo. The coed company produces this change of mind-set. Its values of gender immateriality and integration as essential are targeted to this goal. The values repudiate those present-day cultural norms in business that accept gender segregation as an innate tendency of both sexes. The coed company refutes gender stereotyping and creates an environment in which men and women, even older men and younger women, are free to work closely together without juvenile finger-pointing and suggestive assumptions. Relationships between men and women in such an environment are like those found in an egalitarian family, where parents of either sex can mentor and advocate equally for their daughters and sons. Gender is immaterial in a coed company, and inclusiveness is the norm. With this new mind-set, the mentor/advocacy paradox evaporates.

The values of a coed company have the same effect on the commitment paradox. According to this paradox, a woman who is committed to her job and career is often presumed to have a deficient personal life. A woman with a fulfilling personal life is frequently seen as not seriously committed to her job and career. This particularly mean-spirited paradox is based on the traditional expectations of gender roles that are still often found in today's corporate cultures. Compounding the problem are general societal notions of motherhood and fatherhood that tend to create more intense work/family conflicts for women than for men.

The coed company combats these forces by asserting that a company is a closed environment in which certain values, rules, and protocols prevail. Though the company exists within the broader society and cannot escape being influenced to some extent by that society, it is a relatively self-contained entity that has control over the people who are employed by the company when they are on the job. The values the organization deems most important and the protocols it wants to promote take precedence during the workday. The corporate culture defines what is "politically correct" in its environment. Like the military and educational institutions, companies have unique cultures that coexist with society at large. In a coed company, there are no stereotypical gender roles because gender is immaterial, although this may not be the case in the outside world. There are no preconceptions about motherhood or fatherhood, other than the physical disability involved in pregnancy, that create different personal expectations for men and women. Taking a leave of absence for family medical or parental issues, for example, is not presumed to be disproportionately the responsibility of one gender or the other; nor are the consequences for taking such leaves different by gender. Gender is a nonissue. Hence, there is no place for derogatory presumptions about commitment and the personal lives of working women.

By now, the pattern should be clear. A coed company does not attack the parity paradoxes head-on but severs the historical cultural roots that create the paradoxes. By establishing, articulating, and living the coed values, a coed company makes the parity paradoxes disappear. The daily behaviors and social protocols of the culture enforce a new mind-set. For the bonding paradox, the coed value that integration of the genders is essential will create the antidote. The paradox states that when a woman bonds primarily with her female co-workers, she is segregated and often left outside the power structure. When a woman relates to her male co-workers as "the opposite sex," she rarely builds strong bonds. When a woman tries to bond with her male co-workers as "one of the boys," she tends to alienate both men and women. In a company where integration is essential, sexual segregation is not tolerated in work or in associated social settings. It's replaced by the gender-neutral concept of "work friends," close work associates of either gender. Work friends makes relating to co-workers as "the opposite sex" or as "one of the boys" simply of no significance. The coed value overrides and dissolves the paradox.

The final parity paradox says that employees who imprudently challenge the power structure are often stigmatized and their careers suffer. If women do not challenge, nothing changes. But in a coed company, this paradox doesn't apply. If an organization believes in and effectuates the values that gender is immaterial and that parity between the genders is paramount, the degree of deference required of employees will be determined by their position in the hierarchy, not their sex. Since gender is immaterial, there is no difference between the behavioral expectations of women and those of men; gender roles simply become employee roles. Women who challenge will be treated no more harshly than men who do the same.

Values made real through the daily behaviors of employees and operational processes of a company can be incredibly powerful. In and of themselves, the values of a coed company are deceptively simple: gender is immaterial, integration of the genders is essential, parity between the genders is paramount. Yet, when put in the context of the workplace and brought to fruition through processes, protocols, and acceptable employee behaviors, they create a business culture in which the parity paradoxes cease to exist and true gender parity can be achieved.

Several years ago, we attended a New York Women's

Agenda breakfast at which a CEO receiving an "Honorable MEN-tion" award humbly and almost as a perplexed aside said, "I'm not sure what I did to deserve this, but it does seem to me that the companies that focus the least on women's issues are the ones that are the most successful at giving women opportunities."[8] We too have seen that women thrive in work environments where they are not treated as members of a separate class. This is why, importantly, and perhaps counterintuitively, building a coed company does not focus heavily on the parity paradoxes and the disadvantages they impose on women. In fact, very little attention is given to any specific women's issues at all. That's not to say that a coed company—or for that matter any company—should ignore women who are victims of harassment or discrimination. Every company needs to provide safety and support to its employees. Rather, by establishing the coed values, a coed company aims to neutralize discrimination before it happens.

In language and substance, coed values are gender neutral and apply equally to men and women. They center on creating a culture of equity for all employees in which gender is a non-issue. Instead of trying specifically to advance or even support women—bring them up to men's level—a coed company envisions a corporate culture of parity by removing gender as an issue for both sexes and creating an environment of mutual respect between them. This subtle but pivotal distinction gives the coed company the power to resolve the parity paradoxes and finally level the corporate playing field.

BECOMING COED

A coed company is more than a theoretical construct. It is a reality we've experienced in isolated instances at various points in our careers in the corporate world. But, as far as we've seen, it is a business culture that has not previously been articulated or defined. Identifying and analyzing the parity paradoxes has led us to the cultural root causes of the continuing gender disparity that exists in many parts of the business world. The coed company is our suggestion, our model, for eliminating those root causes and freeing men and women to work together effectively and with parity. Now, with this model in hand, we believe strongly that it is possible to consciously create and sustain a coed corporate environment.

We recognize that changing the culture of a company is no small undertaking. Academics and consultants have written extensively on how to manage and change a corporate culture and the magnitude of the effort required. Lest you doubt that business cultures can and at times need to be reshaped, consider Lou Gerstner, who was brought in as IBM's CEO at a time when its Silicon Valley competitors were running circles around IBM. By realigning IBM's culture, Gerstner transformed an organization with a seemingly insuperable tradition of staid, entrenched employee behaviors into a dynamic modern-day competitor. He unequivocally attests to the importance of managing corporate culture in his book, *Who Says Elephants Can't Dance?* "Until I came to IBM, I probably would have told you that culture was just one among several important elements in any organization's makeup and success. . . . The description would have been accurate, but in one important respect I would have been wrong. I came to see, in my time at IBM, that culture isn't just one aspect of the game—it *is* the game."[9]

The fact that the culture of a behemoth such as IBM could deliberately be changed demonstrates that a coed company can be achieved. But Gerstner was the CEO, operating from a platform of power and position. His success is consistent with what most academics preach about changing the culture. That is, in the top-down power structure characteristic of every corporate entity, the CEO must embrace the change in culture and lead the charge for others to follow. But the vast majority of us are not CEOs or even members of senior management at the companies where we work. So what can a lowly employee do to help make his or her organization a coed company? The answer is simple: plenty.

In the hierarchical system of business, almost every employee has an area over which he or she has dominion. This could be a unit, a team, a group, a department, an office, a division, an operating company, or even an entire corporation. This is the way the system works. Within the area, the employee has the authority and the opportunity to set the tone, to establish priorities, to create a subculture within the larger corporate whole. We suggest that any employee wishing to establish a coed culture should start there—with the domain for which he or she has responsibility.

Whether you're the CEO or the head of the sorting team in the mailroom, the basic ideas for creating a coed environment are the same. By incorporating the following themes into your management approach, you can create a culture change in your area of responsibility:

- *View the problem of gender disparity at work as an issue of corporate culture.* Employee behaviors are driven by the values and norms of a work environment's culture. Individually, men and women are generally not to blame for the gender disparities that persist. They can be let off the hook for past inequities and taught the values and associated behaviors that support a truly coed environment. And they can be held to that standard. Men and women are on the same side in this battle. The culprit is corporate culture.

- *Understand that this is a work issue.* Corporations are closed groups of individuals constituting a business organization with its own values, culture, processes, and protocols. The values you adopt within the corporate walls can be different from those outside the company. You don't need to change the broader society to create a coed corporate culture. But you do need to consciously choose to behave differently at work.

- *Lead constantly by example.* We once heard a management consultant say that the most effective leaders are those who "think it, do it, and then say it." We couldn't agree more. Companies are top-down organizations. Employees take their lead from those above them in the hierarchy. As a leader, you must live the three coed values and model coed behavior in everything you do at work. The credibility of any change effort is only as strong as the behavior of those who lead it.

- *Be patient, but demanding.* Creating a coed company is a long-term commitment that requires constant communication and reinforcement. In time, the coed values and modes of operation will become so ingrained in your culture that they will become second nature.

Beyond your immediate area of authority, there are many co-workers you interact with regularly over whom you have no control. These might include your peers, your superiors, and colleagues of higher and lower rank—those with whom you have no direct or indirect reporting relationships. Introducing the concept of a coed company to these co-workers will be more challenging than doing so within your own area of authority and perhaps may be inappropriate. As we noted in our analysis of the basic business rule of exercising prudence when challenging the power structure, companies expect employees to know their limits in terms of pushing back or introducing new ideas or stepping on the turf of others. Consequently, once you've incorporated the coed values into your own operating style, we suggest that you introduce the concepts carefully to others. Be cognizant of the risks you assume by speaking out— we certainly don't want you to lose your job over this. Talk to peers that you trust, to superiors with whom you have good relationships. Test their reaction to the term "coed company." We have found that this term resonates well with both men and women. Given the realities of the corporate system, we suggest that using the tone of an advocate for change will serve any corporate citizen much better than using the tone of an evangelist. You might consider introducing the concept to the human resources staff, especially if there is a group or an individual that focuses on diversity. If those you speak to are intrigued by the idea of a coed company, give them a copy of this book. Or put them in touch with us. We'd be happy to talk with them.

In December 2004, soccer player Mia Hamm retired. In summarizing her impact on the sports world, the *New York Times* talked about her status in the U.S. sports arena as the greatest soccer player of her time and said:

> That may have been her greatest achievement in winning two world championships and a pair of Olympic gold medals—to escape assessment qualified by her gender.[10]

"To escape assessment qualified by gender" is what we are all looking for in a coed company. Those who believe this is possible, those who strive to incorporate the coed company values into their day-to-day work lives, will grasp the future and make a difference.

NOTES

CHAPTER 1: STILL STUCK ON AN UNLEVEL PLAYING FIELD

1. Adam L. Penenberg, "This CEO Has Silicon Valley Buzzing," *Fast Company*, May 2008, front cover.

2. Patricia Sellers, "The Power 50: 50 Most Powerful Women in Business," *Fortune*, October 15, 2007, p. 77.

3. *Daily Beast*, "The Barrier That Didn't Fall," November 18, 2008, http://www.thedailybeast.com/blogs-and-stories/2008-11-18/the-barrier=that-didnrsquot-fall/ (accessed February 25, 2009).

4. Hillary Clinton, concession speech at the National Building Museum, Washington, DC, June 7, 2008.

5. Catalyst, *1998 Census of Women Corporate Officers and Top Earners* (New York: Catalyst, 1998); *2008 Catalyst Census of Women Corporate Officers and Top Earners of the Fortune 500* (New York; Catalyst, 2008); 2008 *Catalyst Census of Women Board Directors of the Fortune 500* (New York: Catalyst 2008); "Catalyst Quick Takes: U.S. Women in Business," August 2009, http://www.catalyst.org/publication/206/women-in-us-management (accessed September 22, 2009); Bureau of U.S. Census and Bureau of Labor Statistics, U.S. Department of Labor, "Current Population Survey, Annual Averages, 2008," cited in http://www.catalyst.org/publication/132/us-women-in-business.

6. Ibid., *Catalyst Census of Women Corporate Officers and Top*

Earners of the Fortune 500 (New York: Catalyst, 2006–2008). The 2005 census (published in 2006) actually contained data from 1995 to 2005.

7. Ibid., *Catalyst Census of Women Corporate Officers and Top Earners of the Fortune 500* (New York: Catalyst, 1998–2008). Catalyst sometimes includes data for multiple years in a single report.

8. Ibid. (New York: Catalyst, 1998–2007).

9. Ibid. (New York: Catalyst, 1997–2008).

10. Bureau of Labor Statistics, "Highlights of Women's Earnings in 2008," Report 1017, July 2009, http://www.bls.gov/cps/cpswom 2008.pdf (accessed July 2009).

11. Judy Goldberg Dey and Catherine Hill, *Behind the Pay Gap* (Washington, DC: American Association of University Women Educational Foundation, 2007).

12. Ibid., pp. 10, 20.

13. Ibid., analysis of U.S. Department of Education, National Center for Education Statistics, *2000–2001 Baccalaureate and Beyond Longitudinal Study* and *2003 Baccalaureate and Beyond Longitudinal Study*.

14. Ibid.

15. Ibid., p. 2.

16. *Daily Beast*, "The Barrier That Didn't Fall."

CHAPTER 2: SOLVING THE WRONG PROBLEM

1. Jack and Suzy Welch, "What's Holding Women Back?" *Business Week*, February 13, 2007.

2. Lawrence H. Summers, speech at conference titled "Diversifying the Science Engineering Workforce: Women, Underrepresented Minorities, and Their S&E Careers," National Bureau of Economic Research, Cambridge, MA, January 14, 2005.

3. *New York Times*, "At 2 Ivy Campuses, Conflict Is Thriving," January 18, 2005.

4. Sam Dillon and Sara Rimer, "No Break in the Storm over Harvard President's Words," *New York Times*, January 19, 2005.

5. Ibid.

6. Gloria Steinem, "Gloria Steinem Quotes," *Brainy Quote*, http://www.brainyquote.com/quotes/authors/g/gloria_steinem.html (accessed March 6, 2009).

7. Susan Faludi, *Backlash: The Undeclared War against American Women* (New York: Crown Publishers, 1991), p. 48.

8. Rebecca Shambaugh, quoted in *Publishers Weekly*, "Synopsis of *It's Not a Glass Ceiling, It's a Sticky Floor: Free Yourself from the Hidden Behaviors Sabotaging Your Career Success* by Rebecca Shambaugh," Barnes & Noble, http://search.barnesandnoble.com/Its-Not -a-Glass-Ceiling-Its-a-Sticky-Floor/Rebecca-Shambaugh/e/97800714 93949 (accessed March 6, 2009).

9. Barnes & Noble, "Synopsis of *Play Like a Man, Win Like a Woman* by Gail Evans," http://search.barnesandnoble.com/Play-Like -a-Man-Win-Like-a-Woman/Gail-Evans/e/9780767904636/?itm=1 &usri=gail+evans+play+like+a+man (accessed March 6, 2009).

10. John Kenneth Galbraith, *The New Industrial State* (Boston: Houghton Mifflin, 1967).

11. Ibid., p. 147.

12. Ibid., p. 96.

13. Ibid., p.151.

14. Betty Friedan, *The Feminine Mystique* (New York: Dell Publishing, 1984; originally published 1963).

15. Ibid., p. 15.

16. Ibid., p. 348.

17. *United States Statutes at Large*, vol. 86, *Laws and Concurrent Resolutions Enacted during the Second Session of the Ninety-second Congress of the United States of America 1972, and Proposed Amendment to the Constitution and Proclamations* (Washington, DC: U.S. Government Printing Office, 1973), p. 1523.

CHAPTER 3: CAUGHT ON A MALE PROVING GROUND

1. Peter N. Stearns, *Be a Man! Males in Modern Society*, 2nd ed. (New York: Holmes & Meier, 1990), p. 181.

2. Susan Faludi, *Backlash: The Undeclared War against American Women* (New York: Crown Publishers, 1991), p. 65.

3. Deborah Kerfoot and David Knights, "'The Best Is Yet to Come?' The Quest for Embodiment in Managerial Work," in *Men as Managers, Managers as Men: Critical Perspectives on Men, Masculinities and Managements*, eds. David L. Collinson and Jeff Hearn (London: Sage, 1996), p. 83.

4. Robin Ely, quoted in Sarah Jane Gilbert, "Manly Men, Oil Platforms, and Breaking Stereotypes," *Harvard Business School Working Knowledge*, November 27, 2006, http://hbswk.hbs.edu/item/5515.html (accessed October 20, 2009).

5. Kerfoot and Knights, "The Best Is Yet to Come?" p. 83.

6. Michael Kimmel, *Manhood in America: A Cultural History* (New York: Free Press, 1996), p. 318.

7. Michael Kimmel, "Masculinity as Homophobia: Fear, Shame and Silence in the Construction of Gender Identity," in *Men and Power*, ed. Joseph A. Kuypers (Amherst, NY: Prometheus Books, 1999), p. 113. Kimmel's essay was previously published in *Theorizing Masculinities*, eds. M. Brod and M. Kaufman (Thousand Oaks, CA: Sage, 1994).

8. Kimmel, *Manhood in America*, p. 7.

9. Ibid., p. 309.

10. Bill Pennington and Dave Anderson, "Some at Augusta National Quietly Seek a Compromise," *New York Times*, September 29, 2002.

11. Edgar H. Schein, *Organizational Culture and Leadership*, 3rd ed. (San Francisco: Jossey-Bass, 2004), p. 63.

12. *Desk Set*, directed by Walter Lang, Twentieth Century-Fox, 1957.

CHAPTER 4: PARADOX #1: THE TEAM PLAYER

1. Betty Lehan Harragan, *Games Mother Never Taught You: Corporate Gamesmanship for Women* (New York: Rawson Associates Publishers, 1977), p. 65.

2. Bureau of Labor Statistics, U.S. Department of Labor, "Household Data, Annual Averages, Table 39, Median Weekly Earnings of Full-time Wage and Salary Workers by Detailed Occupation and Sex," Bureau of Labor Statistics, 2008, ftp://ftp.bls.gov/pub/special.requests/lf/aat39.txt (accessed February 25, 2009).

3. Brian Lehrer, "Open Phones," *The Brian Lehrer Show*, WNYC, April 2, 2003, http://www.wnyc.org/shows/bl/episodes/04022003 (accessed May 12, 2005).

4. Ibid.

5. Denise DeHass, "2005–06 NCAA Gender-Equity Report," National Collegiate Athletic Association, July 2008, http://www.ncaa

publications.com/ProductsDetailView.aspx?sku=GER06 (accessed September 2009).

6. Judy Goldberg Dey and Catherine Hill, *Behind the Pay Gap* (Washington, DC: American Association of University Women Educational Foundation, 2007), p. 3.

CHAPTER 5: PARADOX #2: MENTORS AND ADVOCATES

1. Quoted in Rey Carr, "Mentors in Business, Industry, Education, Science and Metaphysics," The Mentor Hall of Fame, http://www.mentors.ca/mp_business.html (accessed April 22, 2009).

2. Michael Kimmel, "Masculinity as Homophobia: Fear, Shame and Silence in the Construction of Gender Identity," in *Men and Power*, ed. Joseph A. Kuypers (Amherst, NY: Prometheus Books, 1999), p. 113.

CHAPTER 6: PARADOX #3: COMMITMENT TO THE JOB

1. Thomas J. Peters and Robert H. Waterman Jr., *In Search of Excellence: Lessons from America's Best-Run Companies* (New York: Harper & Row, 1982), p. 17.

2. Elbert Hubbard, "A Message to Garcia," *Philistine*, March 1899.

3. CBS Television, *The Dick Van Dyke Show*, Calvada Productions, October 1961–June 1966.

4. CBS Television, *The Mary Tyler Moore Show*, MTM Enterprises, September 1970–March 1977.

5. *Working Girl*, directed by Mike Nichols, Twentieth Century Fox, 1988.

6. *The Devil Wears Prada*, directed by David Frankel, Fox 2000 Pictures, 2006.

7. Morley Safer, interviewer, "Anna Wintour: Behind the Shades," produced by Ruth Streeter, *60 Minutes*, CBS Television, May 17, 2009.

8. Federal News Service, "Transcript of the Democratic Debate in New Hampshire," *New York Times*, January 5, 2008, http://www.nytimes.com/2008/01/05/us/politics/05text-ddebate.html?_r=1&pagewanted=all (accessed June 18, 2009).

9. Ibid.

10. Faye J. Crosby, *Juggling: The Unexpected Advantages of Balancing Career and Home for Women and Their Families* (New York: Free Press/Macmillan, 1991), p. 15.

11. Bureau of Labor Statistics, U.S. Department of Labor, "Economic News Release, Table A-1, Employment Status of the Civilian Population by Sex and Age," Bureau of Labor Statistics, June 5, 2009, http://www.bls.gov/news.release/empsit.t01.htm (accessed June 8, 2009).

12. Bureau of Labor Statistics, U.S. Department of Labor, "News," Bureau of Labor Statistics, May 27, 2009, http://www.bls.gov/news.release/famee.nr0.htm (accessed June 2009).

13. Quoted in Ronald L. Pitzer, "Research on Father Involvement," Children, Youth and Family Consortium, University of Minnesota, http://www.cyfc.umn.edu/family/resources/AB1011.htm (accessed June 8, 2009).

CHAPTER 7: PARADOX #4: BONDING WITH CO-WORKERS

1. Michael Kimmel, "Masculinity as Homophobia: Fear, Shame and Silence in the Construction of Gender Identity," in *Men and Power*, ed. Joseph A. Kuypers (Amherst, NY: Prometheus Books, 1999), p. 113. Kimmel's essay was previously published in *Theorizing Masculinities*, eds. M. Brod and M. Kaufman (Thousand Oaks, CA: Sage, 1994).

2. Michael Kimmel, *Manhood in America: A Cultural History* (New York: Free Press, 1996), p. 7.

3. Deborah Tannen, *Talking from 9 to 5: How Women's and Men's Conversational Styles Affect Who Gets Heard, Who Gets Credit, and What Gets Done at Work* (New York: William Morrow, 1994), p. 46.

4. Ibid., p. 170.

5. *Random House Webster's Dictionary, Classic Edition* (New York: Random House, 1999), p. 784.

CHAPTER 9: THE COED COMPANY

1. James C. Collins and Jerry I. Porras, *Built to Last: Successful Habits of Visionary Companies* (New York: HarperBusiness/HarperCollins, 1994), p. 122.

2. Thomas J. Peters and Robert H. Waterman Jr., *In Search of Excellence: Lessons from America's Best-Run Companies* (New York: Harper & Row, 1982), p. 75.

3. David Koeppel, "Many Find an Office's Culture Is More Than Dress-Shirt Deep," *New York Times*, June 8, 2003.

4. Carlton Goldthwaite, telephone conversations with Lynn Cronin, April 2006.

5. Catalyst, *The Bottom Line: Connecting Corporate Performance and Gender Diversity* (New York: Catalyst, 2004).

6. Paula Madison, acceptance speech, New York Women's Agenda Star Breakfast, December 5, 2000.

7. *Equal Pay Act of 1963*, Public Law 88-38, *U.S. Code*, Title 29, Section 206(d).

8. New York Women's Agenda Star Breakfast, December 5, 2000.

9. Louis V. Gerstner, *Who Says Elephants Can't Dance? Inside IBM's Historic Turnaround* (New York: HarperBusiness/HarperCollins, 2002), p. 182.

10. Jere Longman, "Mia Hamm, Soccer Star, to Retire Tonight," *New York Times*, December 8, 2004.

BIBLIOGRAPHY

Ackman, Dan. "Sotheby's Brooks Sent to Her Room, But No Jail." *Forbes*, April 29, 2002.

Alkhafaji, Abbass F. *Corporate Transformation and Restructuring: A Strategic Approach*. Westport, CT: Quorum Books, 2001.

Alsop, Ron. "Less Career Satisfaction for Women MBAs." *College-Journal*, from the *Wall Street Journal*, 2004. http://208.144.115 .173/mbacenter/mbatrack/20040209-alsop.html (accessed January 25, 2010).

Appelbaum, Eileen. *Balancing Acts*. Washington, DC: Economic Policy Institute, 2000.

Barnes & Noble. "Synopsis of *Play Like a Man, Win Like a Woman* by Gail Evans." http://search.barnesandnoble.com/Play-Like-a -Man-Win-Like-a-Woman/Gail-Evans/e/9780767904636/?itm=1 &usri=gail+evans+play+like+a+man (accessed March 6, 2009).

Battelle, John. *The Search: How Google and Its Rivals Rewrote the Rules of Business and Transformed Our Culture*. New York: Portfolio, 2005.

Berry, Mary Frances. *Why ERA Failed: Politics, Women's Rights, and the Amending Process of the Constitution*. Bloomington: Indiana University Press, 1986.

Boyett, Joseph H., and Henry P. Conn. *Workplace 2000: The Revolution Reshaping American Business*. New York: Plume, 1992.

Brannon, Robert, and Deborah David. *The Forty-nine Percent Majority: The Male Sex Role*. Reading, MA: Addison-Wesley, 1976.

Brown, Clifton. "At Club in Augusta, Policy of Chairman Remains 'Men Only.'" *New York Times*, November 12, 2002.

Bureau of Labor Statistics, U.S. Department of Labor. "Economic News Release, Table A-1, Employment Status of the Civilian population by Sex and Age." Bureau of Labor Statistics, June 5, 2009. http://www.bls.gov/news.release/empsit.t01.htm (accessed June 8, 2009).

———. "Highlights of Women's Earnings in 2008." Report 1017, Bureau of Labor Statistics, July 2009. http://www.bls.gov/cps/cpswom2008.pdf (accessed July 2009).

———. "Household Data, Annual Averages, Table 39, Median Weekly Earnings of Full-time Wage and Salary Workers by Detailed Occupation and Sex." Bureau of Labor Statistics, 2008. ftp://ftp.bls.gov/pub/special.requests/lf/aat39.txt (accessed February 25, 2009).

———. "News." Bureau of Labor Statistics, May 27, 2009. http://www.bls.gov/news.release/famee.nr0.htm (accessed June 2009).

———. "Standard Occupational Classification (SOC) System." Bureau of Labor Statistics. http://www.bls.gov/soc/ (accessed January 27, /2004).

Carr, Rey. "Mentors in Business, Industry, Education, Science and Metaphysics." The Mentor Hall of Fame. http://www.mentors.ca/mp_business.html (accessed April 22, 2009).

Catalyst. *1996 Census of Women Corporate Officers and Top Earners*. New York: Catalyst, 1996.

———. *1997 Census of Women Corporate Officers and Top Earners*. New York: Catalyst, 1997.

———. *1998 Census of Women Corporate Officers and Top Earners*. New York: Catalyst, 1998.

———. *1999 Catalyst Census of Women Corporate Officers and Top Earners*. New York: Catalyst, 1999.

———. *2000 Catalyst Census of Women Corporate Officers and Top Earners*. New York: Catalyst, 2000.

———. *2002 Catalyst Census of Women Corporate Officers and Top Earners in the Fortune 500*. New York: Catalyst, 2002.

———. *2005 Catalyst Census of Women Corporate Officers and Top Earners in the Fortune 500*. New York: Catalyst, 2006.

———. *2006 Catalyst Census of Women Corporate Officers and Top Earners in the Fortune 500*. New York: Catalyst, 2007.

———. 2007 *Catalyst Census of Women Corporate Officers and Top Earners in the Fortune 500*. New York: Catalyst, 2007.

———. 2008 *Catalyst Census of Women Board Directors of the Fortune 500*. New York: Catalyst, 2008.

———. 2008 *Catalyst Census of Women Corporate Officers and Top Earners in the Fortune 500*. New York: Catalyst, 2008.

———. *The Bottom Line: Connecting Corporate Performance and Gender Diversity*. New York: Catalyst, 2004.

———. "The Catalyst Pyramid: U.S. Women in Business," June 22, 2009. http://www.catalyst.org/publication/132/us-women-in -business (accessed September 22, 2009).

———. "Catalyst Quick Takes: U.S. Women in Business," August 2009. http://www.catalyst.org/publication/206/women-in-us -management (accessed September 22, 2009).

CBS Television. *The Dick Van Dyke Show*. Calvada Productions, October 1961–June 1966.

———. *The Mary Tyler Moore Show*. MTM Enterprises, September 1970–March 1977.

Chambers, Marcia. *The Unplayable Lie: The Untold Story of Women and Discrimination in American Golf*. New York: Golf Digest Pocket Books, 1995.

Clinton, Hillary. Concession speech at the National Building Museum. Washington, DC, June 7, 2008.

Cohen, Philip N., and Suzanne M. Bianchi. "Marriage, Children and Women's Employment: What Do We Know?" *Monthly Labor Review*, December 1999.

Cohen, Theodore F. *Men and Masculinity: A Text Reader*. Belmont, CA: Wadsworth/Thomson Learning, 2001.

Collins, James C., and Jerry I. Porras. *Built to Last: Successful Habits of Visionary Companies*. New York: HarperBusiness/Harper-Collins, 1994.

Collinson, David L., and Jeff Hearn, eds. *Men as Managers, Managers as Men: Critical Perspectives on Men, Masculinities and Managements*. London: Sage, 1996.

Covey, Stephen R. *The Seven Habits of Highly Effective People: Powerful Lessons in Personal Change*. New York: Fireside, 1990.

Creech, Bill. *The Five Pillars of TQM: How to Make Total Quality Management Work for You*. New York: Truman Talley Books/ Dutton, 1994.

Crosby, Faye J. *Juggling: The Unexpected Advantages of Balancing Career and Home for Women and Their Families*. New York: Free Press/Macmillan, 1991.

Cunningham, Mary. *Power Play: What Really Happened at Bendix*. New York: Linden Press/Simon and Schuster, 1984.

Dabbs, James McBride, and Mary Godwin Dabbs. *Heroes, Rogues, and Lovers: Testosterone and Behavior*. New York: McGraw-Hill, 2000.

Daily Beast. "The Barrier That Didn't Fall." November 18, 2008. http://www.thedailybeast.com/blogs-and-stories/2008-11-18/the-barrier-that-didnrsquot-fall/ (accessed February 25, 2009).

DeHass, Denise. "2005–06 NCAA Gender-Equity Report." National Collegiate Athletic Association, July 2008. http://www.ncaapublications.com/ProductsDetailView.aspx?sku=GER06 (accessed September 2009).

Desk Set. Directed by Walter Lang. Twentieth Century-Fox, 1957.

The Devil Wears Prada. Directed by David Frankel. Fox 2000 Pictures, 2006.

Dey, Judy Goldberg, and Catherine Hill. *Behind the Pay Gap*. Washington, DC: American Association of University Women Educational Foundation, 2007.

Dillon, Sam, and Sara Rimer, "No Break in the Storm over Harvard President's Words." *New York Times*, January 19, 2005.

Dowd, Maureen. "The Abyss of Desire." Liberties Op-Ed Column. *New York Times*, January 13, 1999.

Drucker, Peter F. *Management Challenges for the 21st Century*. New York: HarperBusiness/HarperCollins, 1999.

———. *The Practice of Management*. New York: Harper & Brothers Publishers, 1954.

Eichenwald, Kurt. *Conspiracy of Fools: A True Story*. New York: Broadway Books, 2005.

Equal Pay Act of 1963. Public Law 88-38. *U.S. Code*, Title 29, Section 206(d).

Faludi, Susan. *Backlash: The Undeclared War against American Women*. New York: Crown Publishers, 1991.

Fatal Attraction. Directed by Adrian Lyne. Paramount Pictures, 1987.

Faux, Marian. *Roe v. Wade: The Untold Story of the Landmark Supreme Court Decision That Made Abortion Legal*. Updated ed. New York: Cooper Square Press, 2001.

Federal News Service. "Transcript of the Democratic Debate in New Hampshire." *New York Times*, January 5, 2008. http://www.nytimes.com/2008/01/05/us/politics/05text-ddebate.html?r=1&pagewanted=all (accessed June 18, 2009).

Frankel, Lois P. *Nice Girls Don't Get the Corner Office: 101 Unconscious Mistakes Women Make That Sabotage Their Careers*. New York: Warner Business Books, 2004.

Friedan, Betty. *The Feminine Mystique*. New York: Dell Publishing, 1984 (originally published 1963).

Galbraith, John Kenneth. *The Affluent Society*. 2nd ed. Boston: Houghton Mifflin, 1969.

———. *Annals of an Abiding Liberal*. Boston: Houghton Mifflin, 1979.

———. *The Liberal Hour*. Boston: Houghton Mifflin, 1960.

———. *The New Industrial State*. Boston: Houghton Mifflin, 1967.

Garr, Doug. *IBM Redux: Lou Gerstner and the Business Turnaround of the Decade*. New York: HarperBusiness/HarperCollins, 1999.

Gavora, Jessica. *Tilting the Playing Field: Schools, Sports, Sex and Title IX*. San Francisco: Encounter Books, 2002.

Gee, Lisa. *Friends: Why Men and Women Are from the Same Planet*. London: Bloomsbury, 2004.

Gerstner, Louis V. *Who Says Elephants Can't Dance? Inside IBM's Historic Turnaround*. New York: HarperBusiness/HarperCollins, 2002.

Gilbert, Sarah Jane. "Manly Men, Oil Platforms, and Breaking Stereotypes." *Harvard Business School Working Knowledge*, November 27, 2006. http://hbswk.hbs.edu/item/5515.html (accessed October 20, 2009).

Gogol, Sara. *Hard Fought Victories: Women Coaches Making a Difference*. Terre Haute, IN: Wish Publishing, 2002.

Goleman, Daniel. *Working with Emotional Intelligence*. New York: Bantam, 1998.

Graduate Management Admission Council. "August 2003 MBA Alumni Perspective Survey." March 23, 2009. http://www.gmac.com/community/media/p/252.aspx (accessed June 2009).

Gray, John. *Men Are from Mars, Women Are from Venus: A Practical Guide for Improving Communication and Getting What You Want in Your Relationships*. New York: HarperCollins, 1992.

Greenhouse, Linda. "Ginsburg at Fore in Court's Give-and-Take." *New York Times*, October 14, 1993.

Greenhouse, Steven, and Constance L. Hays. "Wal-Mart Sex-Bias Suit Given Class-Action Status." *New York Times*, June 23, 2004.

Hammer, Michael. *The Agenda: What Every Business Must Do to Dominate the Decade*. New York: Crown Business, 2001.

———. *Beyond Reengineering: How the Process-Centered Organization Is Changing Our Work and Our Lives*. New York: HarperBusiness/HarperCollins, 1996.

Hammer, Michael, and James Champy. *Reengineering the Corporation: A Manifesto for Business Revolution*. New York: HarperBusiness, 1993.

Harragan, Betty Lehan. *Games Mother Never Taught You: Corporate Gamesmanship for Women*. New York: Rawson Associates Publishers, 1977.

Harter, James K., Theodore L. Hayes, and Frank L. Schmidt. "Business-Unit-Level Relationship between Employee Satisfaction, Employee Engagement, and Business Outcomes: A Meta-analysis." *Journal of Applied Psychology* 87, no. 2 (2002): 268.

Hawn, Carleen. "The Women of Enron: A Separate Peace." *Fast Company Magazine* 74, September 2003.

Hays, Constance. "Chief of Mattel Steps Down after Reporting Loss in 1999." Business/Financial Desk. *New York Times*, February 4, 2000.

Hewlett, Sylvia Ann. *Creating a Life: Professional Women and the Quest for Children*. New York: Talk Miramax Books, 2002.

Heywood, Leslie, and Shari L. Dworkin. *Built to Win: The Female Athlete as Cultural Icon*. Minneapolis: University of Minnesota Press, 2003.

Hobbs, Frank, and Nicole Stoops. *Demographic Trends in the 20th Century*. U.S. Census Bureau, Census 2000 Special Reports, Series CENSR-4. Washington, DC: U.S. Government Printing Office, 2002.

Hrdy, Sarah Blaffer. *Mother Nature: A History of Mothers, Infants, and Natural Selection*. New York: Pantheon Books, 1999.

Hubbard, Elbert. "A Message to Garcia." *Philistine*, March 1899.

Hymowitz, Carol. "Women Put Noses to the Grindstone, and Miss Opportunities." Marketplace: In the Lead. *Wall Street Journal*, February 3, 2004.

Kerfoot, Deborah, and David Knights. "'The Best Is Yet to Come?' The Quest for Embodiment in Managerial Work," in *Men as*

Managers, Managers as Men: Critical Perspectives on Men, Masculinities and Managements, eds. David L. Collinson and Jeff Hearn. London: Sage, 1996.

Kimmel, Michael. *Manhood in America: A Cultural History*. New York: Free Press, 1996.

———. "Masculinity as Homophobia: Fear, Shame and Silence in the Construction of Gender Identity." In *Men and Power*, ed. Joseph A. Kuypers. Amherst, NY: Prometheus Books, 1999.

Koeppel, David. "Many Find an Office's Culture Is More Than Dress-Shirt Deep." *New York Times*, June 8, 2003.

Koys, Daniel J. "The Effects of Employee Satisfaction, Organizational Citizenship Behavior, and Turnover on Organizational Effectiveness: A Unit-Level, Longitudinal Study." *Personnel Psychology* 54, no. 1 (December 2006): 101.

Kuypers, Joseph A., ed. *Men and Power*. Amherst, NY: Prometheus Books, 1999.

Lehrer, Brian. "Open Phones." *The Brian Lehrer Show*. WNYC, April 2, 2003. http://www.wnyc.org/shows/bl/episodes/04022003 (accessed May 12, 2005).

Levering, Robert, Milton Moskowitz, and Michael Katz. *The 100 Best Companies to Work For in America*. Reading, MA: Addison-Wesley, 1984.

Longman, Jere. "Mia Hamm, Soccer Star, to Retire Tonight." *New York Times*, December 8, 2004.

Lyons, Daniel. "Bad Boys." *Forbes*, July 29, 2002.

Madison, Paula. Acceptance speech, New York Women's Agenda Star Breakfast, December 5, 2000.

Markoff, John. "When + Adds Up to Minus." *New York Times*, February 10, 2005.

Mattel, Inc. "Our Toys." http://corporate.mattel.com/our-toys/default.aspx (accessed September 26, 2009).

Matthews, Martha, and Shirley McCune. *Implementing Title IX and Attaining Sex Equity: A Workshop Package for Postsecondary Educators*. Resource Center on Sex Roles in Education, National Foundation for the Improvement of Education, U.S. Department of Health, Education and Welfare. Washington, D.C.: U.S. Government Printing Office, 1977.

McKenna, Elizabeth Perle. *When Work Doesn't Work Anymore: Women, Work and Identity*. New York: Delacorte Press, 1997.

Meyer, Julie. *Age: 2000*. U.S. Census Bureau October Census 2000 Brief. Washington, DC: U.S. Census Bureau, 2001.

Michaels, Walter Benn. *The Trouble with Diversity: How We Learned to Love Identity and Ignore Inequality*. New York: Holt, 2006.

Mishel, Lawrence, Jared Bernstein, and Heather Boushey. *The State of Working America 2002/2003*. Economic Policy Institute. Ithaca, NY: ILR Press, an imprint of Cornell University Press, 2003.

Mooney, Nan. *I Can't Believe She Did That: Why Women Betray Other Women at Work*. New York: St. Martin's Griffin, 2006.

Morris, Betsy. "The New Trophy Husband." *Fortune*, October 14, 2002.

National Center for Health Statistics. "Live Births by Age of Mother and Race: United States, 1933–98." Centers for Disease Control and Prevention, U.S. Department of Health and Human Services, Division of Vital Statistics. http://www.cdc.gov/nchs/data/natality/mage33tr.pdf (accessed February 14, 2005).

———. "Table 1: Fertility Indicators 1920–2000." Centers for Disease Control and Prevention, U.S. Department of Health and Human Services. Data provided to the authors by the Fertility and Family Statistics Branch of the Population Division of the Bureau of the Census.

NBC Television. *Friends*. Bright/Kauffman/Crane Productions, September 1994–May 2004.

New York Times. "At 2 Ivy Campuses, Conflict Is Thriving." January 18, 2005.

New York Women's Agenda. http://nywa.org/star_halloffame.html (accessed May 12, 2005).

Pande, Peter S., Robert P. Neuman, and Roland R. Cavanagh. *The Six Sigma Way: Team Fieldbook*. New York: McGraw-Hill, 2002.

Pearson, Allison. *I Don't Know How She Does It: The Life of Kate Reddy, Working Mother*. New York: Anchor Books/Random House, 2002.

Pennington, Bill and Dave Anderson. "Some at Augusta National Quietly Seek a Compromise." *New York Times*, September 29, 2002.

Peters, Thomas J., and Robert H. Waterman Jr. *In Search of Excellence: Lessons from America's Best-Run Companies*. New York: Harper & Row, 1982.

Pitzer, Ronald L. "Research on Father Involvement." Children, Youth and Family Consortium, University of Minnesota. http://www.cyfc.umn.edu/family/resources/AB1011.htm (accessed June 8, 2009).

Publishers Weekly. "Synopsis of *It's Not a Glass Ceiling, It's a Sticky Floor: Free Yourself from the Hidden Behaviors Sabotaging Your Career Success* by Rebecca Shambaugh." Barnes & Noble. http://search.barnesandnoble.com/Its-Not-a-Glass-Ceiling-Its-a-Sticky-Floor/Rebecca-Shambaugh/e/9780071493949 (accessed March 6, 2009).

Putzel, Henry, Jr. Reporter of Decisions. *United States Reports, Volume 410, Cases Adjudged in the Supreme Court at October Term, 1972.* Washington, DC: U.S. Government Printing Office, 1974.

Random House Webster's Dictionary, Classic Edition. New York: Random House, 1999.

Rimm, Sylvia. *See Jane Win: The Rimm Report on How 1,000 Girls Became Successful Women.* New York: Three Rivers Press/Crown, 1999.

Rynecki, David. "The 2003 Fortune 500. Golf and Power: Inside the Secret Refuge of the Business Elite." *Fortune*, March 30, 2003. www.fortune.com/ (accessed January 14, 2004).

Safer, Morley, interviewer. "Anna Wintour: Behind the Shades." Produced by Ruth Streeter. *60 Minutes.* CBS Television, May 17, 2009.

Schein, Edgar H. *Organizational Culture and Leadership.* 3rd ed. San Francisco: Jossey-Bass, 2004.

Sellers, Patricia. "The Power 50: 50 Most Powerful Women in Business." *Fortune*, October 15, 2007.

———. "Women, Sex and Power." *Fortune*, August 5, 1996. www.fortune.com/ (accessed February 24, 2003).

SHE SAYS: Women in News. Directed by Barbara Rick. PBS Video. Out of the Blue Films, 2001.

Simmons, Rachel. *Odd Girl Out: The Hidden Culture of Aggression in Girls.* New York: Harcourt, 2002.

Stabiner, Karen. *All Girls: Single Sex Education and Why It Matters.* New York: Riverhead Books, 2002.

Stearns, Peter N. *Be a Man! Males in Modern Society.* 2nd ed. New York: Holmes & Meier, 1990.

Steinem, Gloria. "Gloria Steinem Quotes." *Brainy Quote.* http://www.brainyquote.com/quotes/authors/g/gloria_steinem.html (accessed March 6, 2009).

Steiner, Gilbert Y. *Constitutional Inequality: The Political Fortunes of the Equal Rights Amendment*. Washington, DC: Brookings Institution, 1985.

Summers, Lawrence H. Speech at conference titled "Diversifying the Science & Engineering Workforce: Women, Underrepresented Minorities, and Their S&E Careers." National Bureau of Economic Research, Cambridge, MA, January 14, 2005.

Swiss, Deborah J. *The Male Mind at Work: A Woman's Guide to Working with Men*. Cambridge, MA: Perseus, 2000.

Swiss, Deborah J., and Judith P. Walker. *Women and the Work/Family Dilemma: How Today's Professional Women Are Confronting the Maternal Wall*. New York: John Wiley & Sons, 1993.

Tahmincioglu, Eve. "The 4-Letter-Word Patrol Is in Pursuit." Workplace. *New York Times*, June 27, 2001.

Tannen, Deborah, PhD. *Talking From 9 to 5: How Women's and Men's Conversational Styles Affect Who Gets Heard, Who Gets Credit, and What Gets Done at Work*. New York: William Morrow, 1994.

———. *That's Not What I Meant! How Conversational Style Makes or Breaks Relationships*. New York: Ballantine, 1986.

———. "Wears Jump Suit. Sensible Shoes. Uses Husband's Last Name." *New York Times Magazine*, June 20, 1993.

United States Statutes at Large. Vol. 86, *Laws and Concurrent Resolutions Enacted during the Second Session of the Ninety-second Congress of the United States of America 1972, and Proposed Amendment to the Constitution and Proclamations*. Washington, DC: U.S. Government Printing Office, 1973.

U.S. Food and Drug Administration. "Birth Control Guide." 2003. http://www.fda.gov/ (accessed March 2, 2005).

Vincent, Norah. *Self-Made Man: One Woman's Journey into Manhood and Back Again*. New York: Viking, 2006.

Waite, Linda J., and Mark Nielsen. "The Rise of the Dual Career Middle Class Family." Working Paper 99-01. Center on Parents, Children, and Work, University of Chicago, 1999.

Walsh, Mary Williams. "Where G.E. Falls Short: Diversity at the Top: Can Only White Men Run a Model Company?" Money and Business. *New York Times*, September 3, 2000.

Welch, Jack, and Suzy Welch. "What's Holding Women Back?" *BusinessWeek*, February 13, 2007.

Working Girl. Directed by Mike Nichols. Twentieth Century-Fox, 1988.

Zeitz, Baila, and Lorraine Dusky. *The Best Companies for Women.* New York: Simon and Schuster, 1988.

INDEX

Italized page numbers indicate exhibits